GEORGE LAWSON'S *POLITICA* AND THE ENGLISH REVOLUTION

CONAL CONDREN

Associate Professor, School of Political Science, University of New South Wales

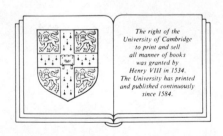

The right of the
University of Cambridge
to print and sell
all manner of books
was granted by
Henry VIII in 1534.
The University has printed
and published continuously
since 1584.

CAMBRIDGE UNIVERSITY PRESS

Cambridge
New York   Port Chester   Melbourne   Sydney

Published by the Press Syndicate of the University of Cambridge
The Pitt Building, Trumpington Street, Cambridge CB2 1RP
40 West 20th Street, New York, NY 10011, USA
10 Stamford Road, Oakleigh, Melbourne 3166, Australia

First Published 1989

Printed in Great Britain at The Bath Press, Avon

British Library cataloguing in publication data
Condren, Conal
George Lawson's *Politica* and the English Revolution. – (Cambridge
studies in early modern British history)
1. Politics. Theories of Lawson, George, d. 1678
I. Title
320.5′ 092′ 4

Library of Congress cataloguing in publication data
Condren, Conal
George Lawson's Politica and the English Revolution / Conal
Condren.
p.   cm. – (Cambridge studies in early modern British history)
Includes index.
ISBN (invalid) 0 521 36642 9
1. Great Britain – Politics and government – 1642–1660.
2. Lawson, George, d. 1678. Politica sacra & civilis.   3. Political
science – Great Britain – History – 17th
century.   I. Title.   II Series.
DA405.c66 1989
320.941′ 09′ 032 – dc20   89-31715 CIP

ISBN 0 521 36642 9

To Averil

CONTENTS

PREFACE

This book arises directly from *The Status and Appraisal of Classic Texts*, a theoretical study dealing with the fate of political texts and the vocabulary of their analysis. As a detailed illustration and adaptation, however, this work is hardly as premeditated as it might seem.

In the earlier book I had argued that there is a poor fit between 'classic' status and what we see as intellectual virtue; and so, there is a certain decorum in the fortuitous way in which Lawson's *Politica* has become the principal grist to a theoretical mill.

In writing *Status and Appraisal*, I made passing illustrative reference to Locke and, having little particular interest in the seventeenth century, I thought it was as well to find out what was currently being written about him. I was shown Julian H. Franklin's *John Locke and the Theory of Sovereignty*, Cambridge, 1978, and, because of its virtuous brevity, I was encouraged to read it carefully. It became clear to me that to assess Franklin's work on Locke one had first to know Lawson's *Politica*, a text I had not previously come across. Reading the *Politica* gradually suggested to me its suitability for a full-scale study. Manifestly an interesting and sophisticated work, it was just as obviously not a 'classic' and was now being proffered in the usual terms as a suitable case for elevation. Had it ever been significant? If so had it been valued as Professor Franklin valued it; and what in the text might have made it of service?

Initially I was encouraged by what I took to be distortions in Franklin's account typical of the standard vocabulary of textual appraisal and promotion he was employing, but I did not know whether it would be possible to sustain an account of the text and its fate in alternative terms. This I believe I have done, although I have minimised cross-reference to my earlier work, so that this study may stand as independently as possible.

However, what also became clear to me as I began this study was that numerous seventeenth-century specialists knew of Lawson and his work and thought that 'doing him' was well overdue. I concluded that there must be some very good reason why they seemed happy to let me try. Was this overwork, generosity, or something worse? That I could be courting disaster by entering a highly populated field of intensely cultivated polemicism has occurred to me more than occasionally.

Despite my native suspicion, the process of educating myself to wear an additional academic hat has been one of the great pleasures of my life, both for the inherent interest, demands and excitement of the subject matter and for the company I have found myself keeping. For the first few years my research and re-education was sustained largely through correspondence with seventeenth-century specialists, all of whom generously answered questions, gave constructive advice and even unsolicited information; and I dread to think I have overlooked anyone in the thanks listed below.

The substance of my book should speak for itself, but there are several points that should be noted here precisely because the reader might share my qualms. First, this is a lost opportunity to deal with the life and thought of George Lawson as a whole. This is, to labour the point, because the study takes its place in the context of a research project that would make a book of such scope inappropriate. In any case, but for the *Politica*, a full-scale study of Lawson would hardly seem justifiable.

Secondly, because Lawson's text is not easily available and has been roughly treated when discussed, I thought it necessary to provide a detailed exposition. Tedious though some may find it, it is designed to deal with a range of minor textual issues and more wide-ranging contextual ones, as well as providing the groundwork for the critical explication of the major problems raised by the work. Those familiar with the *Politica* may well make light work of Part II, those who are not will need to go carefully as a prelude to Part III.

Thirdly, Part III is by far the most difficult of the book. Lawson was not an easy thinker and raises complex historiographical and philosophical issues which do not make for light reading. Throughout, I have tried to keep the argument as simple as possible and this has meant burying in the notes many qualifications and concomitant comments on seventeenth-century political thought and its modern commentators. It was Gilbert Ryle, I think, who remarked that anyone who needed notes (to say nothing of parentheses) in developing an argument, was running into trouble. Part III may be a case in point.

Fourthly, it will rapidly become apparent that in reading Lawson and in trying to frame his text contextually, I have felt the need to go well beyond what we now deem political literature in general and that of seventeenth-century England in particular. Given modern specialisation this raises difficulties. Parts of the text carry a litter of names with which the seventeenth-century specialist and/or political theorist, may not be familiar. So at times the prose is fractured by synoptic descriptions of people and their parenthesised dates, something I find irritating if I am familiar with the subject matter and invaluable when I am not. I have assumed others are as unreasonable. As I am writing for seventeenth-century specialists in political theory and in English intellectual history, I have been arbitrarily selective in giving such guidelines. This is to lurch between teaching grandmother to suck eggs and taking away her rocking chair.

Finally, as this is one of a series of linked studies, there are, especially towards the end, intimations of arguments and concepts I want to take up in the future on a more theoretical level. These concern metaphor and concept formation; the creation of a linguistic domain of the political, and the semantics of its rhetorical manipulation once such a domain is relatively standardised. Given the issues involved, the illustrative comments here, in advance of the theory, are rudimentary. In a perfect world, everything could be done at once and nothing be repeated – except the thanks offered in general to all who have helped. These are now repeated in particular and with great pleasure.

Through correspondence and in many cases through direct discussion, and other kindnesses, especially in the early stages, I should like to thank: Dr Trish Crawford (University of Western Australia), Dr Ian Green (University of Belfast), Dr John Gascoigne and Dr Damian Grace (University of New South Wales), Dr Neil Keeble (University of Stirling), Dr Helen Long (La Trobe University), Dr Geoffrey Nuttall, Dr Margaret Sampson (University of Newcastle, New South Wales), Professor Gordon Schochet (Rutgers University), Dr John Tinkler (University of New South Wales), and Dr Richard Tuck (Jesus College, Cambridge).

Research trips to Britain have been made unforgettably stimulating and thoroughly enjoyable very largely by the friendship and expert help of Harro Höpfl (University of Lancaster), Ian Maclean (The Queen's College, Oxford) and John Morrill (Selwyn College, Cambridge).

Special thanks are also owed to: Felicity and Professor John Pocock (the Johns Hopkins University), Linda and Professor Willie Lamont (University of Sussex) who played such a large part in making my stay at the Folger Library so rewardingly valuable, and Professors Lamont and Pocock for inviting me to participate in the Folger Center for the History of British Political Thought. My thanks also to: the late Sir Jasper More of Linley Hall, Salop, for encouragement, help and hospitality, especially with respect to biographical matters; Jack and Rob Wood, of the Three Tuns, Bishops Castle, who so generously housed me whilst I worked in Shropshire; Mrs Marion Halford of the Shropshire County Records Office; and Ian Roberts of the Yorkshire Archaeological Society. Despite crashing discs and crumbling software, Kathie Meagher managed to get a manuscript to the publishers, a remarkable achievement. Thereafter, Ann O'Quigley copy-edited a trying text with expertise and patience.

The manuscript was read and unquestionably improved by my friends Dr Tony Cousins (Macquarie University), Willie Lamont, Professor Doug McCallum (University of New South Wales), Dr Jonathan Scott (Victoria University of Wellington), the ever constructive and patient Dr Mark Goldie (Churchill College, Cambridge) and finally Averil Condren, who not only improved the prose all the above had criticised, but produced yet another index. Allegra Condren kindly helped with the concordance and with many parenthetical dates.

I am grateful to: Professor Gregorio Piaia of the University of Padua for an invitation to speak on Lawson and Marsilius for the Convegno Internazionale su Marsilio de Padova (1979); the Australian Research Grants Scheme for two awards facilitating research in Britain; the University of New South Wales Arts Faculty for a further grant; the Folger Library and Institute and all involved with the Center for the History of British Political Thought, which is supported by grants from the Research Programs Division of the National Endowment for the Humanities, the Ben Snow Memorial Trust, the George Washington University and the Exxon Education Foundation; and the Australasian Historians of Medieval and Early Modern Europe who are supported by nothing but their generosity and expertise.

I remain responsible for any blunders in the following pages, but with so many professional debts becoming debts of friendship, I am sure I can live with them.

TEXTS USED AND A CONCORDANCE FOR THE *POLITICA*

References to the manuscripts and printed works of George Lawson are in the text. The only substantial manuscript discussed is the 'Amica dissertatio'. A number of other shorter manuscripts attributed to Lawson are also held in the Dr Williams's Library. See Roger Thomas, *The Baxter Treatises*, DWL, Occasional Paper 8, London, 1959. Unless otherwise stated, references to and quotations from the *Politica* are to Starkey's second edition of 1689. This is because, the format being less cramped, it is much easier to work from than the first edition of 1660. It is also more easily available. The differences between the two editions are as follows: the second edition carries no prefatory schema; it has a few misnumbered pages; punctuation varies slightly (the occasional full stop is replaced by a colon); the spelling is modernised (e.g. 'errour' becomes 'error', words ending in 'ie' end in 'y'); the second edition also carries marginal headings. As the 1660 edition is a Thomason tract (E1024(3)), thus on microfilm, I have provided a page number concordance.

During the course of this work I have consulted a number of copies of both editions, largely in search of signs of later use. Thomason's own copy carries no annotations but for his usual indication of purchase date. The 1660 copy held at the British Library of Economic and Political Science (LSE) carries a number of pencil marks, but little or nothing can be extrapolated from them. The same can be said for the volume once owned by William Corker (d. 1702), Fellow of Trinity College, Cambridge, now held in the college library. The annotations on the University of New South Wales 1689 copy by James Winter (?) at least indicate that Lawson was still being read during the nineteenth century.

My thanks are due to the following libraries for access to their Lawsonia: Bodleian Library, Oxford; the Folger Shakespeare Library, Washington; the British Library; the British Library of Economic and Political Science; the Dr Williams's Library, London; the Queen's College Library, Oxford; King's College Library, Cambridge; Trinity College Library, Cambridge; the Menzies Library, University of New South Wales.

CONCORDANCE

1660	1689	1660	1689	1660	1689
1	2	48	83	94	162
2	3	49	84	95	164
3	5	50	86	96	166
5	8	51	88	97	167
6	9	52	89	98	169
7	12	53	91	99	171
8	13	54	92	100	173
9	15	55	94	101	174
10	17	56	96	102	176
11	19	57	97	103	178
12	20	58	99	104	179
13	22	59	101	105	181
14	24	60	102	106	183
15	25	61	104	107	185
16	27	62	106	108	186
17	29	63	108	109	188
18	31	64	110	110	190
19	32	65	111	111	191
20	34	66	113	112	193
21	35	67	114	113	195
22	38	68	116	114	197
23	39	69	118	115	199
24	41	70	120	116	200
25	43	71	121	117	202
26	44	72	124	118	204
27	46	73	125	119	206
28	48	74	127	120	208
29	49	75	130	121	210
30	51	76	131	122	211
31	53	77	133	123	213
32	54	78	135	124	215
33	56	79	137	125	216
34	58	80	138	126	218
35	59	81	140	127	220
36	63	82	142	128	222
37	63b	83	143	129	224
38	66	84	145	130	225
39	68	85	147	131	227
40	70	86	149	132	229
41	72	87	150	133	230
42	74	88	152	134	232
43	76	89	154	135	234
44	78	90	155	136	235
45	80	91	157	137	237
46	81	92	159	138	239
47	81b	93	160		

CONCORDANCE

1660	1689	1660	1689	1660	1689
139	241	187	324	235	403
140	242	188	321b	236	404
141	244	189	325	237	406
142	246	190	325b	238	408
143	247	191	328	239	409
144	249	192	332	240	412
145	251	193	332b	241	414
146	252	194	333	242	415
147	254	195	333b	243	417
148	256	196	337	244	419
149	257	197	338	245	421
150	259	198	340	246	422
151	261	199	342	247	424
152	262	200	344	248	426
153	264	201	345	249	428
154	266	202	346	250	430
155	267	203	349	251	431
156	269	204	351	252	433
157	271	205	352	253	435
158	272	206	354	254	437
159	274	207	356	255	439
160	276	208	357	256	440
161	277	209	359	257	442
162	279	210	361	258	444
163	281	211	363	259	446
164	282	212	364	260	448
165	284	213	366	261	450
166	286	214	368	262	452
167	287	215	369	263	454
168	289	216	371	264	455
169	291	217	373		
170	293	218	374		
171	294	219	376		
172	296	220	378		
173	297	221	379		
174	299	222	381		
175	301	223	283		
176	303	224	384		
177	305	225	386		
178	306	226	338		
179	308	227	389		
180	310	228	391		
181	311	229	393		
182	313	230	394		
183	315	231	396		
184	316	232	398		
185	318	233	299		
186	320	234	401		

ABBREVIATIONS

CSP Dom.	*Calendar of State Papers, Domestic*
DNB	*Dictionary of National Biography*
HSB	Hereford Diocese, Subscription Books
HVB	Hereford Diocese, Visitation Books
DWL	Dr Williams's Library
EHR	*English Historical Review*
HJ	*The Historical Journal*
MFP	Sir Jasper More Family Papers Relating to the 17th Century, held in the Shropshire County Records Office.
SCRO	Shropshire County Records Office
SLSL	Shrewsbury Local Studies Library
GPR	*Giggleswick Parish Records, The Parish Register of Giggleswick, I, 1558–1669* The Yorkshire Archaeological Society 1984, ed. R. W. Hoyle
MPR	Mainstone Parish Records, in SCRO
MoPR	More Parish Records in SCRO; and *The Registers of More, 1569–1812*, The Parish Register Society, London, 1900
Reliq. Baxt.	*Reliquiae Baxterianae*, ed. Sylvester, London, 1696
TSANHS	*Transactions of the Shropshire Archaeological and Natural History Society*
TSAS	*Transactions of the Shropshire Archaeological Society*
Venn *Alum. Cant.*	J. and J. A. Venn, *Alumni Cantabrigienses*
	LAWSON'S WORKS
'Amica diss.'	Amica dissertatio, *Baxter Treatises*, 1 fol. 99–130^b item 9, DWL

xvii

Exam.	*An Examination of the Political Part of Mr. Hobbs, His Leviathan,* London, 1657
Hebrewes	*An Exposition of the Epistle to Hebrewes,* London, 1662
Pol.	*Politica sacra et civilis,* London, 1689
Theo-Pol.	*Theo-Politica,* London, 1659
Magna charta	*Magna charta ecclesiae universalis,* 1665

Part I

HISTORIOGRAPHICAL AND BIOGRAPHICAL PRELIMINARIES

1

Historiography

> Mr. George Lawson was a person of such universal learning and general esteem, that the works that already are extant of him and those that he hath perfected under his own hand for the press, shall stop my pen and supercede my intention of giving a larger character of him.

So wrote the auctioneer Millington, or his phrasemonger, to advertise the sale of George Lawson's books in 1681.[1] It is a pity the pen was stopped and intentions superceded, for within twenty years this man of such learning and esteem was to fall into an obscurity from which only the assiduous ink dippings of the twentieth century have begun, somewhat by accident, to rescue him.

If it was assumed familiarity with Lawson that really stopped the moving pen, it is symptomatic of Lawson's seventeenth-century fate. The apparent dissemination of his ideas and the affirmations of his importance are noticeably discrepant with the willingness of others to enlarge upon him or his work. As we shall see, Baxter, especially, claims he thought highly of Lawson and so did his more politically active friend John Humfrey. Locke certainly knew his work, may well have used it and, implicitly, criticised it; Defoe, as others certainly did, may have paraphrased and popularised it. An eighteenth-century satire, aimed at less than the most arcanely learned, parodied and alluded to Lawson's *Politica* in a way that assumed a continuing public esteem; and one pen still moved in private marginalia when Napoleon was a threat to England. But a learned memorialist prefacing the collected works of Dr John Owen in 1826 could only remark on *a* Mr Lawson who had, like Owen, written an exposition of St Paul's Epistle to the Hebrews. He is quite absent from Benjamin Hanbury's compendious *Historical Memorials Relating to the Independents*.[2] The first history of political thought some thirty years later makes no mention of Lawson either; so I think, by the

---

[1] *Catalogus Librarum*, Printed Books of Sale, 1681–95, London.
[2] William Orme in Dr John Owen, *Works*, ed. W. Russell, 1826, vol. 1; B. Hanbury, *Memorials*, Fisher, London, 3 vols., 1839–44.

1850s, the pens had seized up entirely and the charting of Lawson's significance is made doubly difficult.

I shall suggest, however, that the significance was probably considerable at least until the end of the seventeenth century, and this study should be seen as a partial compensation for the stopped pens of the past. It is also an attempt to rectify the consequences of the more fluid ones of the present.

The uncertain process of rehabilitating George Lawson began, as far as I can tell, with A. H. Maclean's doctoral thesis of 1947, 'The Origins of the Political Opinions of John Locke'. The only copy of this that either I or Cambridge University Library know of disappeared from the university library *circa* 1973. Scholarly paranoia might suggest a cosmic plot to ensure Lawson's obscurity, but Maclean had published an essay abstracted from his thesis in 1949, in which he emphasised strongly the similarities between Lawson and Locke.[3] A few years later, John Bowle gave some attention to Lawson's *Examination*, which he considered the finest of the early attacks on Hobbes. His criteria of assessment were, however, obscure, and the *Politica* remained very much on the periphery of Bowle's vision.[4] Indeed, Maclean's invitation to take Lawson's major work seriously was not accepted for some years. In 1960 Peter Laslett produced the splendid edition of Locke's *Two Treatises* that made possible the gradual resurgence of interest in John Locke, and in this edition he makes passing comment on Lawson, but not of the sort that was to encourage further interest. The overall gist of his remarks is to suggest a Lawson of a less abstract turn of mind than Locke, who coincidentally shares some of Locke's arguments; most readers would have been reassured that Locke was the significant man, comforting not least because there was now a fine edition to work from whereas there was, and remains, no modern printing of the *Politica*.

The most substantial, and now best-known account of Lawson's *Politica* is to be found in Julian Franklin's *John Locke and the Theory of Sovereignty*. It is this work which really took up Maclean's neglected claim. Lawson was heralded as coherent, radical and original, and as *the* theorist who *really* solved – a generation before Locke – the problem of sovereignty in a mixed, or limited, constitution (if such are ever 'solved'). Locke, we are told, too radical for mainstream Whigs, had found the answer to constitutional sovereignty and resistance 'ready-made' in Lawson's *Politica*; and so Locke became 'the source through which Lawson's theory of sovereignty

[3] A. H. Maclean, 'George Lawson and John Locke', *Cambridge Historical Journal*, 9, 1 (1949), pp. 72ff.
[4] John Bowle, *Hobbes and His Critics*, London, 1952; but see M. Goldie, 'The Reception of Hobbes', in *The Cambridge History of Political Thought, 1450–1700*, ed. J. H. Burns, Cambridge University Press, forthcoming, for a more satisfactory discussion.

was transmitted'.[5] It is a depressing thought that these claims are central to any assessment of Franklin's book and precious few reviewers showed any familiarity with Lawson. It would also be fair to say that Franklin's lucid chapter on Lawson can, and has been, taken as a surrogate for the *Politica*. This too has been less than encouraging, as, for all its merits, Franklin's account is forced and full of errors. These issues will be discussed where appropriate; and, as the first part of my conclusion will make clear, Franklin's principal promotional contention, concerning Locke's lifting a theory ready-made from Lawson, is sheer fantasy.

What is of more immediate consequence is that, first, Franklin's work comes at the end of a somewhat hiccoughing move to rehabilitate Lawson marked largely by the attempt to insert the *Politica* into a prearranged his- toriographical tradition between Hobbes and Locke. His identity has been shaped in counter-point to theirs. Take away a faith in the historiographical usefulness of this tradition *per se* and these thinkers become less obvious standards by which to measure Lawson. Nevertheless, if it was originally the importance of Locke that helped draw some derivative attention to Law- son's *Politica*, it is now the remarkable fluidity of Locke studies that reinforces a need for that attention. The conventional patterns of textual relationships and authorial influence are breaking down nowhere as they are in Locke scholarship; a highly schematic tradition of great names is ceasing manifestly to be of much explanatory power or contextual enlightenment and this makes it both easier and more important to give serious attention to the *Politica*. In the first part of my conclusion, I shall pay some attention to Lawson's relationship to both Hobbes and Locke as a means of refocussing on the *Politica*. If anything, my arguments will further complicate the puta- tive patterns of intellectual relationship surrounding Locke and now obscur- ing the nature of his significance.

Secondly, as Franklin's work most clearly shows, the criteria of judgement employed to elevate Lawson into the historiographical firmament of Great Political Thinkers revolves around the standard rhetoric of originality, coher- ence and influence, with a top dressing of the 'radical', uncertainly modified by reference to 'moderation'. All this seems to me to be as unsatisfactory as the tradition into which Lawson is being placed. My own account presup- poses and illustrates a different approach to the historiography of political thought and the appraisal of its texts, which, in the last analysis, recognises both that there is a certain arbitrariness underlying the fate of texts in the

---

[5] Julian Franklin, *John Locke and the Theory of Sovereignty*, Cambridge University Press, 1978, preface, chaps. 3 and 4, quotations from p. 123. James Tully, 'Current Thinking on Sixteenth- and Seventeenth-Century Political Theory', *Historical Journal*, 24, 2 (1981), is uncertain just what relationship is being posited by Franklin. He may have been phased by its simple extremity.

history of ideas and that argumentative 'faults' perhaps more than virtues play a part in the establishment of fame.[6]

There is a sense in which my own early essays on Lawson operated perforce within the terms of the received historiographical context of a pantheon of great thinkers amongst whom Lawson might be given some place. Initially I took issue with Franklin's claims about the logical coherence and originality of the *Politica*, arguing that if it needs to be seen as an appendage to the more famous, Lawson was better seen as a Marsilian than a proto-Lockean;[7] but, as I moved from this sort of *ad hoc* criticism to a more general account of Lawson's *Politica*,[8] others were also moving towards accounts of Lawson's work which were not reliant upon the great tradition, or upon an inherited rhetoric of textual promotion. In discussing Richard Baxter's intermittent dabbling with political and millenial fireworks, William Lamont had a number of interesting things to say about Lawson, who began to assume an important place in Baxter's world.[9] Brian Tierney in a powerful and perceptive argument about the continuity of medieval thought used Lawson as a culminating illustration of his arguments.[10]

The works of Salmon, Schochet and Tuck have discussed Lawson in the context of elaborating historically specific arguments about intellectual movements, to one side of any process of promotion.[11] Schochet, though not touching on the *Politica*, has correctly pointed to Lawson's ambivalent place in the context of patriarchal thought; Salmon managed simply to define Lawson beyond the limits of a tradition of resistance thought in the seventeenth century; Tuck has placed Lawson, perhaps too firmly, within the context of a Presbyterian tradition of rights theory, and this has been further discussed by James Tully.[12] All of these authors have had worthwhile things to say on Lawson, but no overall picture of his major text, or his thought as a whole, has emerged. In all cases this has been due, understandably, to the fact that a certain theme which is partially revealed in Lawson

---

[6] C. Condren, *The Status and Appraisal of Classic Texts*, Princeton University Press, 1985, esp. pt 3.

[7] C. Condren, 'Resistance and Sovereignty in Lawson's *Politica*', *HJ*, 24, 3 (1981), pp. 673ff.; 'George Lawson and the *Defensor pacis*', *Medioevo*, 5–6 (1980), pp. 595ff.; to a lesser extent, 'The Image of Utopia', *Moreana*, 69 (1981), pp. 101ff.

[8] C. Condren, '*Sacra* Before *Civilis*', *The Journal of Religious History*, 11, 2 (1981), pp. 524ff.

[9] William Lamont, *Richard Baxter and the Millennium*, Croom Helm, London, 1979.

[10] Brian Tierney, *Religion, Law and the Growth of Constitutional Thought, 1150–1650*, Cambridge University Press, 1982.

[11] J. W. H. Salmon, *The French Religious Wars in English Political Thought*, Oxford University Press, 1959; Gordon Schochet, *Patriarchalism in Political Thought*, Oxford University Press, 1975; Richard Tuck, *Natural Rights Theories: Their Origin and Development*, Cambridge University Press, 1979. See also J. W. Gough, *The Fundamental Law in English Constitutional Thought*, Oxford University Press, 1955, p. 121.

[12] Tully, 'Current Thinking', pp. 478ff.

has been the principal preoccupation. Lawson, in short, has never really been a focus of anybody's attention. Even Millington tumbled his books indiscriminately with those of three other defunct ministers, and may have stopped his pen in order to say something about them before the proceeds of the sale were to be handed to grieving beneficiaries. Where Lawson has come close to being a centre of attraction, the canvas has been distorted, as I have suggested, by the need to stitch him according to the prior threads of an historiographical tradition of relatively modern invention stretched upon an ill-working framework of appraisal.

For all this, the noticeable interest in the *Politica* has now reached the stage at which Lawson is making his textbook début. Given the riches of the seventeenth century this is an achievement enough to justify a special study. Had Allen's two-volume work on English political thought in the seventeenth century been completed, the début may have been made a generation ago, and the specialist studies may by now have been legion.[13] Only Franklin and Goldie have said anything of the fate of the *Politica*; both have looked, appropriately enough, at the Allegiance Controversy and, of course, at Locke. The crucial point has been whether Lawson was as radical as Locke, or whether it is the radical resistance theorists who use him. Goldie's work is invaluable here but, as I shall suggest, the questions around the use of Lawson have been less than helpfully formulated.[14]

Indeed, there is a sense in which at each stage of this study we have to start again, which is not to suggest any completeness about my argument. This is an exploratory study. Although I am able to add considerably to the little that has been known of Lawson's life, the biographical background – like the historiographical – remains sketchy and I suspect that the 'larger character' that Mr Millington's pen forbore to draw must await evidence now lost forever. In any case, my concern is predominantly with one work,

[13] W. J. Allen, *English Political Thought, 1603–44*, London, 1938. A second volume was intended to run through to 1660; Quentin Skinner, *The Foundations of Modern Political Thought*, Cambridge University Press, 1978, vol. 2, p. 338; Mark Goldie, *Absolutismus, Parliamentarismus und Revolution in England, Handbuch der Politischen Ideen*, vol. 3, *Neuzeit von den Konfessionskriegen bis zur Aufklarung*, ed. I. Fetscher, Munich, 1985. One may now be legitimately surprised, especially given the subject matter, that Lawson's *Politica* rates only a passing footnote in C. C. Weston and J. R. Greenberg, *Subjects and Sovereigns*, Cambridge University Press, 1981, pp. 324–5, and a nod, via Franklin, p. 376.
[14] Mark Goldie, 'The Revolution of 1689 and the Structure of Political Argument', *Bulletin of Research in the Humanities*, 83 (1980), pp. 473ff; and 'The Roots of True Whiggism, 1688–94', in *History of Political Thought*, 1, 2 (1980), pp. 195ff. Richard Ashcraft, *Revolutionary Politics and Locke's Two Treatises of Government*, Princeton University Press, 1986, is the most recent and extreme example, predicated as it is so heavily on the search for 'radicals'. Lawson it seems, is too moderate to provide a useful context for Locke. So, although seeming to build upon Franklin's account, Ashcraft's rather distorting couple of pages on Lawson treats the *Politica* in the marginalising manner of Laslett. This is a pity as there is value in Ashcraft's antidote to Franklin and Maclean.

the *Politica sacra et civilis* of 1660 and 1689. It is this which justifiably has attracted attention as Lawson's most considered and sustained excursus into political theorising. Although formally incomplete (a second volume on administration was to follow), it stands, overall, as a rigorously yet simply argued and acutely perceptive, view of the principles of politics in church and state – especially as they were taken to apply to England and its great upheavals. As such it is difficult to see why it has not attracted more attention, notwithstanding the riches of seventeenth-century political writing. Even here, my own text, like Lawson's, cannot pretend to completeness, that is always fugitive in the history of ideas.

This then is a critical introduction to Lawson's work, through which I aim at some renegotiation of the character and significance of seventeenth-century political thought in general. Immediately, I hope to make Lawson's political thought intelligible; to reveal the problems it seems most designed to confront, the strategies of argument it displays, and the presuppositions which help to make it coherent. Thereafter, I look at its fate in the hands of others in the final stages of the English Revolution. Again the argument is partial, this is because the account I offer is illustrative of what I take to be broader patterns of textual employment, and because those thinkers I discuss are themselves left very incomplete by my concentrating on the fate of the *Politica* through them.

Throughout I assume little knowledge of Lawson but much of the seventeenth century. At every stage of the argument I hope that not only will a more carefully stitched cloth emerge, but also that there will be some partial unstitching of the established ways of weaving images of past texts. Perhaps the whole fabric of the English Revolution and that elusive but richly worked thread of the rise of modern political thought might be reassessed through Lawson's *Politica*. In this respect, a work laid down in time and relatively neglected has advantages of manageability over those monstrous yardages that have been trodden time and again into the scholarly mud.

The place to start is not with the cloth, but with the needle in the haystack, with the life of the man who wrote the book that books are yet to be written about.

2

Biography

In a mysterious and uncharacteristically firm statement, the *DNB* entry on George Lawson insists that he was not a Yorkshireman.[1] If the authors were attacking received opinion, they neither give grounds for their view, nor any alternative birth place for Lawson. He seems, however, to have been born in the tiny Yorkshire village of Lancliffe, a clustering of stone houses thrown against the spectacular edge of Kirkby fell, Ribblesdale and the expansive green surges of Lancashire. What may have been the Lawson home still stands close to the house in which William Paley was later to be born. In a paean of praise to Lawson's *Politica*, Dr John Carr, himself an eminent son of the village and a relation of Lawson's, calls Lancliffe the envy of York, or even Athens, for giving birth to Lawson.[2]

> *Te tantum genuit vicis brevis, anulus orbis*
> *Lancliff, nascenti conscia terra mihi.*
> *Eborac'invideant, vel Athenae . . .*[3]

Hyperbole or not, this tells us clearly enough where to look for the beginnings of George Lawson. The Emmanuel College archives for 1615 record a signature which Venn, who had to cope with numerous George Lawsons from Yorkshire, hazards may be that George Lawson who later became a divine, as well as critic and supporter of the parliamentarian cause.[4] Subsequent handwriting confirms the signature, and Lawson claimed an MA from Emmanuel.[5] On this basis, I turned to Lancliffe at the turn of the century for evidence of birth.

The village and its surrounds seethes with Lawsons intricately intermarried with the similarly large clans of Paley and Carr, but only two George

[1] *DNB*, vol. 11, p. 730: cf. A. H. Maclean, 'George Lawson and John Locke', *Cambridge Historical Journal*, 9, 1 (1949), p. 27.
[2] John Carr, 1632–75. Deputy Regius Professor of Physics, Oxford. He was a pupil of Giggleswick School and attended Christ's College.
[3] The dedicatory poem appears in both editions of Lawson's *Politica*, so any errors could have been corrected.
[4] *Emmanuel College Archives*, chap. 1.4, fo. 129; J. and J. A. Venn, *Alum. Cant.*, vol. 55.
[5] MPR: MoPR; HSB, Mainstone, 1/1/A4/1.

Lawsons are entered in the Giggleswick Parish registers during the appropriate period.[6] An entry for 7 October 1600 records the baptism of George, son of Lawrence, and the more likely entry, dated 2 May 1598 records the baptism of George, son of Thomas, specifically of Lancliffe. Thomas Lawson himself had been born in 1564 and could have been the son of Hugh, Richard or Roland.[7] He had married Ellen Watkinson (born 1569/70) on 1 December 1596. On 9 November 1603 they baptised a daughter, Margaret, and on 14 November 1610 Ellen Lawson was buried. There is no record of George Lawson's early education. He does not seem to have attended the most likely school, Giggleswick, although a good number of the Lawson clan did before going on to Cambridge.[8] The fact that he was admitted as a sizar at Emmanuel indicates that his father was either poor or parsimonious.[9] The whole village may have been in somewhat straitened circumstances at this time, as the larger families had clubbed together to buy out the Darcy family who had acquired much of the Giggleswick area after the Pilgrimage of Grace.[10]

One of the most distorting facets of English seventeenth-century history is that firm evidence of people so often tends to erupt around points of trouble or of administrative punctuation. In this respect record of Lawson's life is typical. He is born, he signs his name on a college register, and from then there is precious little until 1636 when Lawson's title to serve as *stipendierius* at Mainstone in Shropshire is recorded. The entry, however, also states that Lawson had been ordained by the Bishop of Chester in 1619 and reordained in 1624, presumably because of an irregularity with the first ordination; that he had been licensed to serve by the vicar general of the Bishop of Hereford in October 1632; and that on 22 June 1636 he had been licensed to preach by Archbishop Laud.[11]

It seems from this that Lawson, typically, had been on the edges of an ecclesiastical career; a curate and a canon of Hereford, he hovered at the fringes of larger establishments with no living of his own. If this is so, the appointment to Mainstone, probably in 1635, was no great transformation in his fortunes. In 1607, Edward Froysell, then Minister of Mainstone, certified that the church had no glebe lands, and when Lawson was appointed, Mainstone had been appropriated to the distant parish of

[6] *GPR*, Baptisms, 1590–1604. The ubiquity of the name Lawson allegedly arises from the traditional date of the Settle Fair, held on St Lawrence's day. I am indebted to Mr Ian Roberts whose great knowledge of Giggleswick local history has been of much help.

[7] *GPR*, Baptisms, 1560–80. There is a later Hugh, son of Thomas Lawson, up at Christ's Cambridge, in 1650. Ian Roberts, however, suggests that Richard is the most likely father on the basis of the five family trees he has constructed.

[8] Giggleswick School Register.

[9] No degree is recorded. He was admitted 15 June; matriculated, 1615.

[10] Sir Arthur Darcy acquired Lancliffe perhaps, suggests, Ian Roberts because of his loyalty.

[11] HVB, 1636–94, Register of Titles, 14.

Wigmore from which it was served.[12] By this time Lawson was certainly married and living conveniently close to Mainstone, in More.[13] It was whilst he was stipendiary curate in Mainstone that he recorded in a neat semi-italic hand the birth of a son: 'On April 3rd to George Lawson and his wife Anne, a son Jeremiah, baptized on the fifth.'[14] A list of church wardens was drawn up, though not so neatly, in the same hand, for the years 1635–7; and on 10 April 1637 he entered a memorandum to the effect that the parishioners had not (the negative is an interlinear insertion) agreed that those who had purchased tenements and had served as church wardens could represent their tenants in that office.[15] This entry, to which I shall return in a more theoretical context, seems to have been the last thing signed by Lawson as Mainstone stipendiary.

Already, however, Lawson's name was eddying on the edges of the Shrewsbury Ship Money controversy. By 1636, Shrewsbury had yet to be convinced that it really needed to pay money enough to build and equip a 450 ton ship as protection against 'Turks and other pirates in these troublesome times'.[16] Indeed, according to Henry Beaumont, from 1636, petitions for exemption from ship money had gradually given way to outright refusal to pay it. John Trench had claimed that in trying to collect the money he had been systematically abused; and the town council was to be reprimanded for failing to pay all the previous year's levy.[17] Sir Paul Harris, Sheriff of Shropshire in 1638, explained that Shrewsbury's failure to pay up had been caused by a purely local issue, the 'division and factions' surrounding an appointment to St Chads in Shrewsbury.[18] For Shrewsbury people this would have been an important issue. St Chads was an ancient and well established church, which had been collegiate until 1548.[19] At the centre of the divisions were Richard Poole and the Mainstone stipendiary, George Lawson.

A report on the conflict describes Poole as of the (Calvinist) school of Perkins and Downham, but lacking sufficient Greek to warrant appointment to the headship of Shrewsbury School. He was, moreover, a pluralist who

---

[12] W. G. Clark Maxwell, 'The Rural Deanery of Clun in the Seventeenth Century', *TSANHS*, 3rd series (1901–10), pp. 319–20.

[13] HSB, Mainstone, 1, 1632–64, 1/A4/1.

[14] MPR, 3277/1/2. Like most examples of his record-keeping, the entry is in Latin.

[15] *Ibid.*

[16] Henry Beaumont, 'Shrewsbury and Ship Money', *TSAS*, 5th series, 49 (1937–8), p. 34 citing Shrewsbury MSS 6.211.

[17] *Ibid.*, p. 34.

[18] *Ibid.*, p. 34; cf. Kevin Sharpe, 'Crown, Parliament and Locality: Government and Communication in Early Stuart England', *EHR*, 100, 399 (1986), p. 345 for ease with which much ship money was collected.

[19] A. T. Grayton, 'Colleges, Shrewsbury and St. Chads', in R. B. Pugh, ed., *The Victoria County History, Shropshire*, vol. 2.

'by colour of popular election has thrust himself into [St Chads]'.[20] By contrast Lawson is described as 'a very able scholar, well read in the Fathers, Schoolmen, Councils and history of all sorts, a great honourer of Archbishop Laud, and upon all occasions ready to plead for him and justify his proceedings'.[21] Lawson, already licensed to preach by Laud, received his open support, presumably backed up by the patron of Mainstone, the King. The consequent directive was clear enough: Lawson was to become curate and preacher at St Chads and the Bishop of Lichfield and Coventry was to remove Poole.[22] Yet after such a direct command, the colour of popular election stayed fast, and the chastised Poole stayed at St Chads. A hundred years later the church tower toppled.

In the meantime the St Chads affair may not, as intimated by Sir Paul Harris, have been a distracting side-show; it may have been something of a symbolic rejection of royal policy and was at least symptomatic of how difficult it could be to apply royal policy even in what was to prove a strongly royalist town. Any prolongation or escalation of the conflict over St Chads, however, was avoided. A death twenty miles to the south in the village of More afforded room to manoeuvre.

William Biggs, MA, rector of More since 1616, was buried there on 16 March 1637. William Wilson, a temporary curate took his place for a few weeks or so and then Richard More of Linley Hall having the living of More at his disposal, presented it to George Lawson.[23] There are several things to note in this apparently fast-moving and only roughly datable series of events. Most simply, Lawson effectively changed his living from Mainstone to More after 10 April 1637, either having recognised that he could not get St Chads, or preferring the security of More against the possibility of a hostile parish. As he was already living in More, Lawson almost certainly would have been known to Richard More. He might even have asked for the job, although, as I shall suggest below, there is some slight evidence to suggest that, on the margins of another controversy, he may already have commended himself to Richard More.[24]

---

[20] *CSP Dom.*, 1637–8, p. 55. There is something a touch ritualistic about the expression, see Hooker on the general phenomenon, *Laws of Ecclesiastical Polity*, Dent, London, 1965, 5.80.13.

[21] *CSP Dom.*, 1637–8, para. 89. This is perhaps one reason why Lawson is later described as tending towards Arminianism in the *DNB*, and also by Maclean, 'George Lawson and John Locke', pp. 72–3.

[22] *CSP Dom.*, 1637, para. 55.

[23] MoPR, 102–3; Clark Maxwell, 'The Rural Deanery of Clun', p. 320.

[24] The More parish registers are badly damaged by damp (the church had no damp course), and by the results of nineteenth-century alum treatment which has turned much of the parchment black, so when Lawson started to make the entries in a shift away from the vernacular, is not certain, but it was between 10 April and 22 April.

Further, whether by intention or not, More's action in offering Lawson the living was of some benefit to all parties in the dispute over St Chads. The parishioners got the man they preferred; Richard Poole could breathe more easily unless Laud wanted to reopen the issue by putting up another candidate;[25] a cause of hostility to the King could at least be pushed to one side; Laud, although he had not got his candidate into the Shrewsbury living, now saw his man in a secure living at a time and in a place where he increasingly needed vocal supporters; if one takes a broader view, Laud had seen, by Lawson's appointment, a small step taken in the direction of higher educational standards for the clergy. If wider issues were being played out in the St Chads controversy they seem to have been dispersed at Biggs's death and More's action. Yet there remains something superficially odd about Lawson's appointment. Richard More was an unlikely man to help out Archbishop Laud, even indirectly; and if Lawson was so open in praising all things Laudian he seems an odd choice for the rectory of More. To see how, it is necessary to look at the family and the living with which Lawson was to be associated for the rest of his life.

In situation the village of More was not unlike Lancliffe. A post-Dooms-day-Book village some five miles north of Bishops Castle, it lies with the Stipperstone range of hills to the north, the great ridge of Long Mynd to the east, the Clun Forest to the south and the Welsh Hills to the west. Isolated and obscure at first glance, it might not have provided much of a living. Its poverty had been attested in 1291 and again in the Valor of Henry VIII.[26] But the poverty may have been exaggerated. When drawn up, the Valor was arguably unreliable, tending to underestimate the value of livings; and Hill has calculated that there was in any case a five- or sixfold increase in the value of rural livings between 1530 and 1640.[27] Specifically, James had enlarged the charter of Bishops Castle in 1617 which may well indicate the sort of growth and importance of its burgesses that might have created a multiplier effect on outlying villages.[28]

According to tradition, the Lord of More, as constable of the monarch's forces, was obliged to contribute some 200 footmen to any army taken into Wales on a war footing and to act as Royal Standard Bearer. By tradition this responsibility had been with the same family since the thirteenth

[25] Poole was to remain at St Chads until his death in 1644.
[26] J. C. Anderson, *Shropshire: Its Early History and Antiquities*, Willis and Sotheran, London, 1864, p. 474.
[27] Ian Green, 'Career Prospects and Clerical Conformity in the Early Stuart Church', *Past and Present*, 90 (1981), citing Christopher Hill, *Economic Problems of the Church from Archbishop Whitgift to the Long Parliament*, Oxford, 1963, p. 111.
[28] Anon. 'A Note Concerning the Enlargement of the Bishops Castle Charter of Elizabeth by James I, 1617', *TSAS*, 53, part 2 (1950), pp. 252ff.

century.[29] The late Sir Jasper More considered this antiquity somewhat fanciful, his family not buying the estates of More until the sixteenth century. The Richard More who appointed Lawson to his living was the son of Robert More of Linley. He succeeded to the More estates in 1604 and when his cousin Jasper was killed in a duel (1613) these were enlarged by Jasper's Larden estates. During the first decade of the seventeenth century, Richard, a burgess, was active in trade in Bishops Castle. In 1619 he married the sister of Sir Thomas Harris; was elected to the corporation of Bishops Castle in 1623; and was a bailiff of the borough in 1637.[30] Of greater interest, however, are his political and religious affiliations. More has been called a Puritan living in an area of discernible Puritan feeling.[31] The death of his father had prohibited his going up to university, yet it is recorded that by the age of ten he could read the Old Testament in Hebrew;[32] perhaps, like his near neighbour, Sir Robert Harley, he swam 'deep in the tide of fasting and humiliation'.[33]

In 1633, a young farmer, Enock ap Evan of Clun, had somewhat loudly murdered his mother and brother by decapitation. He had done so for no obvious reason. He was tried, condemned, hung and then his body mysteriously disappeared from the gibbet. In a pamphlet called *The Looking-Glasse of Schism* (1635), Peter Studely, one of the clergy of St Chads, had argued that the whole business was the result of a Puritan fanaticism which was rampant in the Clun region. Enock was known not to kneel in church and the disappearance of his body indicated a Puritan plot. More took up the pen to refute Studely's notion of cause and effect and to exonerate his neighbourhood from the charge of puritanism in *A True Relation of the Murders*. Enock, he argued, was a sad young man of no great ability, given to fits of depression. His eccentric distaste for kneeling arose from his belief that in leaving his legs behind, his body would receive uneven spiritual nourishment. After investigation, claims More, he and Sir Robert Howard found that the removal of the body of the murderer was no more than the work of a grieving sister, who had suffered so much that she was given no further

[29] Anderson, *Shropshire*, p. 474; Thomas Auden, *Shropshire*, 5th edn, Methuen, London, 1932, p. 165; Rev B. Blakeway, *The Sheriffs of Shropshire*, Eddowes, London, 1831, p. 215 who is followed by Burke, *Landed Gentry*.

[30] See *DNB* entry on Richard More; Anon., *TSAS*, 57, part 1 (1961), pp. 17–19; F. Lander, 'Bishops Castle Burgesses and Freemen', *TSAS*, 53 (1949), pp. 80ff.; Henry Weyman, 'The Members of Parliament for Bishops Castle', *TSANHS*, 10, 2nd series (1878–1900), pp. 46–7.

[31] W. F. Farrow, *The Great Civil War in Shropshire 1642–9*, Wilding, Shrewsbury, 1929, p. 27.

[32] Weyman, 'The MPs for Bishops Castle', pp. 46–7; Farrow, *Civil War*, pp. 16–17.

[33] George Yule, quoting Froysell on Harley, in *Puritans in Politics: The Religious Legislation of the Long Parliament*, Sutton Courtney, Oxford, 1982, p. 80. Froysell also delivered the funeral oration for More.

punishment. Despite the calm, rational and sympathetic tone adopted by More, he was refused licence to print until 1641, when he had the backing of Parliament. The hostility to Studely, however, is clear, and it is significant that he was prepared to wait and proceed with the matter.[34] Studely, unrepentant and also a firm royalist, was relieved of his living. More also made the official translation of Joseph Mede's *Clavis apocalipsin* (1643), indicating a serious interest in what we might call Puritan eschatology.

In a disputed election, during a period of disputed elections, More was elected to Parliament, as representative of Bishops Castle, along with his fellow justice in the murder enquiry, Sir Robert Howard.[35] More proved to be, as Farrow describes him, 'a strong parliament man'.[36] Although not recorded as speaking in the debates in Parliament, he gave substantial plate to the cause, was a committee man under the auspices of the Scandalous Ministers Act of 1642, and for a while, until his death in 1643, was on the county Sequestration Committee.[37]

Richard More, then, seems to have been a man of considerable religious interests, education, energy and political commitment. Despite his disavowal of 'puritanism', which *A True Relation* treats simply as a term of abuse, his apparent faith and affiliations clearly put him some distance from Laud's 'arminianism'. He would have been an unlikely Royal Standard Bearer for any hostile array winding into Wales. For all its apparent wildness of accusation, Studley's *Looking-Glasse* did reflect a smoking discontent around Clun.

In short, and more immediately to the point, everything that is known of Richard More indicates a hostility to the very things with which Lawson seems to have been associated when More appointed him to the living in his village. He also, no doubt, had sufficient power to rid himself of any priests he might find troublesome. It is, however, possible that Lawson commended himself to More by helping with the composition of *A True Relation*, for at the outset More refers to a minister in his neighbourhood to whom he gave his papers concerning the murder and Studley's understanding of it, and who reduced them to 'a methodicall confutation' (p. 5). Lawson was living in the right place at the right time and he is otherwise unmentioned among the many local ministers whose names are rounded up to form a crowlike gathering of priestly witnesses to different aspects of More's case. Methodical was a word that was to stick to Lawson. For whatever reason or reasons Lawson was appointed (there was rarely that much choice in

[34] Weyman, 'The MPs for Bishops Castle', pp. 46–7.
[35] *Ibid.*; D. Hirst, *The Representative of the People?* Cambridge University Press, 1977, pp. 137ff.
[36] Farrow, *Civil War*, p. 17.
[37] *Ibid.*, pp. 16–17, 117; D. Brunton and D. H. Pennington, *The Members of The Long Parliament*, Archon, Connecticut, 1968, p. 13.

Shropshire) he continued to serve the More family as rector and probably as tutor and educational adviser.[38] In these last capacities Lawson was most firmly associated with Richard More's eldest son.

Samuel More was of Lawson's generation, being forty-seven when his father died. He had been educated at Shrewsbury School and had married his cousin. He had three sons when Lawson was appointed to More: Richard was ten, Thomas nine, and Robert two, just a few months older than Lawson's own son. Lawson, I guess, educated Robert and Jeremiah together.[39] With Colonel Mytton, Samuel More was the principal parliamentarian commander in royalist Shropshire. In what was manifestly a clash of courage and incompetence, he defended Hopton Castle with some thirty men for a month against vastly superior forces despite Hopton's geographically untenable position. On surrender, the frustrated royalists killed all survivors but More (the walls had been defended after a breach), and More's own bitter and moving account of the siege has been reprinted a number of times.[40] Later, in succession, More commanded Montgomery and Monmouth castles in 1645, Hereford (1647) and Ludlow (1646–7).[41] In county committee work he carried on where his father had left off. In the meantime, his son Richard had taken a lieutenancy in Lord St John's regiment (1644), been admitted to Grays Inn (1646) and married a daughter of Sir Isaac Pennington. He was a member of the Committee of Compounding (1646–59) and a member of the Committee for the Advance of Money.

In turn the Pennington marriage linked the Mores with another Pennington son-in-law, John Corbet of Auson and Halson (1609–70) and husband of Abigail. This I believe is the Corbet actively hostile to the King in the Shrewsbury muster-master controversy preceding the outbreak of war.[42] During the war Corbet seems to have worked with Samuel More; he was, at different times, a commissioner for the trial of Charles I, a Councillor of State, a Chief Justice and a Commissioner to keep The Protector from danger. Later, despite the break-up of his own marriage, Richard More the younger was

[38] A long letter written by Richard More the younger to his brother Robert (MFP, SCRO) makes reference to Mr Lawson's educational advice being sought on what might be done with the allegedly useless Robert.

[39] Mauricius Helingus, *Versificatorius*, Nuremberg, 1590, a volume of Greek poetry selections in the More Church Library, has signatures of both boys in what seems to be the same ink with the same pen. Knowing when Robert was born, it was this that led me to look in the Mainstone Parish records around 1635 for the birth of Jeremy (Jeremiah).

[40] See Blakeway, *Sheriffs of Shropshire*, p. 217; cf. Thomas Wright, *The History and Antiquities of the Town of Ludlow*, Proctor and Jones, Ludlow. The original manuscript in the possession of Sir Jasper More is now illegible.

[41] Farrow, *Civil War*, pp. 19, 60, 61, 117ff.; Wright, *History and Antiquities*; R. L. Kenyon, 'The Committee for Sequestration of Estates of Delinquents', TSANHS, 2nd series (1898–1900), pp. 19–22.

[42] Esther S. Cope, 'The Disputes About Muster Masters' Fees in Shropshire in the 1630's', *The Huntington Library Quarterly*, 45, 4 (1982), pp. 271–84.

able to borrow substantial sums from John Corbet's widow.[43] What evidence remains indicates that for over three generations the More family worked in concert at a well-connected level in the parliamentarian cause. In moving from Mainstone to the rectory at More, Lawson then seems to have moved from high to low church; and from marginal court patronage to a world of parliamentary dissidence. There can in addition be little doubt that Lawson was involved with the More family, nor that over the years possibly a close and protective relationship developed between him and its members. It is this as much as anything else that might be seen as helping to submerge Lawson's life in apparent obscurity.

Indeed, during the whole Civil War and Interregnum period Lawson's name seems only to surface in the company of one of the Mores and always in a context of Salopian ecclesiastical politics. At the outbreak of war Farrow estimates that Shropshire was divided into some 194 parishes and that, on the whole, the Shropshire clergy, like its gentry and aristocracy, proved loyal to the King and his church.[44] Nevertheless, in the early days of the war it appears that some 57 of the clergy were prepared to support Parliament's attempt to establish some form of Presbyterian church government. Seventeen of these had been unable to find livings in Laud's Church of England.[45] Within the county there were regional variations. Only one member of the Bishops Castle clergy was a signatory to the loyalist association formed in Shrewsbury in 1642. Even so, in such a county, the clustering of anti-Laudian and Presbyterian clergy around Clun did not always feel secure. Despite the protection of the Harleys, Thomas Froysell fled to the fastness of London, as did George Baxter of Much Wenlock.[46] In the long run, however, most of the clergy maintained their livings, even if at some stage suffering persecution and critical scrutiny.[47] Perhaps this was in part, as Green hypothesises, because many were prepared to keep low and manipulable profiles; it was also no doubt, as he states, because of the difficulty of replacing them.[48]

There is, of course, no reason to assume that the clergy, like the gentry, were required to support either of the two major warring factions. Richard Gough implies that the men of Myddle went to fight for the King because his commissioners arrived in the village first; and after the war had been

[43] Record is in MFP, SCRO.

[44] Farrow, *Civil War*, p. 25.

[45] Auden, J. E. 'Ecclesiastical History of Shropshire During the Civil War, Commonwealth and Restoration', *TSANHS*, 3rd series, 7 (1901–10), pp. 241ff.; 'Clun and its Neighbourhood in the First Civil War', *TSANHS*, 3rd series, 8 (1901–10), pp. 287–336. See also Farrow, *Civil War*, pp. 25–6.

[46] Yule, *Puritans in Politics*, p. 85.

[47] Ian Green, 'The Persecution of Scandalous and Malignant Parish Clergy During the English Civil War', *EHR*, 44 (1979), pp. 526–7.

[48] Green, 'Persecution', pp. 507ff.

traipsing over Shropshire for a good while, a newsheet dated January 1645 claims that about one thousand men from the Bishops Castle region were in arms against both sides of the war.[49] Even allowing for exaggeration, the Clun Clubmen were representative of an important voice in many counties as the war drew on. Their proclaimed allegiance was to country or county and community over and above allegiance to faction or political party and, as I shall suggest, in a number of ways Lawson's own arguments in the *Politica* may be seen as reflecting Clubmen rhetoric. Loyalty to community and country are major themes of the work, and Lawson insists that once war had broken out no one strictly speaking owed allegiance either to King or Parliament.[50] In recognising these and other echoes of Clubmen themes one can begin to see that Lawson's political commitments were not, at least by the time he published the *Politica*, as simple and straightforward as has been assumed, and Samuel More's prove to be similarly elusive or adjustable. Those who stood out against commitment to King or Parliament over and above locality, had an ecclesiological extension in the clerics who, through variable balances of self-interest and principle, managed to maintain their livings despite competing claims of religious policy issuing from the warring parties. Lawson was one of them, and his Erasmian principles of religious comprehension and his insistence on the prime clerical duty of teaching the word to the flock and curing souls in need is the rationalising, or principled, voice that represents that unmartyred majority.

However many might have wanted Shropshire to stay aloof from the war, there were too many families with firm commitments and, being on the route from Ireland to London, the county was strategically too important to escape involvement. In ecclesiological terms, despite the loyalism of the majority of the clergy, Shropshire was one of the few counties in which something of a Presbyterian *classis* system was able to operate – thus doctrinal issues must have been brought very much alive at the local level.[51] Lawson was certainly concerned with such matters, as fragments of correspondence and an exchange of animadversions with the hyperactive pen of Richard Baxter indicate.[52] The men knew each other directly, but on one occasion at least, a third clergyman, Francis Tallents (1619–1708),

---

[49] Richard Gough, *A History of Myddle*, ed. D. Hey, Penguin, Harmondsworth, 1981 edn; J. S. Morrill, *The Revolt of the Provinces: Conservatives and Radicals in the English Civil War, 1630–1650*, Allen and Unwin, London, 1976, pp. 46, 98.

[50] Morrill, *Revolt*, at length for a fine discussion of Clubmen.

[51] See, at length, W. A. Shaw, *A History of the English Church During the Civil Wars and Under the Commonwealth*, Longman, London, 1900, 2 vols.; more specifically, Yule, *Puritans in Politics*, on whose analysis I am drawing here.

[52] Baxter, *Treatises*, DWL, 'Quaeries Touching Some Propositions in the Assembly's Confession of Faith', vol. 2. fols. 208–10, item 39, 4.; 'Amica dissertatio', vol. 1, fols. 99–150b item 9; for further details and untitled items see Roger Thomas, *The Baxter Treatises*, DWL Occasional Papers, 8, London, 1959.

acted as courier between them.[53] It is generally from the period of ecclesiological experimentation ushered in by the Long Parliament's abolition of episcopacy that Lawson and Baxter's intellectual association seems to date: more specifically, it may date from as late as Baxter's *Aphorisms of Justification* (1649) to which Lawson replied.[54]

Shropshire was divided into six *classes*, the sixth containing some 34 of the old Shropshire parishes around the Bishops Castle region, including More. George Lawson, along with Thomas Froysell, who had re-emerged from the metropolitan woodwork, George Barkley of Mainstone, Richard Heath, an oriental scholar of Hopesay, Edmund Lewis of Chirbury and Anthony Hawke of Stretton are named as fit ministers for the system.[55] How effective this handful was in making the system work is not known. The lay involvement, however, was impressive as it included Samuel More of Linley, the governor of Ludlow since the virtual end of the war in Shropshire, and his physician son Thomas, whom I suspect to have been a friend of Lawson's encomiast.[56]

According to Yule only the fourth *classis* in Shropshire operated, though it did so very effectively until 1660, and Lawson himself was later to give a succinct but general explanation for the failure of the *classis* system as a whole.[57] From the beginning it was a compromise between different models of reform; it had too many enemies; its status, along with the formally abolished episcopacy, was uncertain; there were insufficient men qualified to make it work, and Parliament had insufficient trust to delegate any genuine authority (*Pol.* 252–6).

Despite difficulties, Lawson had clearly been prepared to work along with the mooted reforms, and by being named as a minister fit to be of the sixth *classis* he had manifestly taken the Solemn League and Covenant.

In 1648 a petition was sent from a large number of worried Shropshire clergy fearing the collapse of the fledgling *classis* system and its replacement by the anarchy, as it was seen, of Independency.[58] One can hardly doubt that this reflected *The Heads of the Proposals* and fears arising from the army coup of 1647. More directly it may have reflected changes in the balance of ecclesiastical politics in the county and the workings of the com-

[53] Baxter, *Letters*, DWL, vol. 2, pp. 161–3, letters dated 24 April 1653 and 7 January 1655–6. It seems Lawson had sent papers commenting on arguments by Baxter. According to Tallents, he expected a reply, according to Baxter he did not.

[54] The *Aphorisms* did cause a stir not least because they touched on issues of acute importance since the abolition of episcopacy. In the *Reliq. Baxt.*, p. 107, Baxter remarks that the most important reply was by Lawson, but it is not clear if they knew each other already.

[55] But not the Rev T. Cobly of Widdicombe. I have abstracted the details from Auden, 'Ecclesiastical History', p. 269.

[56] *Ibid.*, pp. 269–70.

[57] Yule, *Puritans in Politics*, pp. 229ff. and 263.

[58] Auden, 'Ecclesiastical History', pp. 270–2, for details of the signatories.

mittee system. Of the sixth *classis*, only Froysell of Clun and Barkley of Mainstone signed the petition. The majority, Hawke, Heath, Lewis and Lawson, are absent from the list. Lawson may already have come to the conclusion that Presbyterianism could not work and he probably believed that he should himself co-operate with any serious attempt at on-going reformation. This it seems was not simply quietism. After the execution of Charles I Lawson not only accepted the Engagement of October 1649 but, according to Baxter, wrote an Engagement tract, which Baxter found underwhelming.[59] Perhaps Lawson was unimpressed too, for it seems not to have been published.[60]

In 1654 the ominous-sounding *Ordinance for the Ejection of Scandalous Ignorant and Insufficient Ministers and Schoolmasters* came into being. In a sense it was part of a continuing process of attempts to improve the standards of the clergy, and to capitalise on the increasing numbers of better-educated men seeking orders, although it could be, and was, exploited for political ends. As Green remarks, scandal could run the gamut from drunkenness to political attitudes not acceptable to Parliament. The arbiters of scandal were potent men.[61] For whatever reason, fairness of the inquisitors, or shortage of replacements, or simply a dulling lack of scandal, Shropshire was not a county in which the clergy suffered unduly under the Triers, as they became called.[62] Twenty-one commissioners were appointed for the county as a whole, Samuel More amongst them, and twenty-one ministers assistant. These included George Lawson, Richard Heath and the ubiquitous Froysell. It is, moreover, certainly possible that in counties such as Shropshire a real shortage of clergy made flexibility vital if people were to be served at all. It may be indicative that in 1655 we find Lawson making the entries in the register for the parish of Lydham, which lay between More and Bishops Castle. The hand seems hurried; uncharacteristically the entries are in English. Auden claims that all the ministers assisting the Triers were Independents, but Yule, more convincingly, is sceptical.[63] Froysell, along with perhaps nine others, had initially been hostile to Independency. As Lawson's *Politica* seems to indicate, Presbyterianism itself at the beginning of the war in fact encompassed overlapping clusters of religious belief, and one did not have to be committed to a system to work with it. Unless his own views changed remarkably, Lawson could not be counted as an Independent. One could be, as Lawson was in time to become again, an established Church

[59] Baxter, *Reliq. Baxt.*, pp. 107ff.
[60] Julian Franklin, *John Locke and the Theory of Sovereignty*, Cambridge University Press, 1978, pp. 129, 130. For discussion see Introduction to Part II.
[61] Green, 'Persecution', p. 509; Yule, *Puritans in Politics*, pp. 150–1.
[62] Green, 'Persecution', p. 526; Auden, 'Ecclesiastical History', pp. 285–6.
[63] Auden, 'Ecclesiastical History', p. 284; Yule, *Puritans in Politics*, e.g., p. 230.

of England minister and still want scandal eradicated and educational standards raised. The ghost of Laud would have walked with some of the affirmations of principle involved, if not with their administrative means of application.

In 1656 Samuel More was elected, like his father before him, as MP
for Bishops Castle but was excluded as a danger to the ailing and financially
troubled Protector, along with such familiar names as Sir Arthur Hesilrige
and Anthony Ashley Cooper. More's exclusion is puzzling. Had he been
a safe Cromwellian, there is little doubt that Corbet could have vouched
for him. Yet there is equally no evidence of any inseparable rift between
the More and Corbet families. The precise nature of, or shifts in, More's
political affiliations cannot be read from the general pattern of his actions
and previous involvements. He may like many country gentlemen have been
hostile to Cromwell's financial wielding of the *Instrument*. He may have
been a republican and hence disquieted by the *Humble Petition*. He may
have been, or have become, hostile to the Independency associated so
strongly with the Protector, and these possibilities are not mutually exclusive.
It is, at any rate, in the period from about the time of Samuel More's exclusion
until his eventual death some six years later that Lawson's belated literary
career flowers. As the two men may have been close, it is reasonable to
suppose that they were of much the same mind. If More thought as Lawson
was to write in 1660, he was not enamoured of Cromwell and did want
a settlement. Certainly, having been excluded from Parliament, he returned
to Shropshire to await the election of 1658. What part, if any, he played
in the Restoration is unknown; but More seems to have acquired a parliamentary reputation for being something of a time-server[64] and in 1660
he was able to make his peace with Charles, being confirmed in his Commonwealth offices, which he held until his death.

Surviving evidence makes it clear that Lawson had been writing and circulating manuscripts certainly since 1649, but it was largely in the hectic
five-year period ending with the full restoration of the Church of England
that Lawson published. A manuscript, possibly an early version of the *Politica*, was lost at the printer's around 1657 (see below) and during this year
he was persuaded to bring out the *Examination of the Political Part of
Mr. Hobbs, His Leviathan*. The *Theo-Politica* appeared in 1659, bringing
to fruition some of the more theological themes that had been explored
in fragmentary and *ad hoc* manuscripts written up to ten years before. In
addition, by 1660, Lawson had written (or rewritten) a very substantial
treatise on politics in two discrete parts. The first, standing on its own

---

[64] B. D. Henning, ed., *History of Parliament: The Commons III Members M-Y, 1660–1690*,
Secker and Warburg, London, 1983, pp. 95–6.

as a theory of political relationships and offered as a suasive to peace and permanent settlement in church and state, appeared as the *Politica sacra et civilis*. The second part, an application of his principles to the problems of administration never came out and no manuscript is known. The first part attests sufficiently to Lawson's capacity to come to terms with a restoration at the level of high theory; as Samuel More's behaviour is testimony to a capacity for practical adjustment.

In 1662 Lawson published his largest theological treatise. Appropriate to its difficult subject-matter, *An Exposition of the Epistle to Hebrewes* is long, heavy and opaque, but even more thoroughly than the *Theo-Politica* it carries themes of theological interest to Lawson since his early discussions with Baxter. In May Samuel More died, and Lawson himself may have been ill or considerably affected for his handwriting in that year is uncharacteristically shaky and uncertain. Three months later he signed his acceptance of the Act of Uniformity, which confirmed him in his living within a national Church of England. How difficult physically and/or morally it was, one cannot tell. The *Politica* affirms clearly enough that Lawson wanted a national ecclesiastical settlement with a reformed episcopacy and a parish-based clergy; but the Act required the abduration of the Solemn League and Covenant, and seemed implicitly to require acceptance of principles that the Lawson of 1660 might have found unacceptable. For whatever reasons, the oath of acceptance signed on 21 August, is in two different inks with a clear false start, in what could almost be the hand of a semi-literate.[65] The mass of ministers in Shropshire were also prepared to swear allegiance to King, episcopacy and the Book of Common Prayer; sixteen could not and these include several members of Lawson's own circle of ministerial friends and colleagues – Froysell of Clun, Richard Heath and Francis Tallents. In all, seven of the twenty ministers assistant to the Triers lost their livings, Lawson had probably worked with them all. In a personal passage that could almost be speaking prophetically to men such as Tallents, Heath and perhaps Froysell, Lawson had written:

I do not write this out of partiality or prejudice: for some of that party (Independents) are my special Friends, and I dearly love them; some are pious, prudent, and learned, and I honour them much: Yet I desire them seriously to consider what they do, and also so far as they can to forcast, what is likely to be the issue, if they do not unite more firmly amongst themselves, and combine with other pious Ministers, and people of God, both in Worship and Discipline (*Pol.* 309).[66]

---

[65] HSB, 3, 1661–91, 1/A4/3 does not list Lawson as signing, but he did sign the subscription rolls from which the books were copied. His entry is obscured by stitching.
[66] The appeal here seems to affirm strong support for Baxter's efforts at establishing voluntary associations of ministers in the late 1650s.

Lawson, recovered from the traumas of 1662, published a redaction of the *Theo-Politica* in 1665, the *Magna charta ecclesiae universalis*, and died eventually in 1678. His burial is entered on 12 July as 'George Lawson clerk'. The Letters of Administration list the accoutrements appropriate to a comfortable country life: wall hangings and carpets (in 'the best parlour'); damask amongst the table cloths and napkins; holland sheets and pillowcases; the appurtenances of a well-equipped small farm; two beds in the maid's room; cabinets, trunks and large tables; and a study of books apparently valued at £150.

Anne Lawson, his wife of over forty years, was buried on 14 August two years later. In May 1681 Jeremy Lawson auctioned Lawson's books, perhaps in part to pay for the posthumous republication of the *Magna charta ecclesiae universalis*, which it seems had done something to make Lawson's theology and moral guidance more accessible.[67]

In many respects what little is known of Lawson fits the pattern of a typical seventeenth-century cleric. He was one of the wave of better educated men who sought a career in the church from the beginning of the century. And if, after university, he did not return to his native region, he settled eventually in a very similar one. Before this, and also quite typically, he seems to have spent a considerable and uncertain time on the edges of a secure living. Again this living was not as poor as older and official records might indicate. Like the majority of the clergy at the outbreak of war, he showed that, for whatever reasons, he was prepared to work with a changed system of church government; like the majority at the Restoration he was prepared to work within the re-established national church as well.[68] Unlike so many, however, he lived long enough to provide a pattern of conformity throughout the whole troubled period. Few had the opportunity to have loyalties so tested. Whether one accepts Curtis or Green on the average length of incumbency (27 or 19 years, respectively), Lawson's career was far longer than average.[69] It runs from the low church policies of Abbot, through the ceremonialism of Laud, followed by Presbyterianism and Independent experimentation to the re-establishment of an episcopalian Church of England. Superficially this might suggest that Lawson was like the archetype, the Vicar of Bray.

This, however, would be at least too simple. To begin with, he seems to have been actively involved in his church. He did, moreover, expound carefully and in detail theological and ecclesiological principles, which, as

---

[67] *Catalogus Librarum*, Sale Catalogues of Books, 1681–95, London.
[68] For these general characteristics, see Green, 'Career Prospects', pp. 71ff.
[69] M. H. Curtis, 'The Alienated Intellectual in Early, Stuart England', *Past and Present*, 23 (1962); cf. Green, 'Career Prospects'.

we will see, encompass the full scope of his conformity without necessary contradiction within the extraordinary vicissitudes of English protestantism. He may, of course, have been in practice an ecclesiastical trimmer as Samuel More may have been a political one. Equally, however, the principles Lawson enunciates may have guided him and were a sufficiently abstract formulation of allegiance and priority to encompass diversity of specific action. It is misleading, as it may be with More, to tie him to a firm party commitment. 'I am', insisted Lawson, 'of no party as party' (*Pol.* Epist.) and, notwithstanding the prejudicial connotations of 'party', this claim must be taken seriously. Lawson's life, like More's, shows a capacity both for involvement and only contingent commitment to the specific causes through which he worked. The views and guiding principles, or the rhetoric through which each could justify changes of course, were probably widespread. Lawson was unusual in articulating common presuppositions and priorities. In the *Politica* he insists that specific causes must be judged by performance and dubious means can contaminate the ends to which they are allegedly directed. He also specifies a hierarchy of loyalty to God and community before specific institutions, causes and persons. This is at one both with Leveller and Clubman notions of priority. There is, however, nothing idiosyncratic or inconsistent in this. Such principles generated a universal rhetoric; what divided men was nicety of application. Samuel More was parliamentarian governor of Monmouth Castle when the putative one thousand strong band of Clubmen were gathering not far from his home. What divided him from them at that time was possibly only the belief that Parliament still did sufficiently represent the community. This neither stopped him changing his mind later when confronted by a different Parliament, nor would it have made him inconsistent to do so. This is to indicate only how Lawson's principles might be applied.

Much the same, however, can more confidently be said of Lawson himself. His affirmed loyalties to ecclesiastical and secular causes and institutions were bounded by their approximation to a notion of community interest. Whether, in short, the *Politica* in this biographical context should be seen as an affirmation of a pattern of consistent principle which helps explain widespread conformity, or whether his work is the remnant of a well-trimmed sail, we cannot know. It is the difficulty of penetrating rhetoric that we should never overlook.

In the year of Anne Lawson's death, Samuel More's eldest son was, like father and grandfather before him, seeking election to Parliament. Perhaps to help pave his way he rebuilt the war-damaged tower of Shelve Church and gave the village of More itself an extensive library of 350 volumes. Most churches would have had a handful or so pertinent books, and small church libraries were not uncommon; but as the majority have been dispersed or gathered into diocesan libraries their significance is difficult to establish and easy to ignore.[70]

The continued existence of the bulk of the More Library, plus evidence of the larger whole from which it was taken, surrounding documentary evidence, and some remaining indication of the nature of Lawson's own library, make an interesting exception. The result is of direct if indeterminate relevance to understanding the immediate intellectual context from which Lawson's own work had emerged, and of more general significance in establishing a picture of intellectual life in seventeenth-century England.

Richard More drew up an eight-clause document to ensure that the donated library was used as intended, for the encouragement of a (new) preaching minister (Daniel Wall) and for the education of the inhabitants of More.[71] The church-wardens were given responsibility for checking the books, and the locks and keys of the presses in which they were to be kept. The rector also had keys but, with the exception of More himself or of his assignees, there were no borrowing rights and even the exceptions were required to borrow any book only in the presence of a church-warden, who was to note particulars, and it was to be returned within one month 'to the same place from whence it was taken'. The safe continuity of the library was to be ensured even ceremoniously by the requirement that church-wardens account for themselves and their responsibilities on every annual change of office – in the presence of the rector and inhabitants.[72]

The gift of the library was an important matter, and its contents seem to have been chosen with care. The original cataloguers remark on the catholicity of theological works, and the daunting standards of erudition which seem expected are hardly less remarkable.[73] The library was used as intended for a while, perhaps well into the early eighteenth century, for it is only then that the church-wardens show signs of the illiteracy that would have prohibited them carrying out their responsibilities.[74] There is a running tally of books borrowed and returned (though some are now no longer in the library). There are variable signs of usage. Some works

---

[70] W. G. Clark Maxwell, 'On the Library of More Church, Salop', *TSANHS*, 3rd series, 7 (1906), pp. 115ff.; and 'The Church Library of More', *TSANHS*, 3rd series, 9 (1909), pp. 21–2. C. Condren, 'More Library, Salop' (appendix with F. Carleton), *Library History* (1987), pp. 141ff. for a fuller discussion.

[71] MFP, SCRO.

[72] MFP, SCRO; Condren, 'More Library', for analogues and the distinctiveness of More's actions.

[73] Clark Maxwell, 'On the Library', p. 17. The catholicity of selection is less likely to reflect breadth of taste, or perhaps even theological confidence (*pace* Clark Maxwell) than the need to be thoroughly well prepared against opponents.

[74] MoPR. William Nicholas and Henry Yop, church-wardens in 1729, sign with crosses. See also 1732, 1736, 1761, 1764, 1766, 1767, 1768, 1774.

(notably volumes of Calvin), seem much read while others were almost untouched – nine volumes of Cesare Baronio's *Annales ecclesiastici* (1589–1601) look virtually unopened.

It would seem that the explicit reason for the gift reflects the fact that George Lawson was dead and, as a preaching minister, he was proving difficult for Daniel Wall to follow. This indicates in turn that there was some expectation, at least by Richard More, that the inhabitants of the village should have available to them considerable intellectual resources, which had been lost around the time of Anne Lawson's death, and that the village church should function as a focal point for intellectual life. That there was an intellectual life in such a small and isolated village might cause surprise. It perhaps begins to indicate what the rise in literacy in the seventeenth century could mean.

Lawson's personal library must have been very considerable indeed, and Richard More's own holdings, from which the More volumes were selected, were impressive. A catalogue of his books drawn up around 1690 lists some one thousand separate items classified under the headings of divinity, medicine, tragedy, poetry and comedy, law, dictionaries, geography and history, and miscellaneous.[75] The medical collection probably came to him on the death of his brother Thomas, and no doubt many volumes came via his father and grandfather. The list is incomplete as it does not include his own copy of Lawson's *Examination*, which is still at Linley Hall. The medical collection has curiosities (*The Anatomy of the Jointed Worm*) but it also includes theoretically and historically important works by Fallopio, Scaliger and Cardano. The geography and history works are extensive with Venetian statutes, the works of Machiavelli, Savonarola, Thomas More and Tacitus. The extensive theology holdings include Erasmus, Laud, Stillingfleet, Luther, Grotius, Abbot, Chillingworth and Plato next to *The Beehive of the Romish Church* (1623). Poetry, apart from its Greek, Latin and Italian authors, is a treasure-house of English early or first editions: Carew, Milton, Donne, Herbert, Cowley and Marvell.

All this indicates that at least when Lawson wrote he lived in a rich intellectual ambience; and throughout, in discussing the intellectual context and broad inheritance from which the *Politica* emerges, I have very largely monitored hypotheses with reference to the works which these libraries indicate would have been available to him.

If one turns to the indirect provenance of the More Church Library itself, this too is suggestive. A variety of owners are listed in the surviving volumes. The most commonly found signatures are of Thomas Pierson (a well-known preacher in the region at the turn of the century) and Christopher Harvey,

---

[75] 'A Catalogue of My Books', MFP, SCRO.

poet, and sometime Fellow of Brasenose.[76] Various members of the More
family are listed as owners – the library includes Richard More the elder's
copy of Mede's *Clavis Apocalypsin*. William Biggs (Lawson's predecessor)
owned one book, and several volumes of Lawson's own library – indicating
a circulation of books between Lawson and the Mores – found their way
back to More Church. What is perhaps more surprising is that a number
of volumes seem to have been owned or borrowed by villagers of lower
social standing. Checking names with parish registers one can see that a
John Ward, possibly a servant of Lawson's, owned one volume;[77] members
of the Owen family owned others, as did the Lloyds. One Lloyd-owned
volume has noted in it 'borrowed by my father'. Other names that can
be cross-checked with the parish records are John Barker (d. 1638) and
Guilliam Bright (d. 1634). Richard Heath of Hopesay at one time owned
a volume which could well have found its way to the library via Lawson
or Samuel More.[78] In the context of the seventeenth century the village
of More hardly approaches the eye, a flea-like dot on the provincial map,
it was at the demographic, economic and political periphery of the country.
In many ways such a marginal location no doubt makes sense, but we should
be cautious about extending the easy metaphors of centre and periphery
from political and economic life, to intellectual life. After all, the majority
of Members of Parliament who converged on London in 1640 to make
Westminster the political centre of the country, returned to provincial or
peripheral homes, perhaps like the Mores, to read, collect, exchange and
make available books in their locality. The majority of the ten thousand
or so ministers in England were also in more or less provincial livings.
By no means all had such extensive resources as George Lawson; but if
More and its environs is any guide, there may even have been no intellectual
centre.

John Morrill remarks upon the ambiguity of the notion of country which
could mean either England or county.[79] This was an ambiguity which facilitated a dual rhetorical appeal in arguments of loyalty and allegiance. If
seen in purely political or economic terms this must look a trifle odd, because
the notions of centre and periphery make clear sense. But if this were not
the case in terms of the intellectual structure of the country, then the ambiguous currency of argument is more understandable. It may be said that
rather than exaggerating the importance of the provincial periphery in trying

[76] Clark Maxwell, 'On the Library of More' notes many of these.
[77] There is a reference in MFP, SCRO to a John Ward working for Mr Lawson, but the
Wards were a large clan who favoured the name John.
[78] For more details see Condren, 'More Library'. Dorcas Owen (d. 1712) was Richard More's
mistress and mother of his children thus the estates went to the sons of Robert More.
[79] Morrill, *Revolt*, p. 14.

to explain the English Civil War, Morrill has rather drawn attention to one of two complementary aspects of community rhetoric made possible by the widespread diversity and depth of English intellectual life and increasing literacy. Hobbes at least thought that the universities provided centres of intellectual life, and that their control, through the dissemination of right doctrine, was the way of eradicating false opinion throughout the country. This notion, and the implied causative role of the universities in disrupting the kingdom in the first place, begins to look naive. The curricula of the universities had remained stable, even 'medieval' during the seventeenth century; and if the More region was typical, between them Lawson and the Mores may have had a library fit to rival a small college without any curricular restrictions. If there was no clear intellectual centre and if the war was a war of opinion, control of the mind of the country, with cheap print, newspapers and chapmen hurrying in the dark, was never a possibility.[80]

One must be careful in reading fragments from a single case, in some ways More was untypical, not least because literacy seems to have declined there during the eighteenth century; but the overall impression provided is of a very rich intellectual ambience in which George Lawson worked. It becomes easy to see how he could display such a breadth of learning and cite his authors with such accuracy. Moreover, the background provided by this motley remains of books, scribbled signatures and catalogues, in turn suggests that Lawson himself could assume an extensive local audience as well as a national one for his work. Here the amphibolous rhetoric of country and county come together in a different way. The *Politica* is written in an informal style, with intimate expression suggestive of verbal delivery. This may be just transitional convention as the world moved gradually away from an oral culture. Lawson also claims that he is writing not for the learned, who in any case know more than he, but simply for ordinary minds. This too might be convention, a part of the rhetoric of modesty which was necessary to the establishment of most writers' credentials.[81] It is also possible, however, that the informality and apparently modest disclaimer reflect the degree of originally verbal delivery for the interested inhabitants of More. Again, penetrating the rhetoric is the problem, but the residue of literacy raises the possibility.

In writing the *Politica*, Lawson – despite the obscurity of his origins, the safe political isolation of his living – was by no means intellectually bereft. This meant that, in effect, he could without any resultant tension appeal to local and national allegiance at the same time and hope to be

---

[80] Cf. Sharpe, 'Crown, Parliament and Locality', who seems not to question the metaphors of centre and periphery when applied to communication and the dissemination of ideas.
[81] Annabel Patterson, *Marvell and The Civic Crown*, Princeton University Press, 1978, pp. 181–3 for pertinent comments on the modesty *topos*.

listened to, at different levels, in different regions. He could speak in a language of country and appeal to county. The concept elaborated to embrace these differences, was that of community – one of the most resonant and diversely co-optable of terms in English seventeenth-century political discourse. It was indeed a potent term in the armoury of the Levellers, the Diggers, the Clubmen, as well as in the more refined garb of Jonson, Cleveland and the Cavalier poets. For all such people, the denial of community (as Cleveland denied it to the Scots who 'ramble not to learne the Mode/How to be drest . . .') was a denial of human civilisation and the most legitimate of social relationships.[82] Lawson articulates what a discordant association of names, such as Overton, Marvell, Cleveland, Lovelace, Harrington and Lilbourne had in common – verbally at least. Through his own co-option of the communal inheritance, he enunciated a pattern of abstract principles, used them to muffle the spectre of the English Revolution in civilising dress; and had them seem to display the pattern of his life and of his protectors.

[82] A. D. Cousins, 'The Cavalier World of John Cleveland', *Studies in Philology*, 78, 1 (1981), pp. 66ff., quoting 'The Rebel Scot', in *The Poems*, eds. B. Morris and E. Withington, Oxford, 1967, p. 85.

Part II

AN EXPOSITION OF LAWSON'S
POLITICA

INTRODUCTION

Early in 1660, John Starkey, bookseller at the Mitre, near St Pauls, put Lawson's *Politica* on the market. George Thomason acquired his copy in May, the month in which the final terms for the return of Charles II were being worked out, and in which the twilight power of the Presbyterians in the Convention Parliament finally guttered.

The *Politica*, then, appeared towards the end of that brief and explosive recrudescence of political speculation associated with the demise of the Commonwealth and the Restoration of the Stuarts.[1] Starkey was responsible for six other volumes in 1660; Tyton could boast some twenty-six, more than double his output for 1657 when he sold Lawson's *Examination*. But these were both small fish.[2] The extraordinary and concentrated bulk of political works, ranging from bawdy verse and broadside to heavy tome, itself indicates a widespread awareness of a distinct crisis of settlement. Yet hitherto, Lawson's *Politica* has been associated with the last troubled months of Oliver Cromwell's regime. It has been thought to have been written in 1657 around the very time when Lawson's patron was licking his wounds after rejection from Cromwell's last Parliament, a very different context.

Franklin suggests that the work may have been conceived even earlier, possibly growing from a lost Engagement tract, which he has tentatively identified as *Conscience Puzzled* (1650).[3]

Franklin's dating of the *Politica* is tied closely to his interpretation of the work in which he sees a hostility to the possibility of a Stuart Restoration; a plea to the nobility to stay loyal to Cromwell's Commonwealth and even a support for the *Humble Petition and Advice*. But for the fact that the *Politica* was undoubtedly long in gestation I believe Franklin to be mistaken

---

[1] There is no systematic treatment of the literature of these years, but during them seventeenth-century book production probably reached its peak. I estimate that, including broadsides, voluminous Quaker materials (untouched by Thomason) and satire and poetry of an overtly political nature, some 4,500 items were printed. See Averil and Conal Condren, 'A Political Bibliography of the Settlement Controversy 1659–60: An Initial Computer Study', *The Bibliographical Society of Australia and New Zealand Bulletin*, 9, 3 (1985), pp. 208 ff.

[2] See Paul G. Morrison, *Index of Printers, Publishers and Booksellers in Donald Wing's Short-Title Catalogue of Books 1641–1700*, University of Virginia, 1955.

[3] Julian Franklin, *John Locke and the Theory of Sovereignty*, Cambridge University Press, 1978, pp. 129 and 130; Baxter, *Reliq. Baxt.*, London, 1696, 1, p. 107. Richard Ashcraft's dating for the *Politica c.* 1640s (*Revolutionary Politics and Locke's Two Treatises of Government*, Princeton University Press, 1986, pp. 310–11) is the most anachronistic, and requires reading Lawson's retrospective ruminations on the Interregnum in a prophetic idiom. Naturally, no evidence is provided for such a mislocation, the only function of which seems to be the convenience of treating Hunton and Lawson together.

on all counts. In some measure the work carries the marks of the Engagement
Controversy and coheres with Lawson's unpublished manuscript materials
dating from *circa* 1650.[4] The existence of substantive unpublished materials, however, invalidates Franklin's assumption that if Lawson wrote an
Engagement tract, then he would certainly have published it; and, as I shall
indicate later, there is a significant linguistic difference between *Conscience
Puzzled* and the *Politica*. More important, there are no sound reasons for
tying the *Politica* specifically to 1657, and none at all for supporting this
date with hints of affiliation erroneously gleaned from the text. By the time
he published the *Politica*, Lawson was not a confirmed Commonwealth
man, and certainly no Cromwellian.

In the *Examination* (Epistle to the Reader), Lawson offers partial explanation for the brevity of his critique of Hobbes:

I had formerly finished a Treatise . . . which if it had not been lost by some negligence,
after an *Imprimatur* was put upon it, might have prevented and made void the
political part of Mr *Hobbs*: and though one Copy be lost, yet there is another,
which may become publick hereafter.

Now if, as Franklin and I have previously assumed, this refers to the manuscript later published as the *Politica*, there are several things still to be noted.
Despite Lawson's complaint, printing could be a speedy and efficient matter
in the seventeenth century; but, as Tyton published the *Examination* in
1657, Lawson's statement would seem to imply either most expeditious
writing and dispatch of the *Politica*, or a date before 1657. If then, the
missing manuscript referred to in the *Examination* is the *Politica*, there
is nevertheless a difference between written in and completed by, which
we have conflated.[5]

In any case, Lawson's statement is ambiguous. It is not clear if the manuscript would have made void *Leviathan* itself or a longer critique of the
work. The former possibility would obviously indicate a date of composition
prior to 1651. It would also mean that the missing work is not the *Politica*
as it came to be published in 1660 – for the text contains too many references
to events and other texts post-dating 1651. If the latter possibility is correct

---

[4] These are scattered amongst the *Baxter Treatises*, DWL, vols. 1, 2, 4, 5, 6, 7; see Roger
Thomas, *Catalogue of the Baxter Treatises*. The relevant material mostly seems to date
from *c.* 1649–50; see especially, 'Amica diss.', vol. 1 fols. 99–150[b].

[5] I had simply assumed 1657 or an earlier date, 'The Image of *Utopia* in the Political Writings
of Lawson', *Moreana*, 69 (1981), pp. 101–5; '*Sacra* Before *Civilis*: On the Ecclesiastical
Politics of George Lawson', *The Journal of Religious History*, 11 (1981), pp. 524–35; Franklin, *John Locke*, writes of the *Politica* being finished by 1657, p. 53, and thereafter as written
in that year. The missing manuscript may not have been the *Politica*, though I think it
is.

and the missing manuscript is the *Politica*, then the work was still unquestionably revised between 1657 and 1660.

Lawson's account of separation seems in part to be a commentary on Dr John Owen's *Of Schism* which was not published until 1657; and there are references to Lawson's previously published works, the *Examination* and the *Theo-Politica* which appeared in 1659 (*Pol.* 11, 158, 325). As I shall indicate (see p. 175) there are differences of tone, emphasis and conceptual elaboration between the *Examination* and the *Politica* and these may plausibly be seen as the results of revision.

It is, of course, impossible to say how complete the revision was. The last chapter of the *Politica* is scrappy and repetitive and the work has no discussion of events in 1659. But perhaps Lawson thought that raking over the most recent coals of discord was senseless. Even so, if the work is a plea to stay loyal to 'the present government', as Franklin has it, it is a peculiarly belated plea even for an isolated Shropshire vicar.[6] Franklin, in fact, cites a number of passages to show that Lawson was a Cromwellian and the distortions involved will be treated in the context of discussing Lawson's understanding of the Civil War and Interregnum. It is enough now to indicate that the passages Franklin cites do nothing to support a 1657 dating for the *Politica*. Lawson's appeal to the *magnati* of England (*Pol.* Epist.) is not a plea to stay loyal to the present government but is a call to help achieve a settlement in a hostile and politically corrupt environment.[7] His attitude to Cromwell is far more ambivalent than Franklin suggests by misreading references to the Isle of Wight Treaty and the *Humble*

---

[6] The work also sounds little like those explicitly defending the 'Good Old Cause' and the Commonwealth in 1659–60. See e.g. Baxter, *A Holy Commonwealth*, arguably if marginally a defence of the Good Old Cause; more centrally, Henry Stubbe, *An Essay in Defence of the Good Old Cause*, London, 1659; John Milton, *The Ready and Easy Way to Establish a Free Commonwealth and the Excellence Thereof*, 1659; Anon. *A Coffin for the Good Old Cause*, but the expression was slippery. For a valuable survey, Barbara Taft, 'That Lusty Puss The Good Old Cause', *History of Political Thought*, 5,3 (1984), pp. 446 ff. There is however a further curious puzzle concerning dating. In the *Exposition of the Epistle to Hebrewes*, 1662, Lawson makes reference to the *Theo-Politica* and to his *ecclesiastical and civil politics* (the *Politica*?) but as if it were yet to appear. This may be a printing error, or it may mean that *Hebrewes* also predated the *Politica*.

[7] Franklin, *John Locke*, p. 58, seems to misread future for present tense in referring to Lawson's comments on overseas politicians 'fearing our union and agreement'. Lawson states clearly that the politicians are making it their business to continue differences between us. Ominous overseas disruption inhibiting settlement was in the air in 1659-60. See e.g. Anon., *A Letter written from the City of Florence*, 1660; Thomas Campanela, *A New Machiavell*, with an admonitory preface (what else?) by William Prynne, 1659. For a survey of the literature originating, or allegedly originating, from abroad, and using this to claim some authoritative advisory perspective, see Carolyn A. Edie, 'Good News From Abroad: Advice to The People of England on the Eve of the Stuart Restoration', *Bulletin of the John Rylands Library*, 67, 1 (1984), pp. 382 ff. Lawson's overtly political catalogue of current corruptions makes a somewhat eccentric plea to stay loyal to the present government, although *Pol.* 186, gives a more rosy view of the Interregnum.

Petition.[8] If, as Franklin notes, Lawson considered the exclusion of the Stuarts[9] (*Pol.* 93–5), he also backed away from the possibility, and he seems to hold out some hope of a restoration (*Pol.* 367) – a gesture more attuned to 1659 than to 1657.

Lawson had been a parliamentarian during the Civil War and was certainly an Engager. But much blood had flowed beneath the bridge since 1649 and neither Lawson's theory, nor Samuel More's conduct, runs simply into the still waters of a Commonwealth commitment fixed in 1657. By 1660 when a revised *Politica* was printed, Lawson was intellectually capable of accommodating himself to a restoration, just as the excluded Samuel More was about to have his offices confirmed by Charles II.

What at this stage, then, emerges from this interplay of putative dating and uncertain political commitment? First, we cannot use what turn out to be rather misleading hints of political allegiance to establish a firm date of writing. Secondly, this may not be just a technical difficulty but, as I shall suggest, something that is intimately related to the way in which Lawson's whole theoretical enterprise developed. Thirdly, it seems likely that while much of the theoretical substance of the work significantly pre-dated the publication in the context of the 1660 settlement crisis, the principles of Lawson's politics as they first appeared in the *Examination* were not only refined and expanded, but adjusted to fit that crisis. The character and extent of the changes will become clear in the process of explicating the main lines of argument in the *Politica*.

Like Locke's *Two Treatises*, with which it has been so closely associated, the *Politica* may have been written in one political context (we cannot say which), revised and published in another, and despite a continuity of precept, carried a new persuasive force. In effect this means, at least for Lawson, that we cannot really separate date of publication from date of creation. The *Politica* as we have it must be placed towards the end of the settlement controversy rather than prior to its beginning. But the work is best seen as a settlement tract in a much broader sense – and here I would certainly concur with Franklin. It is an abstract thesis pertinent to a distinctive family of settlement crises which reverberated through seventeenth-century Britain. Lawson understood his work as such a conspectus; and if it shows vestiges

---

[8] Franklin, *John Locke*, p. 60. this is discussed below. He also hypothesises that Lawson's acquaintances would have been discussing the possibility of Cromwell's royal transmogrification in the early 1650s. He does not say who these acquaintances might have been, but from what I have been able to discover of Lawson's circle (Baxter, Froysell, Heath, Tallents, Samuel More) there is no reason to think that such an idea would have been greeted with any enthusiasm.

[9] Franklin, *John Locke*, pp. 58, 60.

of the Engagement Controversy following the execution of Charles I and was published just prior to the Restoration of his son, the *Politica* was also fittingly republished in his last active year by John Starkey in 1689. It may be that, rather than any displayed commitment to the Rump or Cromwell, it was in part Lawson's political aloofness at the level of party affiliation that made his work germane to the constitutional problems of the seventeenth century as a whole. If it also fitted with his patron's views, it displays those attitudes which facilitated the traumatic but relatively blood-less shifts from Commonwealth to Stuart Restoration and to Williamite regime.

In each of the three great settlement crises, the language of debate and justification was noticeably similar. With each change of regime came ques-tions of allegiance and the sanctity of existing oaths; questions of consent and conquest; of obedience, rebellion and resistance; of constitutional dissol-ution and reform; of natural right, tyranny, fundamental law, sovereignty and patriotic integrity; trust and contract. In a sense this family of crises, developing from and then living under the shadow of the English Civil War and its powerful mythology, may be seen as establishing or entrenching a quasi-modern English language agenda and style of political argument. Yet the specification of the relevant political and ecclesiological events was largely a function of an already well-worn political vocabulary which we would most readily think of as medieval and un-English. The questions and terms which we are apt to see as modern came in a context of concern for a religious settlement which, by and large, was held to have priority over, or to be the *sine qua non* of, the more secular settlement of the political nation.

As Lawson shared such priorities and used a pervasive rhetoric appropriate to their articulation, even if he did not display all his contemporaries' passions, it may be useful to conclude this introduction to the exposition of the *Politica* with a map of religious discourse in which to locate his work as a whole and the *Politica* in particular.

The seventeenth century was one of systemic religious controversy and a time of tolerably sustained mayhem in the name of divinely sanctioned peace. The controversy was diverse just as the mayhem was widespread. It ran the gamut from the niceties of defining divinity to the notorious semiotics of sectarianism. With respect to the religious dimension of Lawson's work as a whole the following rough areas of dispute should be outlined.

At the most abstract level, theological argument dealt with a cluster of questions surrounding the nature of God. The most important of these concerned predication and its consequences; the grounds for knowledge of God and the limitations of discourse about postulated divinity.[10] Such arguments drew on a rich theological, logical and linguistically sophisticated inheritance dating back to the Church Fathers. The terms of debate had been set down chiefly in the thirteenth and fourteenth centuries by writers such as Scotus, Aquinas, Ockham and later Suarez. Such men and their works were used irrespective of their associations with any particular visible church; men whose legacy, shorn of their own theological priorities, was to form the basis of much modern philosophy. One could almost say at this level that the major doctrinal and political divisions between Catholic and Protestant were, as such, an irrelevance – certainly an unreliable guide to intellectual location.

A second area of dispute concerned the relationship between God and creation as a whole, and this could provide, by necessarily predicating the universe as providential, an immediate context for the relationship between God and humanity. This area in turn dealt with such questions as the nature of mankind, the fall, sin and grace, the significance of the crucifixion and the role of faith and works. It is this area of dispute which most clearly marks the point at which theology became moral theology and specific positions on its questions begin to make relatively consistent sense in terms of ecclesiological labels. This third area of moral theology flows naturally into a fourth which comprised the issues of sacramental theology and ecclesiology. On the basis of what was known by whom of the nature of sin and salvation, so the very notion of a church, its role and form in society, and its treatment of the sacraments could be legitimated. At the nexus of ecclesiology and moral and sacramental theology, one finds the most obvious way in which religious belief directly subsumed political argument and impinged on matters of state. It was also at the junction of these distinguishable areas of dispute that overt post-Reformation differences in religion were most difficult to reconcile – at which religion became manifestly 'ideological'. It was here that people stood and shouted stridently with the abusive vocabulary of sectarianism and certainty; here that we have the most tangible and easily perpetuated encapsulations of religious differences concerning music, church murals, the significance of the surplice, the positioning of altars, and altering the praying position. Needless to say, even without the case of Enock ap Evan, such symbolic lines of religious dispute could take on and sustain significance far removed from any theological principles to which they might ultimately and deviously be related.

Now germane to, and lying beneath all these fluid areas on this map

---

[10] See, for example, Pufendorf's succinct survey of the well-worn issues, as a preliminary to political discussion in *De officio hominis civis libri duo*, 1673, 1.5.; *The Westminster Confession*, ed. W. Carruthers, Presbyterian Church of England, London, 1903, chap 2.; Milton, *Paradise Lost* in *Poems* ed. Helen Darbishire, Oxford University Press, 1988, 10, 799 ff.

of holy waters, was the Bible. On the surface it provided a common point of reference, an authoritative vocabulary, a reservoir of proofs and precepts, illustrations and imperatives. Precisely because of this it was eristically vital that it be co-opted and hence through longstanding strategies of manipulation it gave forth as much heat as light. Dispute arose over the status of its books and the relationship between Testaments; over the way in which it could be read, and over whose readings might carry authority; over how and how far it was a book of guiding rules; how far it left areas of human activity within a realm of indifference (*adiaphora*). Dispute continued, of course, over its relationship to other sources of knowledge both pagan and Christian in origin. Ironically, it was probably least relevant and seems least relied upon in the most abstruse realms of theology; most used and contested in the more political regions of religious belief. *Par excellence*, the Bible was a political text.

As a whole, Lawson's thought flows through all the permeable areas I have loosely distinguished here. In the early unpublished manuscript material, most notably his 'Amica dissertatio', in the *Theo-Politica* (1659), and *Exposition of the Epistle to Hebrewes* (1662), he operates at the first level in the idiom of Aquinas, Ockham and Augustine, and at the second and third levels of dispute. In all these works, with varying degrees of emphasis, he is explicitly concerned to indicate what can literally be known of God, and on a basis of Augustinian awe and Ockhamist scepticism, to specify the significance of the fall, the crucifixion, the nature of sin, divine law and punishment, and the interpretation of the Ten Commandments. As these arguments often lead into abstruse ramifications, in the *Magna charta ecclesiae universalis* he attempted a more popular and edifying reduction of them – ever conscious of the requirements, and assumed limitations, of his audience, as he maintains he is of his capacities. In the *Examination*, his first known published work, he operated more consistently around the third and fourth levels of dispute, dealing with the difficult nexus of politics and religion. Hobbes is taken to task for his Erastianism, his conceptions of law, government, sovereignty and for the atheistic implications of *Leviathan*.

As Lawson accused Hobbes of being a great simplifier, we can expect the *Politica* to be a difficult text. So a synoptic overview might be useful before embarking on a detailed exposition.

In the context of Lawson's *oeuvre*, the *Politica* may be seen as an expanded appendix to his discussion of the Fifth Commandment in the *Theo-Politica*. It is an exploration of the biblical *loci*, love thy neighbour (for Lawson the communal imperative) and honour thy father and thy mother (the political one). These interest Lawson principally as they come into conflict. But the work is also an elaboration of much that is in the

Examination. As my exposition of the *Politica* will make clear, however, there are important differences between the two works. These will be reviewed in chapter 15.

Within the broad context of religious dispute I have outlined, the *Politica* focusses on God and human society in a narrow sense, elucidating the tensile claims of community authority and political power. The relationship between the state and the community may briefly be explicated with reference to more familiar, if later, demarcations. In some way Lawson's distinction resembles Tönnies's notions of *Gemeinschaft* and *Gesellschaft*, though not seen as types of society prearranged in developmental sequence, so much as defining aspects of the same universal phenomeonon, political society. In this way Michael Oakeshott's more recent distinction between *societas* and *universitas* is particularly suggestive. This is perhaps hardly coincidental, as he is explicitly abridging what he takes to be early modern understandings of the European state.[11] Lawson's community (especially his secular community) has the essential marks of the Oakeshottian *societas*. It is a 'fellow-ship' held together by loyalty (Lawson and Oakeshott share the same terminology), but lacking a uniform substantive purpose. Instead, it subsumes a diversity of socially organised practices and enterprises. Lawson's *politica*, his state or commonwealth, is a more purposive order of subjection, close to Oakeshott's *universitas*. Its *telos* is to maintain the common good through the subjection necessarily lacking in the community. It is this purpose and the obligations attendant upon it that hold it together. A political *community* is thus an order of hierarchical obligation imposed upon the loyalty of equal fellowship. Pertinently, Oakeshott remarks of his chosen metaphors, *societas* and *universitas*, that, although each is inadequate on its own, yoked together they help reveal the ambiguous character of the modern European state, which he calls 'an unresolved tension between two irreconcilable dispositions'.[12] Microcosmographically this points both to the structure of Lawson's argument and to its principal problems.

Further, Lawson's argument is an attempt to make the genus *politica* clear by bringing into analogical relationship its species, institutionalised church and secular state. Only through the interplay of church and state, each a different compound of communal and political identity, can the full complexity of political society and its tensions be revealed; the language appropriate to their understanding be refined; and the nature of obligation, sovereignty, loss of power, fulfillment of duty, exercise of right, all be made clear. Lawson's discussion of these portentous issues is always conducted

---

[11] Michael Oakeshott, *On Human Conduct*, Oxford, Oxford University Press, 1975, pp. 199 ff. It is an interesting coincidence that Oakeshott, I understand, supervised Maclean's thesis which rediscovered Lawson.
[12] *Ibid.*, pp. 200–1.

with one eye firmly on the problem of achieving a national political and ecclesiastical settlement, which he claims has been hampered both by ill-will and by ignorance of the basic principles of government. And so he is obliged to confront the happenings of the Civil War and its aftermath and to assimilate them to his analogical model.

Within the overall conceptual structure of the work, the organisation is relatively straightforward. The first eight chapters deal with God and his relationship to communities, the imposition of political order upon them, the loss, gain and transference of political power – these issues being taken up first with respect to civil society, and then with respect to its ecclesiastical analogue. Lawson's preoccupation with such issues in a specifically ecclesiastical context, however, is fully shown in the following six chapters which deal with the location of the power of the Keys within visible churches. This *topos* Lawson takes to be the principal issue of church government, one directly analogous to that of sovereignty in the secular state. The final two chapters return to the themes of the first chapters, though dealing with them under the heading of subjection and its limits rather than power. The penultimate chapter concerns civil subjection; the final one subjection within a church. Throughout, though somewhat unevenly, his theories are interlaced with his understanding of Britain's Civil War and its aftermath. The discussion of these events will be held over until the more abstract dimensions of his text have been elucidated and discussed.

As will become increasingly apparent in exposition and the separate discussion of particularly difficult or significant topics, Lawson's endeavour to persuade an audience to political and religious peace on very selective (ultimately theological) grounds, together with the systematically analogical structure of the work, conspire to bring the rhetorical plane of discourse and the interplay of religious and political metaphors very much to the fore. At this early point, I should stress that I mean to convey nothing prejudicial by reference to rhetoric and the attention I give it in Lawson's work. It indicates rather that I am asking questions organised around the apparent attempt of a man to persuade an audience of certain beliefs through his writing. The text, then, is not seen as a simple doctrinal edifice, or an abstract logical structure but as a weave of tactics, strategies and repertoires of language that might have aided his stated purpose. As it stands, this is inordinately vague, but it seems best to display the rhetoric of Lawson's *Politica* through exposition, and above all through the following analysis, rather than by trying to treat it *in abstracto*.

A related point is that the interplay of metaphors (which can hardly be ignored given the self-conscious analogical structuring of the work) should not be seen as some sort of top-dressing to the conceptual meat of his argument. On the contrary, it is only through examination of Lawson's metaphors and the possibilities and difficulties which they create, that we can really specify his argument. They must provide a textual *explanans* for his theory and its broader significance. I take them to provide something of an Ariadnean twist of thread for the whole of this study, one which will be used to tie it all together in the final chapter.

3

God and human society

The Epistle to the *Politica* informs the reader that, inquiring into the causes of present disaster and divine judgement, the author discovered (after much study of political authors and the political parts of the Bible) that the causes were as much religious as secular.[1]

Sins and impenitency have brought down God's judgement, but ignorance and error in matters of government have also caused division (*Pol.* Epist.).[2] More specifically, Lawson emphasises what he takes to be much confused thinking about secular and ecclesiastical communities. These Lawson sees as linked by common principles of politics, distinguished by complementary aims and the differing adaptation of the rules of government. They are, in short, distinct but not separate, and by laying them side by side Lawson hoped to make clear the nature of each. Lawson's modern readers are more willing to separate than to distinguish and so his conceptual technique has allowed the undue isolation of the secular and the imposition of a distorting modernity upon his text. For not only are his secular doctrines suspended in a net of theological conviction, but also the distinct realms of church and state were perceived by him to be mutually informing. In this I believe he was quite typical. The whole text may be seen as being teased out from the first sentences of the work, which authoritatively declaim the theological basis of all Lawson's thought and the principles which structure the taxonomies of church and state.

---

[1] A common view in 1659–60 seems to have been that religion was both a cause of trouble and the key to settlement; see e.g. *A Coffin for The Good Old Cause*, p. 5; *England's Settlement* ... pp. 15ff; John Eliot, *The Christian Commonwealth*, preface. Such works were at one with a wide range of earlier writings, see e.g. Joseph Hall, *A Modest Offer*, 1644, reprinted, 1660, pp. 2–3. Lawson may have arrived at such a view himself only after finishing the *Examination*, which seems to play down the importance of religion in the war, see p. 32. The change in Lawson's view, if there was one, is discussed below.

[2] This explicitly providential frame, together with what Franklin somewhat archly calls a plea for moral rearmament, was again standard fare. See, Abraham Nelson, *A Perfect Description of the Antichrist*, 1660; J. Collens, *A World in Season*, 1660, pp. 4–5; *Berith Anti-Baal*, 1661, for the author of which repentance is the only remedy; and the repetitive outpourings of writers such as Daniel Baker, and Edward Bagshaw the younger.

Propriety is the ground of Power, and Power of Government; and as there are many degrees of Propriety, so there are of Power: Yet as there is but one Universal and absolute Propriety, so there is but one supreme and universal Power, which the most glorious blessed, and eternal God can only challenge as his due (*Pol.* 1, see also 51, 114).[3]

Conventional, firm and confident, this statement belies doubts Lawson entertained about the problems surrounding the predication of God, just what such hypothetical assertions entailed, and whether human intelligence could ever really capture an adequate notion of divinity. Such doubts had been explored at length in the unpublished 'Amica dissertatio' and were to be voiced again in his *Exposition of the Epistle to Hebrewes*. However, as the *Politica* is largely restricted to questions of power relationships within human societies, the power of God provides the obvious point of departure if not the only one (*Pol.* 72). Indeed, the standard notion of an omnipotent God furnishes the most important theological axiom for the *Politica*; touched on intermittently, it is reiterated as Lawson begins his conclusion (*Pol.* 411). The corollary of God's ultimate power is the restricted and contingent nature of all other power relationships and rights of propriety. He who creates all may also dispose as he will (*Pol.* 1–2; *Exam.* 57).

Here, though obliquely expressed, is the same image of God the maker as we find, for example, in Anthony Ascham, in *The Westminster Confession* and later in Locke, and the presupposition (which Tully has emphasised so clearly) that making bestows special rights over the things made.[4] But to forestall any anticipation of doctrinal cosiness, it should be reiterated that the sharing of an abstract theological precept did not necessarily lead to a community of political opinion. God the uniquely powerful and creative proprietor is a *topos* Lawson's *Politica* also shares with the magisterial neo-Hobbesian treatise of John Hall (1627–56) *Of Government and Obedience* (1654). For Lawson an uncertain and variable world of human relationships lies in the shadow of God's creative omnipotence. The world conspires to be both providential and, from our limited understanding, fortuitous. It is in this way that Lawson can conclude that politics is but a branch

---

[3] This reaffirmation of a standard precept (see e.g. J. Althusius, *Politica methodice digesta*, 1614 edn, ch. 18, ed. C. J. Friedrich, Harvard University Press, Cambridge, Mass., 1932) may in part be in opposition to what James Tully has called Grotius's radical simplification of the vocabulary of property, *A Discourse on Property*, Cambridge University Press, 1982 edn, pp. 70–1; H. Grotius, *De Jure belli ac pacis libri tres*, trans. F. W. Kelsey, Oxford, Clarendon Press, 1913, 1925, bk. 1, ch. 2; but see also *De jure prolegomena*, for a discussion more at one with Lawson's presuppositions and formal preamble. See also Locke, MSS E7, Lovelace Collection, Bodleian Library, Oxford, for an opening passage strikingly similar to Lawson's, also discussed below, and Philip Hunton, *A Treatise of Monarchy*, 1643, pp. 2–3 where government is specified as participation in divine majesty: John Hall, *Of Government and Obedience*, 1654, 1.8.

[4] Tully, *A Discourse*, at length.

of divine providence, both civil and ecclesiastical matters 'belong unto Theology' (*Pol.* 2, 48); and at the same time stress the contingent nature of human affairs, as will be discussed below.

To specify the crucial problems within the realm of human politics, Lawson passes rapidly from the nature of God and his universe to that of man, providing a ground-clearing survey of man's relationship with his creator and fellows. His notion of human nature is synoptically set down with corroborative texts from Augustine, Cicero and Aristotle. God has endowed man with rationality, which embraces a capacity to understand something of his laws and justice, free will and a strong socio-linguistic instinct. Man (he cites the inevitable Aristotelian tag) is a political animal, and with his capacity for language the need to socialise can be fulfilled. The creature is alas also fallen, and is governed by God's strict justice, offset by 'the sweet mercy of Christ' (*Pol.* 20). Despite then a familiar and edifying conjunction of texts,[5] Lawson never lets us forget the propensity to fall over our feet of clay. He has less than an optimistic view of the future, and a willingness on occasion to blame all on wholesale moral turpitude. In theory government is legitimated by bringing to fruition the advantages of association, making them 'firm and lasting'; more immediately, 'we are ready every moment to fly asunder and break in pieces, if we were not kept together rather by the sword of an Army, than by any civil Power and Policy, or good affection; this is a sad condition and a just judgement upon us for our sins' (*Pol.* 19). He offers loosely, as it were, a Hobbesian present trapped in a Lockean eternity.

God has also endowed man with a capacity for temporal and spiritual life – the universality of the latter being indicated by the fact that all people have some sense of religion (*Pol.* 28).[6] It is these capacities, shaped by the ends of the common good and salvation respectively, that are reflected in Lawson's distinction between civil and ecclesiastical society.

Ultimately both social forms are governed by God, but secular government is usually indirect. Some of God's sovereignty is held by his viceregents, the 'higher powers' of Romans 13. Spiritual government, however, is directly by Christ. Unlike secular society, there is for Lawson a sense in which all churches are absolute monarchies. As a corollary, the extent of government in each form of society is different. Drawing on the ubiquitous distinction between transient and intransient acts, which had been converted into the evangelical insistence on a firm line between internal and external govern-

[5] Brian Tierney, *Religion, Law and the Growth of Constitutional Thought, 1150–1650*, Cambridge University Press, 1982, pp. 35–6.
[6] Cf. James Harrington, *Aphorisms*, nos. 33, 35–7, 39, 40, in *Works*, ed. J. G. A. Pocock, Cambridge University Press, 1977; William Bray, *A Plea to Stay Loyal to the People's Good Old Cause*, 1659, p. 9.

ment, Lawson claims that human government touches only externals.[7] It is limited to social relationships and mortal existence. Internal matters of the soul and conscience are reserved for the tribunal of God (*Pol.* 3).

The broad composite world of external social relations is specified by Lawson in order of increasing complexity: from 'families' and 'vicinities' (that is localised linguistically similar groupings of families existing in some degree of co-operation) to 'occasioned multitudes', that is, more specialised organisations existing for specific substantive ends. These are corporations in a narrow sense of the term. Here Lawson could be following or extrapolating from any number of writers, quite possibly from Althusius, *Politica methodice digesta*, whose discussion of the *collegium*, or *universitas*, is markedly similar.[8]

All of these groups can be subsumed by Lawson's central notion of a community, which seems close to the Althusian *jus symbioticum* or to the Oakeshottian *societas*. Lawson's community is a mature and established aggregation of other groupings and it is directly important because it alone can give rise to a commonwealth or state; and it is only with a state that one has strictly an order of political subjection. This whole set of common classifications is used to give a narrowly defined neo-Aristotelian scope to political activity.

Initially Lawson's discussion of the notion of a church does not directly parallel that which leads to the concept of a community. First, he distinguishes between the church triumphant (in everlasting peace) and the church militant. In its mystical form the latter comprises the community of 'real saints' having 'fellowship in Christ' (*Pol.* 15). The members of this church, living and dead, are known only to God. In its visible form, the church militant consists of all those who outwardly profess faith, it comprises both wheat and chaff, 'therefore we find a *Judas* in the Colledge of Apostles' (*Pol.* 32).[9] The notion of the visible church is further broken down into universal and particular (essential for any Protestant), and it is at this point that the refined notion of a church enters fully into the mundane and parallels secular social relationships. The universal church is introduced as simply the sum of all professed Christians living, who *ipso facto* accept their subjection to Christ and their reciprocal relationships to each other as brethren

---

[7] Marsilio of Padua, *Defensor pacis*, 1324, ed. H. Kutsch, Berlin, 1958, 1.4, on its importance in evangelical thought. See also Harro Höpfl, *The Christian Polity of John Calvin*, Cambridge University Press, 1982, e.g. pp. 52–3, 26–7. Even so absolutist a thinker as Filmer employs the distinction, see James Daly, *Sir Robert Filmer and English Political Thought*, Toronto University Press 1979, p. 108.

[8] Althusius, *Politica methodice digesta*, chap. 4, but his terminology is more fluid than Lawson's; Michael Oakeshott, *On Human Conduct*, Oxford, 1975, pp. 203–6 for a contemporary use of Althusian terminology for a distinction similar to Lawson's.

[9] Cf. Hooker, *The Laws of Ecclesiastical Polity*, Dent, London, 1965, 3.1.4; *The Westminster Confession*, ed. W. Carruthers, Presbyterian Church of England, London, 1903, chap. 25.

through this subjection. Particular churches are specific forms cut from the universaĺ fabric, they are legitimate socialised variations within the scope allowed by biblical indifference.[10] What differentiates all forms of church from the diversity of secular relationships is that all are 'occasioned multitudes'. A church is always some community of the professedly faithful organised towards, or participating in, the substantive end of everlasting peace. As I have noted, for Lawson churches are also absolute monarchies. Despite these crucial differences, Lawson insists, 'Church government presupposeth the rules of Government in general, therefore he that will know the latter must understand the former' (*Pol.* 11).[11]

Despite seeming to provide little more than a contextualising rehearsal of what Lawson assumes can be taken for granted, his position would already have been considered contentious by some. It is in contradiction to patriarchalism in the strict senses of that term in that, although it takes the Fifth Commandment as the quintessentially political imperative, it does not regard the family as the paradigm of political organisation.[12] In enmeshing politics in a context of theology, Lawson reaffirms a traditional relationship recently challenged in different ways by Hobbes and Harrington.[13]

Moreover, Lawson's co-option of a notion of community would have had its opponents – indeed it may be seen as a reply to a position that had been clearly drawn up and designed to discredit the evocative rhetoric of community. Bishop John Maxwell (1590–1647), *Sacro-sancta regnum*

[10] Hooker, *Laws*, 3.1.10–14; 3.2.1–2; *Westminster Confession*, chap. 25.

[11] Hooker, *Laws*, 3.1.1.14 on churches as forms of government.

[12] Again, like a good deal of the early part of the *Politica*, Lawson may be extrapolating from a work such as Althusius's *Politica methodice digesta*, which was specifically critical of the political implications of the metaphor of the family. In Althusius's case, the rationale seems to be provided by Ramist methodology – less evident, for example, in a writer like Rutherford, *Lex Rex*, 1644 (though the criticisms remain) and certainly modified in Lawson. More immediately, Lawson's position was in opposition to writers like Thomas Tompkins, *The Rebel's Plea*, 1659 and E. Bagshaw, *De monarchia absoluta*, 1659. The opposition is not entirely clear cut, for in the *Theo-Politica* Lawson's acceptance of the Fifth Commandment as a metaphor for the political, brings family and polity closer together. The ambivalence created by this image is well noted by G. Schochet, *Patriarchalism*, Blackwell, Oxford, 1975, pp. 181–2 with respect to Lawson's *Examination* and *Theo-Politica*. See also Daly, *Filmer*, who usefully distinguishes anthropological, legal and analogical familiarism, e.g. p. 152.

[13] Quentin Skinner, *The Foundations of Modern Political Thought*, Cambridge University Press, 1978, 2, pp. 341–2 claims this to have been challenged by both Buchanan and Althusius. David Wootton 'The Fear of God in Early Modern Political Theory', *Historical Papers, Canada* (1983), pp. 79–80 has been highly critical of the reading of Buchanan. With respect to Althusius, what, following Ramus, was at issue was the logical structure of distinguishable intellectual domains. He was concerned more with conceptual irrelevance rather than a clear and concrete separation. This I think is rather different from the questioning of the nexus of theology and politics to be found in Hobbes and Harrington, inasmuch as each, albeit in differing ways, saw the scientific as providing the essential frame for the political, rather than seeing the political as having an abstract logically independent identity of its own.

majestas (1644), and John Hall, *Of Government and Obedience* (1654), by a sort of methodological individualism combined with a highly reified notion of power, had both asked how it was possible for individuals who do not have power to be seen as giving or entrusting it to governments. The young Locke was to adopt a similar position. In the meantime, Lawson's theory of political society presupposes, in contrast, that in God's providential universe we never have sufficient power to be isolated individuals. Rather, community is always assumed as the only notion that can precede a concept of the political. On this basis, the principal concern to emerge from the opening sections of the work, with respect to both state and church, is with the nexus of community and 'politica' in the context of subjection to God. The rules of government which Lawson discusses are for the benefit of the individual caught in the middle of this conceptual web.

Set down schematically, methodised as Lawson would have said,[14] the *Politica* is a discourse on the diagram below:

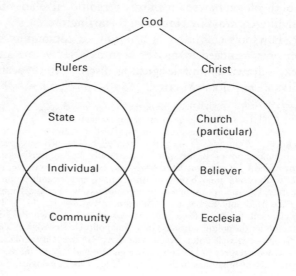

[14] The references to method and to being methodical may well allude to the public law theory surrounding the work of Althusius, who proclaims in his title his methodical exposition. It may also refer to Ramist methodological reforms which had such an impact on writers such as Bodin and Althusius; but by the time Lawson was writing, reference to method had become a more diversified claim to intellectual seriousness. It is central to the writings of Bacon, and of course Hobbes; but Baker's *Chronicles of the Kings of England* (on which I suspect Lawson drew for historical material) also makes a claim on the reader's attention through its new method. Lawson himself is later praised for his methodical head by Baxter and by Humfrey. On the diversity of method and reference to it in the early modern period, see Neal Gilbert, *The Renaissance Concept of Method*, Columbia University Press, 1960.

4

Community and political power

Lawson's discussion of the concept of community *per se* is couched in the terminology of secular society and politics; thus the received vocabulary of politics constitutes an area of metaphorical expansion for Lawson's ecclesiology. The community itself is provisionally styled a 'common or public society of Men' (*Pol.* 13). Above all, it is a society immediately capable of political form (*ibid.*). This identification is authenticated by reference to Aristotle, Cicero, Augustine and Forsterus (Johann Forster? 1495–1556) for Hebrew etymology.[1] This social *matter* awaiting only the political *form* presupposes language, religion and a diversity of established custom and social sub-groupings. The ecclesiological analogue is identified in similar terms. It is an association of Christian believers ready to receive the form of organised office and discipline which defines a particular visible church (*Pol.* 35, 44). Moreover, it is no mere family or congregation (*Pol.* 32–5), but, like its secular analogue, 'an association joined as one', capable of unity of concerted action (*Pol.* 16). Thus, analogically, it is one made of many members, 'as in an organical body' (cf. *Exam.* 21); and (the analogy is tightened to a metaphor) it is 'one person morally conceived' (*Pol.* 16; *Exam.* 30). Ecclesiologically it is 'morally one Person spiritual: and as such, may act and do many things ... they receive a Power and Ability to act as one Person for the special good of themselves' (*Pol.* 34). As the power comes from God, it is not surprising to find that, in both its secular and ecclesiological manifestations, the community exists in a context of divine law which it is bound to observe (*Pol.* 17, 33–4); it is thus required to be rational and just in order to be a proper community. This is stressed by Lawson as he circumscribes the importance of consent in communal life. All communities involve express or tacit consent but villains, 'even

---

[1] *The Politics, Republic* and *City of God*, respectively. The reference Forsterus is presumably to his Lexicon of which there is a copy in the *Catalogus Librarum* but which is not amongst the twelve works on Hebrew etymology in the More Church Library. It could also be to his polyglot Bible. The argument follows Marsilian and Althusian corporate elaborations on Aristotle.

devils' (*Pol.* 17), are capable of forming a purely 'rational association'.[2] Community status requires justice (adherence to divine law), which consent itself cannot bestow. In short, and this becomes central for Lawson, community is a divinely sanctioned society worthy of consent. 'And this Union is so firm, not because of Man's Consent, but God's Precept and Institution, to which it shall be conformable' (*Pol.* 34). On this basis consent operates as a derivative criterion of legitimacy; in this general sense, Lawson's notion of community is at one with the Levellers, Clubmen, Ben Jonson, the Cavalier poets, Althusius and numerous others.

More specifically, the distinction between express and tacit consent is necessitated by the size and structure of the Lawsonian community, for his model is clearly a Roman law corporation (cf. *Exam.* 21). Express consent seems to be the defining capacity of the *cives* who enjoy liberty and equality: there is no human subjection amongst them 'all are fellows' (*Pol.* 26). In the religious context, the *cives* (believers) are free and equal before each other, and are subject only to Christ. Before Lawson articulates the entailed freedom and equality of the *cives* or complete members, however, he has already distinguished them from members who are only *virtualiter et diminute* (*Pol.* 24). These 'virtual' members (women, children, aliens and servants) are subsumed by *cives*, members *formalite et plene* (*Pol.* 24). The *cives* are not accountable to the virtual members, indeed they enjoy a *plena potestas* on their behalf, and hence virtual members can only be seen as giving tacit consent.[3] Even among the complete members, however, some are more equal than others. These are the *eminenter cives* 'who by reason of their descent, Estates, Parts, Noble Acts, are not once members but somewhat more, as being fit for Honour, Offices and Places of Power if once a Commonwealth be constructed' (*Pol.* 25). To such *eminenter cives*, even the complete 'may give their suffrage virtually' (*ibid.*). Lawson's use of the term virtual so soon after introducing the notion of virtual membership suggests strongly that the *eminenter cives* are not simply potentially important, but are ostensibly 'more than once members' who may represent the *cives* as the *cives* represent the human beings that numerically make up the community. This communal hierarchy is carried over directly into Law-

---

[2] This would seem to indicate that Lawson, somewhat unusually, along with the Muggletonians, did consider an atheistic society to be a possibility. See David Wootton 'The Fear of God in Early Modern Political Theory'; *Historical Papers*, Canada (1983), pp. 61ff.

[3] Cf. Marsilio, *Defensor pacis*, 1324, ed. H. Kutsch, Berlin, 1958, 1.12.4, for almost identical phrasing (Lawson may in effect be translating here); but the general point is almost ubiquitous: see e.g. Grotius, *De jure belli ac pacis libri tres*, trans. F. W. Kelsey, Clarendon Press, Oxford, 1913, 1925, 1.3.6, for variant terms; J. Althusius, *Politica methodice digesta*, 1614 edn, ed. C. J. Friedrich, Harvard University Press, Cambridge, Mass., 1932, chaps. 5–6, which again seem to hover over the *Politica*; Philip Hunton, *A Treatise of Monarchy*, 1654, p. 4, for virtual rather than tacit consent.

son's ecclesiology. Ministers he considers to be *eminenter cives*, though they are of less importance than their secular analogues.[4]

As I shall suggest, Lawson had a vested persuasive interest in portraying the community as, by definition, large, sophisticated and hierarchically structured; and something of such complexity required the employment of corporation theory and its defining notions of representation and consent if his own theory was to remain both conceptually manageable and in touch with the perceived realities of the country for which he was writing. Even so, the heart of the community may be said to lie in those free and equal *cives* who stand synecdochically (*Pol.* 340) for the larger grouping which enjoys all the attributes of civilisation but for the strictly political ones pertaining to a formal order of subjection. Thus although 'this association conduceth much unto [the] safety, help comfort [of the *cives*] and furnish them with many things not only necessary, but convenient . . . yet without a form of government, these advantages would not be firm and lasting' (*Pol.* 19). Experience, he adds darkly, we have readily before us 'so many and great are our differences' (*ibid.*).

As with his discussion of community, Lawson opens his account of the settled power structures of church and state in the vocabulary of secular politics. The discussion of politics *per se* merges imperceptibly into that of the secular state; and the closeness of the ecclesiastical analogue is established by the terms through which the visible church is defined as 'a Spiritual Commonwealth' (*Pol.* 108). In both realms a constitutional form is defined as 'an order of Superiority and Subjection in respect to Power' (*Pol.* 47); and the power is not mere force. Coming from God, power is good in itself (*Pol.* 51; *Exam.* 13). Force stands in opposition to God's will, and would be inappropriate to the community's needs for peace and happiness (*Pol.* 50–2; cf. *Exam.* 8, 9, 22).[5] One wonders, logically, how sheer force can exist, though its conceptual importance for Lawson will prove to be central – even if its employment is (appropriately) arbitrary. What Lawson builds into his notion of power looks, conventionally enough, much like an extrapolation from the complementary predicates (power and justice) he has already provided for his concept of God; and the difficulties of the

[4] Cf. H. Stubbe, *A Letter to an Officer in the Army*, London, 1659, pp. 49ff., for whom the superior physical power of the few creates hierarchy, and the few are required to protect those they subsume. Lawson's point can be seen conceptually, if not historically, as preparing the ground for an answer to Filmer's attack on consent as a criterion of political legitimacy. See James Daly, *Sir Robert Filmer*, Toronto University Press, 1979, chap. 4.
[5] The distinction between power and force was standard. See e.g. Samuel Rutherford, *Lex Rex*, 1644, question 9 where force is the 'Licentious deviation' of power coming from Satan; Locke, MSS E7, p. 1, Lovelace Collection, Bodleian Library, Oxford. Reformation disputes had brought it to the fore as a means of avoiding the indiscriminate embrace of Romans 13. See e.g. Quentin Skinner, *The Foundations of Modern Political Thought*, Cambridge University Press, 1978, 2, pp. 217–18 on the *Magdeburg Confession* of 1550.

power/force distinction are themselves consequent upon the difficulties of divine predication. For Lawson the central point is that although resisting God's power is quite illegitimate (this gives a role for the term rebellion), resisting pure force is not. From power and force, good and evil, then, comes the imperative to discriminate between resistance and rebellion. A political sovereign holding power as God's viceregent becomes like a god (*Pol.* 51). Such a ruler (or group of rulers) by definition possesses majesty and the acts of majesty are to govern, command, to bind to obedience and punish with the requisite power to carry out threat (*Pol.* 51–2, 98; *Exam.* 8–9, 23).[6] Such a sovereign by the mere fact of existence also definitionally creates a body of subjects. The terms subject and sovereign are reciprocally defining, they are 'relates' (*Pol.* 50).[7] Subjects, through nominal definition, are seen as subjected and the relationship between subject and sovereign is thus the creation of the form of superiority impressed (imprinted, moulded) upon the communal matter (*Pol.* 12, 13, 16, 35, 46).[8]

If one isolates this strand of sovereignty and subjection, Lawson seems to be setting up an awesome and irresistible power capable of an enormous diversity of acts, amenable to the sort of complex taxonomy of administrative classification, which – as Thomas More might have remarked – rulers do not need to be told about (cf. *Exam.* 155). Lawson tosses off a stream of names of those who have elaborated and discussed such classificatory systems: 'Angelicus, Bodin, Clapmarius, Grotius, Besoldus, Arnisaeus', the omnibus 'others', and the anonymous squabbling casuists. These are mentioned partly it seems to impress upon the reader Lawson's own credentials

---

[6] Cf. Marsilio, *Defensor pacis*, 1.10.4; 1.12.6; *Westminster Confession*, chap. 23; Peter Martyr Vermigli, 'Commentary on Romans 13', in *Political Thought*, ed. R. Kingdon, Droz, Geneva, 1980; John Hall, *Of Government*, 1.9 whose specification of the powers of viceregents (p. 43) resembles Lawson's.

[7] Hall, *Of Government*, 1.6; Hooker, *Laws*, purely in the context of ecclesiology, 'the names of all church officers are words of relation' 5.80.3; Hunton, *A Treatise*, p. 1; John Milton, *The Tenure of Kings and Magistrates*, in *The Prose Works of John Milton*, ed. J. Max Patrick, Doubleday, New York, 1967, p. 366, 'We know that King and Subject are relations, and relatives have no longer being than in the relation …' The point is made in Ramus's *Logic*, chap. 13; Christopher Besold, *De magistate in genere*, in *Operis politici*, Strasburg, 1626, 1.1.2, cited in Franklin.

[8] Stubbe, *A Letter*, p. 57 for similar imagery. Brian Tierney, *Religion, Law and the Growth of Constitutional Thought, 1150–1650*, Cambridge University Press, 1982, pp. 97–8, intimates that Lawson took the imagery from Jean Gerson, but Lawson claims not to have read him. The vocabulary of form and matter had been widespread since Aristotle. The general understanding of sovereignty as distinct from community again looks much like Althusius, *Politica methodice digesta*, preface, chap. 1. See Alberigo Gentili, *De jure belli libri tres*, 1608; Clarendon Press, Oxford, 1933 edn, 1.15, for the analogy of states as citizens much as Lawson uses the word because of the absence of subjecting parties. It is a passage in which Cicero looms large.

for continuing the discussion; partly to indicate that his claim is only to be providing a more precise variation on long-standing themes. As these writers (insofar as they are even known now) would mostly be regarded loosely as absolutist, the effect is to dramatise the power that flows from God through kings. Grotius is praised for his brevity and style (*Pol.* 53)[9] but it is to Christopher Besold (1577–1638), German theorist of public law, a writer for whom Lawson showed scant respect in the *Examination*, that he turns briefly for a more refined nomenclature of sovereignty. Besold distinguishes between *real* and *personal* sovereignty: the former being invested with the people (for Lawson the people as a community); the latter with the prince (or for Lawson any governmental form).[10]

Real majesty for Lawson amounts to the capacity to form or change a constitution. *Personal* majesty is the power of sovereigns requiring obedience. Then somewhat harshly Lawson tells us that Besold says nothing about *real* majesty; and, with an almost visibly dismissive wave of the quill in the direction of Arnisaeus *et al.*, he makes bold on his own behalf, classifying the acts within the domain of *personal* majesty. These range from issuing forth with armies to issuing coin of the realm. In standard Bodinian form, stress is placed on legislation, taxation, judgement and the execution and suspension of laws. Broadly, he concludes, the acts of *personal* majesty fall into the categories of legislative, executive and judicial (*Pol.* 68–71), a division of powers about which he entertained doubts in the *Examination*.[11] *Personal* sovereignty itself may take on different forms, but whatever its shape and structure it is indivisible and is thus, like the community beneath it, essentially corporate (*Pol.* 71) – a point taken up later in the century, and marginally noted in some copies of the *Politica*.

[9] Presumably, Grotius, *De jure*, 1.3.6, paraphrasing Aristotle, *Politics*, 4.14. See also Besold, *De magistate* 1.1.1–2.
[10] Besold, *Principium et finis politicae doctrinae* and *De magistate*, both in *Operis politici*, cited in Franklin. It is not clear if Lawson has any particular text in mind. See Julian Franklin, *John Locke and the Theory of Sovereignty*, Cambridge University Press, 1978, pp. 64f. Bodin, *The Six Books of the Commonwealth*, 1.7.8 divides sovereignty into two forms; Althusius, *Politica methodice digesta*, 11–13, 14, uses the nomenclature of *real* and *personal* but with reference to tax collecting and other duties.
[11] The distinction apparently dates back to Hervaeus Natalis, *De potestate pape*, Paris, 1647, see Tierney, *Religion*, p. 45. According to C. C. Weston and J. R. Greenberg, *Subjects and Sovereigns: The Grand Controversy over Legal Sovereignty in Stuart England*, Cambridge University Press, 1981, such a stress on legislation and execution would make Lawson modern rather than old-fashioned. But this too seems to be well embedded in medieval ecclesiastical argument. On Pope John XXII's authority stemming from legislative power see C. Condren, 'Rhetoric, Historiography and Political Theory', *The Journal of Religious History* (1984), pp. 30–3. See also Hunton, *A Treatise*, pp. 25, 40; he was effectively attacked by Filmer (Daly, *Filmer*, pp. 49–50). Hunton has since been rendered more clear (and Lawsonian) than the text warrants by C. H. McIlwain, 'Philip Hunton: A Forgotten Worthy', in *Constitutionalism and the Changing World*, Cambridge University Press, 1939, pp. 174–5.

Lawson's Althusian–Besoldian terminology ushers in the most central and troublesome aspect of his constitutional theory, which will be discussed in full below. Immediately, however, one can say that the notion of *real* majesty located in the pre-existing community counterbalances Lawson's stress on the strength of the sword. Indeed, *real* majesty, inseparable from the community (*Pol.* 58; *Exam.* 10), is in a sense greater than *personal*, for it is an antecedent power to model the state (*Pol.* 57, 71).[12]

Thus when a form of government is dissolved, if there is 'a failer [*sic*] of Succession, the Power of the Sovereign doth dissolve unto them by the law of nature, rather it was always in the people' (*Pol.* 58).[13] The explicit correlate is that the power of *real* majesty embraces the right to dissolve a settled constitution in a just and necessary cause (*ibid.*); but Lawson is careful also to disengage his own position from what he takes to be established resistance theory, exemplified by writers such as the Scottish jurist George Buchanan (1506–82) and a Protestant leader of the Low Countries, François Junius (1545–1602). To such names he might well have added Althusius, Beza, and the monarchomachs. All those writers are wrong, he asserts, who suggest that such powers to dissolve exist in a body of subjects (*Pol.* 58): 'Subjects as Subjects cannot do it, because of their Subjection and Obligation, whereas the Community as a Community is free from any Obligation to any particular form' (*ibid.*; *Exam.* 15, 16).

At this point, it is instructive to move to the ecclesiastical dimension of Lawson's argument. Here, despite parallels of terminology and conceptual relationship, there are important changes of emphasis which lessen the incipient tension created by Lawson's terminology and concepts. To begin with, the notion of ecclesiastical majesty is housed in the image of the Keys of the Kingdom of Heaven; like that of the sword, it conveys an element of coercion. The power of the Keys is a matter of binding and loosing (*Pol.* 109–10), which is to govern. More specifically it involves the control of

---

[12] Cf. Besold who, as Franklin suggests, *John Locke*, pp. 66–7, seems to use the distinction more to indicate a share in government rather than an authority prior to it. Althusius, *Politica methodice digesta*, chaps. 9 and 18 makes the distinction between forms of majesty in terms of ownership and usage. See also Besold, *De magistate*, 1.1.4 where personal majesty *capus est non totum Corpus*. The possible differences between Lawson and Besold are discussed below (pp. 98–101).

[13] Stubbe, *A Letter*, pp. 49ff.; broadly similar Althusian affirmations are found in the Leveller manifestoes. Milton, *Tenure*, p. 353, provides an unequivocally aggressive affirmation: 'the power of Kings and magistrates is nothing else, but what is only derivative, transferred and committed to them to trust from the people to the Common good of them all, in whom the power yet remains fundamentally'; Rutherford, *Lex Rex*, question 9, specifies a residual power against tyrants in the Reformation/Althusian tradition; Hunton, *A Treatise*, pp. 17–18, though with a less clear notion of residual community. As John Hall, *Of Government*, 2.1, p. 87, perceptively remarked, community was usually associated with a notion of trusteeship.

discipline, the rights of admonition and excommunication, and such things as the administration of church property. Such a power is as extensive as any visible church in which it is located. In contrast to the state, however, Lawson emphasises 'the very narrow scantling' of all ecclesiastical power (*Pol.* 108). Visible churches are directly governed by Christ, thus there is less scope for human dominion. Moreover, as churches are concerned with spiritual ends, they are organised largely around those intransient acts which come directly before the tribunal of God. Such a uniform lack of power amongst visible churches enables Lawson to emphasise their equality and divisibility (*Pol.* 112).

Lawson distinguishes between the primary and secondary power of the Keys. The primary power resides in the community of brethren forming the church and it is said to be primitive, total and supreme – uncompromising terms not used of its secular analogue. The secondary power of the Keys is said to be derivative, partial and subordinate; demeaning terms not used of secular *personal* majesty. Church ministers, who come closest to being the ecclesiastical equivalent of God's viceregents in the secular domain (*Pol.* 113) are seen as accountable officers with only advisory status and moral authority.[14] So, a hierarchical relationship between constituent authority and administrative organisation is clearer in Lawson's ecclesiology than in his secular theory.

Lawson's discussion of majesty flows easily into the problem of the acquisition of power in church and state. As civil power usually comes indirectly from God via the community, it is initially established through consent or even election (*Pol.* 82, 84). Ideally, or paradigmatically, God creates a governmental form through the rational election of the community but, for Lawson, this obviously most legitimate of states receives scant attention, because it is manifestly rare. In fact, most governments originate in conquest or usurpation (*Pol.* 83, 87–8),[15] so election dwindles into an element of communal consent. A just war may reduce a people to voluntary submission; and the conqueror may then take the people under his protection as subjects.

[14] Cf. Marsilio, *Defensor pacis*, 2.13–16 on the ideal character of priests and 1.19 upon their lack of coercive power. For Lawson ministers are Christ's deputies, and even in some respects above angels but they do not hold the Keys. *Contra* Baxter, *A Treatise of Episcopacy*, 1681, chap. 2. who takes up the issue with Lawson as expressed in the *Theo-Politica* in which Lawson argues the case more powerfully.

[15] Cf. A. Ascham, *On the Confusions and Revolutions of Government*, 1649; F. Guicciardini, *Ricordi*, ed. E. Pasquini, Garzanti, Milan, 1975, p. 48; though Lawson could not have known this; Marvell, *Horatian Ode*, 'So when they did design / The Capitols first line, / A bleeding Head where they begun, / Did fright the Architects to run, (67–70). This alludes to the decapitated head under the foundation of the capitol, a *figura* for the head of Charles. See also N. Machiavelli, *Il Principe e Discorsi*, Feltrinelli, Milan, 1973 edn, 1.9, following Livy on Rome's foundation on fraticide.

Such governments, adds Lawson a shade redundantly, are apt to be despotic and absolute (*Pol.* 83). The consent here, if minimal by modern standards, is of importance for Lawson.[16] The choice may only be between submission and extermination, but in a providential universe, where the afterlife is a priority, it remains a genuine choice. Moreover, consenting to a conqueror in such a universe, may well be consenting to God, 'and that princes are divested of majesty and people of liberty, and fall under the power of Strangers, it's from the judgement of God, punishing them for their crimes' (*Pol.* 83).[17] The difficulty with conquest is that the motives and ambitions of the conqueror are usually suspect; even the behaviour may be unpalatable and obnoxious; but the power is from God and thus in itself good (*Pol.* 83–4). But here, where it seems immediately relevant, the distinction between power and force is not reintroduced.

Usurpation differs from conquest because, first, it occurs from within a community and, secondly, unlike conquest, it is never just according to *human* law (*Pol.* 86).[18] Nevertheless, 'there are few titles now, especially such as are successive in a line which did not at first begin in usurpation' (*Pol.* 87).[19] Lawson raises the question of resistance to usurpation, but even in an extreme case there is no unwavering commitment, indeed perhaps even a commitment at all, for we must consider, he says in the advisory idiom of Polonius, how far a usurper is perhaps a tool of God, and in resisting him we resist God (*Pol.* 89) – a phrase redolent of *Westminster Confession* submissiveness (chap. 10). Resistance even if formally allowable might be a remedy worse than the disease (*Pol.* 89; *Exam.* 19 for similar phrasing). What may be usurpation in terms of positive law may not be in the context of divine (*Pol.* 89). In any case, it may not be possible to keep our old oaths of allegiance, and thus in time an aura of legitimacy

[16] Grotius, *De jure*, 3.8. It is misleading to say that Lawson simply confuses allegiance with submission, as does Richard Ashcraft, following Franklin, in *Revolutionary Politics and Locke's Two Treatises of Government*, Princeton University Press, 1986, p. 311.

[17] Another standard theme germane to the Civil War and exploited by the *de facto* theorists, e.g. Ascham, in *Confusions* and *Conscience Puzzled*, 1651. See John Wallace, 'The Engagement Controversy, 1649–52', *The Bulletin of the New York Public Library*, 68 (1964), pp. 384–5. A common source is likely to have been Vermigli, 'Commentary on Judges, 3: 29–30' and 'Commentary on Genesis' in *Political Thought*, pp. 100, 109–10. It was however a dangerous and double-edged doctrine. See Daly's lucid discussion in *Filmer*, pp. 114ff.

[18] Franklin overlooks Lawson's insistent distinction in his discussion of *Conscience Puzzled* and Lawson's possible authorship of the tract, *John Locke*, pp. 61, 129. The author of *Conscience Puzzled* refers to England as a conquered nation in 1650. The author of the *Politica* would have regarded this as wrong. Franklin's guess as to authorship needs Lawson to have changed his language.

[19] Ascham, *Confusions* and later stressed by Hume, 'Of the Original Contract', *Political Essays*, ed. C. Hendel, Liberal Arts Press, New York (1953?), p. 47.

will gather around new-found power.[20] Finally, Lawson reiterates the well-worn distinction (dating from the Italians Bartolus of Saxoferrato, d. 1357, and Coluccio Salutati, d. 1406) between one who comes to power as a usurper and subsequently rules well, and one who acquires power legitimately and then rules as a usurper of more power than 'either God will or Man can give' (*Pol.* 90).[21]

Thus one can always find good enough reasons for accepting usurpation, though there may always be good reason for resisting it. Usurpation definitionally denies rights '[and] some tell us that there is no Right which may not be defended' (*Pol.* 93). The people, he states, do have the right to defend themselves even against a *personal* sovereign acting as a usurper. A resistance theory after all then? Not quite, at least it is still alloyed with a *de facto* willingness to submit. And, he adds, the people as subjects cannot resist (a point elided in Starkey's marginal gloss, *Pol.* 93); it is only when the sovereign forfeits power by usurpation that the people *qua* people may challenge him (*Pol.* 106–7). Even then, prudence and providence must be weighted against political right; it may still be wiser and more just, as it were, to lie down and be counted (*Pol.* 107; *Exam.* 19). However we behave, we remain assured that the political world is capricious and uncertain, and reading God's intentions through it is both essential and difficult. The acquisition of political power is almost invariably another's loss; and whom God is using for what purposes remains obscure. This we do know, that power sits but lightly and briefly upon the shoulders of men; spades change to sceptres and sceptres into spades (*Pol.* 99). None should take up power without being willing to lay it aside, for loss is inevitable and the means to this loss ingeniously diverse. Natural causes, usurpations, conquests, and civil wars may all amount to dissolutions or 'failures' of succession (*Pol.* 90). Hence the Machiavellian, or Guicciardinian, contingency of human affairs is used to underline the vital importance of the reconstituting and settling capacities of the *real* majesty of the community, though even that may be destroyed.

This emphasis on uncertainty is missing from Lawson's ecclesiology, and as the acquisition and loss of ecclesiastical power is less morally imponderable, it is treated more shortly and simply. As churches are governed by

[20] Cf. Hunton, *A Treatise*, p. 18; it was to become a standard *de facto* theme, which runs through to Hume, formalised by his stress on habit. See Wallace, 'Engagement Controversy'; J. G. A. Pocock, *Obligation and Authority in Two English Revolutions*, Victoria University of Wellington Press, 1973; Quentin Skinner, 'Conquest and Consent' in *The Interregnum*, ed. G. E. Aylmer, Macmillan, London, 1972; Condren 'A Cloath of Fading Colours: Hume, Reid and the Inheritance of Contract', *Australian Society of Legal Philosophy*, 10 (1986), pp. 63f.
[21] Cf. Coluccio Salutati, *De Tyranno*, chap. 1 (1400); Bartolus, *De tyrannia*, chap. 2; Althusius, *Politica methodice digesta*, 18; Peter Martyr Vermigli, 'De tyrannide perferenda a piis hominibus' ('Commentary on Genesis 34') in *Political Thought*, p. 106.

Christ, there can be no regimes legitimated by time. Here the *de facto* ethos evaporates; acceptable usurpation and conquest become contradictions in terms. In this sense, paradoxically, the ecclesiastical universe is less informed by providence than the secular.

Certainly there is flexibility and diversity of church form within the ambit of biblical indifference, but churches must conform to the elective paradigm in their initial ordering (*Pol.* 123); and any arrogation of the community's rights to the primary power of the Keys must be a direct affront and disobedience to Christ (*Pol.* 126–8). Usurpation and conquest are not entertained as possible means to God's ends. We know where we are, and are now confronted with the unequivocal point of Lawson's distinction between power and force, somewhat blurred in the secular context. Ecclesiastical usurpation or conquest constitute force, and the brethren must obey God in the face of such force by some act of separation, the analogue of secular resistance. What little there is of ecclesiastical power is quite lost by its conversion into force, and in the last analysis this gives a clear-cut nature to the believer's necessary response. It thus becomes all the more vital for Lawson to specify what is encompassed by biblical indifference to church form and to defend his location of the primary power of the Keys in the community. Church and state form stand analogous and Lawson turns next to the varieties of *personal* majesty in state and church as an adjunct to his defence of the *real* majesty of the ecclesiastical community.

The necessarily reciprocal acquisition and acceptance of political power may be institutionalised in different ways (*Pol.* 130). Lawson then, like the Catholic Thomas More, the Church of England Richard Hooker and the Scottish Presbyterian Samuel Rutherford and the broadly 'Presbyterian' tradition, held that God commanded mankind to be ruled, but authorised no specific governmental structure (*Pol.* 147).[22] But circumstances had changed the general force of the precept. When Rutherford was writing, such a principle was easily directed against the Stuart monarchy or more specifically its apologists (Bishop Maxwell's *Sacro-sancta* was the ostensible target); but in 1659–60, its reiteration could provide a ground for settlement that could encompass the family's restoration.

The anonymous *A Short Discourse Upon the Desires of a Friend* (1659) had not unreasonably depicted monarchy and republicanism as embattled

[22] Rutherford, *Lex Rex*, questions 9 and 13; Richard Tuck, *Natural Rights Theories: Their Origin and Development*, Cambridge University Press, 1979, pp. 144–5, for Lawson as being a part of this broad grouping. The term is potentially misleading as to some extent it would have to cover Thomas More's *Epigrammata*, 83, 205. See Damian Grace, 'Thomas More's *Epigrammata*: Political Theory in Poetic Idiom', *Parergon* n.s. (1985), pp. 115ff. It would also only ambivalently include Lawson.

contenders for the title of best government, urging the establishment of a government to compose all differences. The tract reflected the common presupposition that the key to a settlement lay in finding the correct institutional form for the country.[23] In contrast, Lawson's whole discussion of governmental types seems designed to defuse that burning issue. Initially, Lawson stresses that when he speaks of *personal* majesty he means to include along with monarchy 'all Aristocratical and Polyarchical Sovereigns who are many physically, but considered as one person morally' (*Pol.* 71).[24] The more detailed treatment is held over, which structurally reinforces the impression that such matters are of secondary importance. When the discussion is reopened Lawson, operating with the received and minimal classifications of monarchy, aristocracy, democracy and free state, proceeds to destabilise and adjust them to English circumstances.

Initially the ground is prepared by anglicising also the hierarchical structure of his concept of underlying community. The difference of status between *cives* and *eminenter cives* is now amended to a threefold distinction between the merely free, the nobility and the supremely eminent, an adaptation of Althusian corporate federalism perhaps. These distinctions, though not tied exclusively to English circumstances, are then related to the commons (who may vote); the gentry and (lesser) nobility; and those magnates of such importance that they, above all, may be looked to for leadership in the settlement of the nation (*Pol.* 131–2; cf. *Pol.* Epist.).

With respect to the forms that may be imposed upon the community, all are diverse and fluid. Despite some 'imperious Dictators and Masters of words' (*Pol.* 135) monarchies are not necessarily absolute (cf. *Exam.* 17).[25] Although the Spanish, French and Polish monarchies tend to this extreme, those of Sweden and Denmark do not. The King of England (present tense) is different yet again (*Pol.* 135). Shifting clearly towards real definition he argues that words and definitions cannot determine the power of kings and the usual definition in terms of the governance of free men according to law could apply to any form (*Pol.* 135–6). What really matters is whether monarchy *tends* towards despotism and whether it is balanced by any other component within the ambit of *personal* majesty. Despotic government can be just but it is uncertain and may easily degenerate into

[23] See, e.g., John Milton, *The Ready and Easy Way to Establish a Free Commonwealth and the Excellence Thereof*, 1959; Anon., *The Grand Concernments of England*, 1659; Anon., *Parliament's Plea*, 1659; E. Bagshaw, *The Rights of the Crown*, 1660; John Eliot, *The Christian Commonwealth*, 1659; John Couch, *England's Jubilee*, 1660.
[24] Cf. Althusius, *Politica methodice digesta*, chap. 9.
[25] Cf. Grotius, *De jure*, 1.3.13; the allusion seems to be to Hobbes. It may draw on Althusius criticising Bodin. See Demetrio Neri, 'Antiassalutismo e Federalismo nel pensiero di Althusius', *Il Pensiero Politico*, 12, 3 (19) p. 403.

a violation of properties and persons.[26] The wise despot will govern as if restricted.[27]

Aristocracy is the rule of the best, and as a closed 'oligarchy' it is a fitting term for the Venetian system, but generally such aristocracies degenerate into tyrannies of the few (*Pol.* 142). Democracy, the rule of the *plebs* is the worst form of government, and despite the definitional energies of Aristotle, hardly worth studying (*Pol.* 144).[28] The pure forms then are all pushed to one side or elided.

Lawson's synoptic designation of the best state is couched in the sort of language which is redolent of free state, classical republican associations. Like Aristotle's idealised notion of a polity (later co-opted to democratic theory) it is one in which 'all jointly should be Sovereign and every single person a subject' (*Pol.* 82). But when Lawson turns at greater length to governmental form, the free state (now discussed explicitly) is only 'may be' the best (*Pol.* 145) and itself comes in a variety of unspecified forms. Experience of the pure forms of monarchy, aristocracy, democracy, he tells us, on the authority of Machiavelli, had led men to settle on a mixture of elements drawn from them all. The free state is one in which none of the pure forms dominates in the assemblage, and in making this point Lawson gradually slips into describing the component parts as kings, peers and commons (*Pol.* 146–7). This is a long way from all jointly being sovereign and each a subject. The distinctive vocabularies of free-state republicanism and mixed monarchy have been largely run together.[29] For all practical purposes this amphibolous ideal encompasses any variation of rule by king, lords, commons or even (given a consular or protectoral component) a republican elite which might be settled on the community. Lawson may be seen, then, as appropriating and subverting the hitherto divisive vocabulary of republican and parliamentarian commitment in order that a settlement should not founder.

Any genuine settlement had also to be an ecclesiastical one and Lawson clearly saw that the job of accommodating religious differences was more difficult than coping with secular ones. His aim is to suggest the desirability of a national church which is portrayed as an analogue of the free-state-mixed-monarchy ideal and is similarly rooted in a widely based Key-clutch-

[26] A variant of a locus in Aristotle, *Politics*, 15, 1286b; Marsilio, *Defensor pacis*, 1.11.7; 1.16. The judgement in terms of the end of the relevant activity, though ultimately Aristotelian, may more immediately be a sign of well-digested Ramus.

[27] Following John of Salisbury, *Policraticus*, on Trajan, or perhaps Grotius, *De jure*, 1.4.6; Hunton, *A Treatise*, pp. 6–7.

[28] Standard fare, but although Harringtonians had a higher regard for the word democracy, they assimilated it to the role of a body of *cives* which might still exclude *plebs*.

[29] Henry Wright, *A First Part of the Disquisition of Truth*, 1616, pp. 10f. had also accommodated Machiavelli's discussion of the Roman blend of pure forms to English constitutional practice.

ing community. In this way the fluidity of Lawson's institutional vocabulary reinforces the parallels between church and state.

If, then, Lawson may be seen as belonging to a Presbyterian political tradition he was not an ecclesiological Presbyterian, for he applied the general precept about the contingency of governmental form to church as well as state. In the ecclesiological context the question was not which governmental form is required by the Bible, but, as for writers like Hooker, Andrewes and Erasmus, which diversity of forms come within the tolerance of biblical indifference. Throughout the extensive discussion, the crucial criterion of permissible arrangement is whether the right of the community as the primary holders of the Keys is being challenged.

5

The Keys

The first church forms discussed, albeit briefly, are broadly monarchical. In consecutive chapters (9 and 10) Lawson deals with the papacy *qua* church form and as claimant to the power of the Keys; and then with the claims of secular monarchs to head a church. The papacy began as a permissible church form necessitated by the sheer growth of the Christian community.[1] But this was illicitly converted into a pseudo-monarchy. It became institutionalised force arrogating unto itself the Keys of the community, challenging the true monarchy of Christ and threatening the equality of visible churches by conflating the notions of universal and particular church (*Pol.* 261f.). It is thus a supreme example of the fallacy of transmission which will be found operating in the aristocratic claims of episcopacy and Presbyterianism. Peter and his successors are worlds apart, but it is the assumption of direct lineage of office which bolsters papal claims. The remarkable survival of this designated usurper at no point elicits a providential explanation from Lawson and the only role for the papacy in a cosmic context is as a possible Antichrist (*Pol.* 441).[2]

The claims of civil authority symbolically associated with monarchy are taken more seriously. Here Lawson treads a pencil-thin path of abstraction between the claims of Erastianism and the incipient possibility of thoroughgoing independence. One extreme threatened a settlement devoid of integrity, the other any national settlement at all. The crux of the problem, however, arose from the fact that all commonwealths quite properly make laws affecting religion in the name of peace and the public good (*Pol.* 204–5).[3] To go beyond external and indifferent matters, however, is to usurp the power of the Keys. Thus a king as titular head and guardian of the

[1] Cf. Marsilio, *Defensor pacis*, 1324, ed. H. Kutsch, Berlin, 1958, 2. 15–18; 22–26.
[2] For other scattered comments on the papacy see *Politica*, 277, 440 ff.; it is not clear whether Lawson regarded the papacy as Antichrist. Those who use him later in the century draw out much more fully a hostility to Catholicism.
[3] Cf. Locke, MSS Lovelace Collection, Bodleian Library, Oxford, discussed below, pp. 189–90. Cf. also *The Westminster Confession*, ed. W. Carruthers, Presbyterian Church of England, London, 1903, chap. 23.

common good is one thing, as one who binds, loosens and excommunicates is quite another. Henry VIII made precisely this shift, says Lawson, not by sound argument, but by metonymous sleight of hand (*Pol.* 204), transferring his legitimate claims *qua* secular monarch to the spiritual realm. The claim increased his revenue at the expense of his plausibility. This Thomas More understood: 'and to touch it roughly, as he did, might cost him dear, as it did'.[4] What is important in this whole question is that the categories of temporal and spiritual are neither merged together, which is the error of the Erastians (*Pol.* 210–13; cf. *Exam.* 138–9), nor separated entirely. This, as Lawson will urge at greater length, is the error of those who would fragment the country in the name of spiritual freedom: 'though a Minister, as a Minister have no power but that of Word and Sacraments: yet from thence it will not follow, that the Church hath not a power spiritual *distinct* [my italics] from that of the State in matters of Religion' (*Pol.* 213).

Lawson's general point here may be seen as largely formal, and certainly the precept of a balance between the claims of a distinct church on the one hand and a peace-keeping *personal* majesty on the other, as in the *Westminster Confession*, could be understood in strikingly different ways. Precisely because of this, such a formulation might aid a settlement. As Lawson himself admits, he had been able to take the Oath of Supremacy understanding it to leave spiritual matters untouched. And two years after publishing he was able to swear to all the other oaths of the newly established episcopal Church of England.

In chapters 11 and 12, Lawson turns to what he considers to be aristocratic forms of church government. Given the oceanic controversies surrounding the claims of episcopacy and Presbyterianism, Lawson trips nimbly over a mitre-bobbing sea of troubles. The terms bishop and presbyter are, he argues, intimately linked (*Pol.* 215) and bishop in particular has different meanings depending on context (*Pol.* 217). To begin with, like Hobbes in *Leviathan*, 42, Lawson claims that, in the New Testament, bishops are synonymous with presbyters as officers of a church. Only later is the term bishop 'appropriated to one who was more than a presbyter' (*Pol.* 215). Even such a relative superiority was not necessarily permanent. The crucial point for Lawson, however, is that the term bishop refers to humanly ordained officers presupposing a prior church community. Hierarchical bishops are occasionally to be found in the early church and it is upon their existence that those 'zealous for episcopacy' base their case that bishops are *jure divino* and thus possessors of the Keys.[5] They are mistaken. All

---

[4] On Lawson's treatment of More, see C. Condren, 'The Image of *Utopia* in the Political Writings of George Lawson', *Moreana*, 18, 69 (1981), pp. 1901 ff.

[5] Specifically *contra* M. A. de Dominis (Spaletensis), *De republica ecclesiastica*, see also Hooker, *The Laws of Ecclesiastical Polity*, Dent, London, 1965, 5. 98.

Christ's apostles were essentially equal; hierarchy is of human origin designed to meet human problems; there are no special episcopal powers of ordination; all priests are in spiritual essentials equal (*Pol.* 219).[6] Even Lancelot Andrewes (1555–1626) is taken to task for resting his case for episcopacy on a fallacy of transmission.[7] And where Andrewes cites Lawson's own much admired and cited Ireneus and Tertullian, these are deemed to be but 'human voices with an humane and Fallible faith' (*Pol.* 226).

Although bishops are widespread and anciently established, arguments concerning their *jure divino* claims from both universality and antiquity are insufficient for prescription in matters of divinity (*Pol.* 227–8). In sum, secular habits may create a legitimacy, spiritual ones may not. In the light of these general arguments concerning episcopacy as a church form *per se*, Lawson turns to English episcopacy. He stresses both the changes in the role and status of bishops and their partial dependence on secular power, bringing out the contingent and largely administrative nature of their office. His account is thus a specific illustration of the general proposition that bishops are a part of a particular order of ecclesiastical subjection. Their claim to be more than this is degeneracy (*Pol.* 229–30).

What then is at stake is not the legitimacy of episcopacy *per se*, but the status of a political form of church. Those zealous for episcopacy have, as it were, confused a specific manifestation of *personal* majesty with *real* majesty, and in an ecclesiastical context this is a challenge to Christ. All offices it seems have a tendency to rise above their proper sphere (*Pol.* 442). As with monarchical, so too with aristocratic claims to the Keys; succession of persons without doctrine means little, it is a form of *ad hominem* argument (*Pol.* 237) needing doctrinal backing. Conversely, alluding to Tertullian, succession of doctrine on its own may be enough (*Pol.* 236). This intimation of the ultimate legitimacy of separation, fundamental to Lawson's ecclesiology, will give a special poignancy to his discussion of independency. But first he turns from Tweedledum to Tweedledee.

Where episcopacy has been sloughed off, he writes, presbytery now reigns, yet both confuse a workable form of government with divine right (*Pol.* 239). Here Lawson's use of secular terminology patently structures ecclesiology. He even invokes a Polybian criticism of pure governmental forms. Again, the variety of meaning for the term under discussion is stressed. There are preaching presbyters, who because they have been held to be synonymous with bishops receive little further discussion. Then there are

---

[6] Cf. Marsilio, *Defensor pacis*, 2.15, who Lawson specifically follows. This seems to be the most cited passage from the *Defensor* during the seventeenth century, and obviously no wider knowledge of Marsilio was necessary to have some access to it. See David Calderwood, *The Prelate and the Pastor*, 1628, and R. A., *A Letter to a Friend*, 1662, who quotes most extensively. On this tract see discussion below, p. 144.

[7] Lancelot Andrewes, *Tortura Torti*, 1616, at length.

ruling elders to whose claims most of his attention is devoted, and finally there is a discussion of Presbyterianism in England, which, as it is integral to Lawson's understanding of the Civil War, will be held over. With respect to the claims of ruling elders, Lawson points out that they do not appear until quite late in the New Testament (Acts 11.30) and it is difficult to say if they have any jurisdiction, as has been assumed. Those who make such a claim have confused honour given *to* with government *by* elders (*Pol.* 241).[8] Such obscure and doubtful origins do not provide a firm foundation for the claim that primitive presbytery provides a required model for all modern churches (*Pol.* 244).[9] Certainly they cannot be shown to be the primary subject of the Keys – their existence presupposes a prior *ecclesia*.[10] This is so whether we see the presbyters as officers, or as representatives (*Pol.* 244ff.), and it is from this community that they derive their power, and to which, as officers at least, they are ultimately answerable.[11] Whether as representatives they are answerable to or stand for the underlying community is a moot point (see below), which is not helped by Lawson's analogy with Parliament – that its members may be considered as officers individually, but as representatives *en masse* (Pol. 246–7). Lawson fleshes out his case against Presbyterianism by considering two syllogistic formulations of its claim, concluding, as he has already, that Presbyterianism is a human, permissible and aristocratic form of organisation contingent upon a prior religious community.

What matters above all for Lawson is not antiquity of formal office, purity of form, or discipline, but the profession of The Word by a visible community and the propagation of that Word by its priests. In ecclesiology community has an overwhelming and consistently emphasised priority over governmental form. If this is so, there is a very thin line between a national Church of England and Independency of the most fragmenting sort. The maintenance of this line depends upon the very notion of the community as the primary subject of the Keys. The final dimension of its defence, and the reinforcement of the line between a national church settlement and ecclesiological fragmentation, is provided by Lawson's somewhat miscella-

---

[8] He seems to have had in mind here Melvillian doctrine associated with Gillespie and Bucer. Interestingly, Lawson holds that the Fifth Commandment, taken in a sufficiently large sense, is the quintessentially political one, and in the *Theo-Politica* the distinction between honour and government is markedly blurred.

[9] Cf. T. Bilson, *The Perpetual Government of Christes Church*, 1593, Lawson's own copy of which is annotated and corrected in his hand, but the annotations may post-date the publication of the *Politica*. The unusually sickly looking ink conforms to that found in the later parish entries in his encumbency.

[10] Cf. Thomas Hooker (of New England), who is held to score over Rutherford on this point, though himself is held to be astray in seeing all officers as jurisdictional; *Pol.* 245.

[11] *Contra* Bilson, *Perpetual Government*, Epistle.

neous, and misleadingly titled, chapter 13 devoted to the claims of democratic church forms.

In fact Lawson cannot find any warrant for democracy in the Bible, and is not even sure that anyone has defended such a view.[12] The chapter title 'Whether the Power of the Keys be primarily in the people' would seem almost to be determined by the force of secular nomenclature, the chapter's content by the shortcomings of the forms he has already discussed. Above all it specifies in greater detail the nature of the church and the common confusion between community and political form. Here he distinguishes between the whole church and a secondary church by way of representation (*Pol.* 263). 'The primary (church) is the proper subject of real power, the Representative of personal' (*Pol.* 263). What had, in the preceding chapter been a somewhat ambiguous association between office and representation – given Lawson's previous association of representation with underlying community – is now rather different. Lawson seems to collapse the distinction between *personal* majesty of office and the representatives of the community. Moreover, Lawson immediately defines the church *qua* community (excluding its virtual members) in the idiom of his ideal secular form, the free state. 'All jointly and the whole doth rule, every several person though Officer, though Minister, though Bishop, if there be any such, is subject to the whole, and to all joyntly' (*Pol.* 263).

Despite the terminology of state form, Lawson immediately refers to this as a 'Community' (*Pol.* 263). The collapse of the distinction between officer and representative seems therefore to prepare the ground for the collapse of the parent concepts of community and *polity*. So, Lawson's church emerges like a rabbit from a dialectical hat as a political community. Lawson has appropriated the Italianate idiom of free state politics to an English ecclesiastical settlement. The church as the 'subject' of the Keys is defended with reference to two biblical cruxes: 'I will give unto thee the keys of the Kingdom of Heaven', from which he remarks sardonically, there have been 'Chymical extractions of all sorts of Governments' (*Pol.* 265). In this context he argues that Peter should be seen properly as standing for the church as a whole – as a representative. Here Lawson is reverting to the notion of a representative, as distinct from an accountable officer. And what is given to the church through Peter is doctrine above discipline. The second crux is John 20, 22–3, 'Receive ye the Holy Ghost, whosoever sins ye remit, they are remitted unto them, and whosoever sins ye retain, they are retained' (*Pol.* 267). After a series of appropriate distinctions, Lawson

---

[12] Lawson has not apparently read the Brownists (the followers of Robert Browne) who were so accused. David Blondel is regarded as not really guilty of democracy and Robert Parker, *De politica ecclesiastica*, Frankfurt, 1616, who accuses Morellius, it is suggested, leans a little that way himself; *Pol.* 258–9.

concludes that the remission must be considered provisional, and the matters of the soul cannot be open to the scrutiny of merely public discipline (*Pol.* 269). However far priestly authority extends, it still presupposes belief, office and community (*Pol.* 269). The principal function of a priest is to tend souls, and convert – which is not a matter of gathering churches out of churches 'under pretence of a purer Reformation' (*Pol.* 270). Thus he begins to defend the parish within a church against the discrete congregation (*Pol.* 298).[13]

Given the lack of biblical injunction, he argues the preoccupation with discipline and form has an inevitably fragmenting effect upon an ecclesiastical community, which is politically disastrous and a reversal of spiritual priorities (*Pol.* 270–1). Andrewes, who had earlier been criticised, is now turned against the misguided sect ideal and its disciplinary fastidiousness.[14] A church as a visible particular requires faith and teaching, it must embrace both wheat and tares; it must focus on the afterlife and use the best men there are amongst its priests and laity for its leadership.[15] Its political form is thus negotiable, for there are few rules and requirements in the Bible and much that is indifferent; and with a dangerous and potentially counter-productive lurch towards reason of church, he remarks that even the rules might be waived aside by the Apostles in extraordinary circumstances, and this may be precedent enough for us (*Pol.* 295).

At this stage one can see Lawson defending a narrow theological point on a wide front. Although uncompromising on the location of the Keys, the effect is to legitimate a wide variety of churches. The issue of ecclesiastical, like that of secular, form is diffused and through similar strategies of argument. It is this latitudinarianism which may be seen as making sense of his own accommodating conduct over a long career, and which theoretically reflects a long-standing Erasmian objection to fighting on punctilios. Here too, one can see how Lawson can avoid party labels, manipulate writers with critical discrimination, and suggest a free state model of a church as amphibolous and as diffusing as his model of mixed government. Any church form might do for a community at a pinch, as long as it did not lock itself in an implausible and ossifying rhetoric of divine origin. To accept its own human shape was to accept a capacity for change and the accommodation of those who needed it. As I shall argue, after the Restoration this was to strike a chord with such reluctant non-conformists as John Humfrey. The more immediate and, for Lawson, less appetising corollary was that

---

[13] A different route to Hooker's conclusions, *Laws*, 5.80.3–4.

[14] Andrewes, *Tortura*, described as 'that most learned and exact piece far above his other works', *Pol.* 271, 275; cf. Hooker, *Laws*, 3.1.

[15] This use of lay talent for administration is something Lawson approved of, presumably from his experience with Presbyterian ecclesiology.

such a human church might lack sufficiently potent reasons to stop those wishing to separate from leaving. Superficially, if a gathering or congregation was seen as a community, the arguments for a national church would have to become dangerously Erastian. In the last of the chapters devoted to the Keys and ecclesiological settlement, Lawson directly confronts the sect ideal which he must do without denying the right to separate. To this end he exploits the sociological sophistication of his notion of community and the aura of divine sanction that has surrounded it from the beginning.

Chapter 14, which concerns the permissible extent of a church, is somewhat disingenuously introduced as a digression. In fact, it is the culmination of the whole argument devoted to the question of the Keys and an ecclesiastical settlement. His position is directed against Independency.

The Congregationalists are difficult to attack in general, he writes, as they seem to agree only in their hostility to parishes and representative ecclesiology. It is almost impossible to find a single name for them (*Pol.* 305). However, their faith in the necessity of uniform and direct participation is erroneously located in biblical precedent. Thus synogogue does not uniformly refer to a congregation and neither does *ecclesia* (*Pol.* 309–13). Indeed, the latter on occasion refers to a church meeting through its representatives (*Pol.* 315).[16] Thus representation is permitted.[17] The Congregationalists have confused the need for worship in one place with order and discipline being similarly restricted (*Pol.* 316–17).[18] In any case, historical precedent does not itself give binding precept (*Pol.* 320).[19] The results, he insists, of trying to put Congregationalist misconceptions into practice have been schism, disruption and dereliction of Christian duty. Separatists unchurch churches in the name of conversion and abandon the sinners (*Pol.* 307–8, 324b). God (Lawson plays a precious providential ace) has already punished some of their congregations (*Pol.* 309) and sooner or later they must reverse the slide into fragmentation. Yet, he remarks in a passage already cited, 'I do not write this out of partiality or prejudice; for some of that party are my special Friends . . . I desire them seriously to consider what they do, and . . . forcast, what is likely to be the issue, if they do not unite more firmly amongst themselves, and combine with other pious Ministers . . .' So the fist upon the pulpit becomes an open palm in the

---

[16] The most specific point of attack here is Robert Parker, *De politica ecclesiastica*. But more generally Lawson is descanting upon the lengthy dispute during the 1630s between Parker and Thomas Hooker, like Lawson an Emmanuel man, who left Europe for New England 1641? and died 1647.

[17] Cf. Richard Hooker, *Laws*, 5.80.

[18] Although sharing a similar pattern of precept, the target here may be John Owen, *Of Schism*, 1657.

[19] Very much the burden of literature having difficulty in co-opting an authoritative past. Hooker, Hobbes, Selden, all provide variants on the theme.

choir offering a national church, a mean between the claims of universalism and the Congregationalists.[20] Given Lawson's broad notion of a community this seems now to be the only option. A congregation arises from something smaller than a community; a universal visible church is something far larger. Moreover, a church arising as a political organisation from a proper community thus stands in the shadow of the divine sanction enjoyed by a community. Itself only convenient and permissible, a church arising from a community is blessed.

Speaking of a national church Lawson says, 'I will here suppose the major part ... [of the population] to be Christians, and the association and incorporation to be made by tacit or explicit consent, which sometimes may be confirmed by the Laws of the Supreme Power' (*Pol.* 325b). All are subject to the whole 'either properly taken or virtually for a Representative of the whole ...' (*Pol.* 328b). With this resurfacing of the extensive notion of community emerges also Lawson's early sense of representation as distinct from office-holding within an administration. Shown to be permissible, the practical advantages of a national church are legion: it is less open to schism, may draw on great talent and have augmented communal wisdom (*Pol.* 333).[21]

A national church finally takes its place in Lawson's *Politica* exemplifying his distinction between community and polity. He finds numerous institutional analogues, whilst theoretically he cites the authority of Marsilio in a crucial passage: 'Marsilius in his *Defensor pacis* determines the Power of Legislation to be *in populo, aut civium universitate*. Yet he grants that the Laws may be made *per valentiorem partem* or their Trustees; and that what is so done by them is done by them all' (*Pol.* 340–1). Lawson correctly stresses, as modern commentators have usually overlooked,[22] the corporate nature of Marsilio's *valentior pars* and the particular way in which it represents the *legislator humanus*, without being answerable to it. On this theoretical basis, it is easy for Lawson to see the national church as coextensive with the commonwealth which arises from a prior community in its secular capacity. Notwithstanding this, the right of separation still cannot be denied.

[20] The papacy has, for Lawson, almost irrevocably tainted the notion of a universal visible church, although he does admit the possibility of synodic organisation, as at Nice or Chalcedon (*Pol.* 304). Following the high church theologian Dr Thomas Jackson, the most that can be hoped for is a league of friendship between particular churches. This is prefigured in *Pol.* 43–4.

[21] His presupposition that increased numbers increases wisdom is found also in Marsilio, *Defensor pacis*, 1.13.

[22] For a discussion of this see C. Condren, 'Resistance and Sovereignty in Lawson's *Politica*,' *HJ*, 24,/3/ (1981); 'George Lawson and the *Defensor*', *Medioevo*, 6 (1980). My doubts as to whether Lawson is referring to Marsilio's unstressed notion of an *ad hoc legislator* (accountable to a formal body) or the *valentior pars*, which seems not to be, reflects the equivocable status of representation in the *Politica* as a whole, which is discussed below.

Lawson is suggesting rather that separation is at present not desirable nor necessary and that a church lacking communal sanction lacks an aura of divine blessing. Overall, with his distrust of his fellow clerics, his unwavering emphasis on the community as the repository of the Keys and his acceptance of the need for externals to be controlled, he is closer to Harrington's civil religion than to Baxter's national church.[23] Let God judge the Pope, he concludes, let bishops be reduced to their ancient functions, let presbyters be satisfied with being 'officers, or at the best Representatives' and 'Let the People not be wronged, or any ways deprived of that right, which is theirs by rule of the Gospel' (*Pol.* 350). Such a peroration seems an odd prelude to two chapters on the importance of subjection.

[23] See Mark Goldie, 'The Civil Religion of James Harrington' in *The Languages of Political Theory in Early Modern Europe*, ed. Anthony Pagden, Cambridge University Press, 1987, esp. pp. 207, 215–17.

6

The limits of subjection

In the final chapters Lawson returns to reiterate the themes surrounding subjection and sovereignty. Although there is repetition there is also elaboration – not always consistent with earlier discussion and there are shifts of emphasis.[1]

The creation of hierarchical orders of subjection is of divine ordination through God's power (*Pol.* 353–4). Submission, a recognition of God's commands encapsulated in the Fifth Commandment and in Romans 13, is required across a full range of human relationships. That between sovereigns and subjects is paradigmatic of those between parents and children, husbands and wives, masters and servants, teachers and scholars.[2] All involved in such relationships, however, are equally subject to God. It is of course this reiterated proviso which generates the quintessential problem of the human condition for Lawson, that defined by the clash between obedience to a remote God and to an immediate sovereign who only participates in and uses God's power (*Pol.* 355, 411 ff.).[3] What is emphasised now, however, is that understanding this is largely a matter of having an adequate battery of appropriately discriminate classifiers. It seems that if we have not the terms to delineate the notion of subjection it is difficult for us to see the pattern of our obligations. Thus Lawson says of Bodin, he '*mistakes much* by confounding *Civis (et) subditus*. For though every Subject be *Civis*, yet every *Civis* is not a Subject' (*Pol.* 356; cf. 26). As Lawson

---

[1] Cf. Philip Hunton, *A Treatise of Monarchy*, 1643, who at the outset more elegantly suggests that as sovereignty and subjection are relational terms one can discuss all pertinent issues under the auspice of one of them.

[2] Cf. T. Bilson, *The Perpetual Government of Christes Church*, 1593, Epistle, for the same specification of relationships. It is this form of assertion which made so plausible the metaphorical interplay between family and polity, providing a thin end of a patriarchal wedge. It dates from John Chrysostom, *Homily 23 on Romans 13*, which was not always cited. But see, Peter Martyr Vermigli, 'Commentary on I Kings 18:15–18', in *Political Thought*, ed. R. Kingdon, Droz, Geneva, 1980, p. 92.

[3] Cf. J. Althusius, *Politica methodice digesta*; and John Ponet, *A Short Treatise of Politic Power*, 1556, for the notions of government as a trust. See Lawson, at length, in *Theo-Politica* for further use of these terms.

reiterates, the term *civis* does not entail ordered subordination within a governmental form; the term *subdites* does (*Pol.* cf. 26). Lawson underlines the conceptual difference by discussing it through an implied temporal shift redolent of contractual connotations. Men 'deprive' themselves of unlimited liberty which they 'had' as *cives*; they 'divest' themselves of some power, 'resign' themselves to a superior will (*Pol.* 357); cf. *Exam.* 16–18, 23).[4] Yet not all is lost. The notion of *civis* is neither redundant nor obliterated in this change, as Locke also was to insist, and as Spinoza was to argue, any more than community is lost in the creation of polity. So the firm distinction between *real* and *personal* majesty remains, the latter being but entrusted and held by a 'representative' (*Pol.* 258b). The tensions of a ramified theological principle set out in the first sentence echo at the end and Lawson approaches the sticking point of resistance twice more.

First, drawing on Henningus Arnisaeus (d. 1636) he suggests that political subjection is bounded by the public good (*Pol.* 258b, 359).[5] 'No rational people will subject themselves but upon condition of Protection ... and so to better their Estate; For power being ordained of God, was intended for the good of the parties to be governed' (*Pol.* 359).[6] His initial response to the hypothetical violation of these bounds is uncharacteristic. He runs together resistance and rebellion, thus making them similarly improper, and suggests passive suffering as the only alternative to obedience (*Pol.* 360–1). There seems little intimation of this choice in the ecclesiological context, except that he urges us to accept the imperfection of human churches. With respect to usurpation again, there is perhaps more stress on the advisability of passive acceptance (*Pol.* 364–5; *Exam.* 19), though only in a secular context. It is rash to bandy about the term usurper whenever the acquisition of power does not fit our own fancies (*Pol.* 365). Conversely, he adds, we should not sail with every prevailing wind. Lawson, in fact, seems to be circumscribing a rhetoric which may degenerate into special pleading; and attempting to provide a criterion for its use, he specifies a hierarchy of loyalty expressed in the terminology of treason. Ignoring obli-

---

[4] Cf. Henry Stubbe, *A Letter to an officer in the Army*, London, 1659. Lawson makes no references here to contract, though it is accepted in the *Examination*, and passingly mentioned in the *Politica*, p. 101, in the context of the coronation oath.

[5] Arnisaeus, *Constit. Pol.*, chap. 12; again an echo of Althusius, and earlier Italian writers on the rhetoric of the communal good, it is a very common point: e.g. Hunton, *A Treatise*, p. 65: Henry Stubbe, *An Essay in Defence of the Good Old Cause*, London, 1659, pp. 11–12. But cf. John Hall, *Of Government*, 2.1. p. 93 where the 'publick good' is argued to be not a thing but a 'bare political notion'.

[6] Cf. the more explicit treatment of *Exam*; John Milton, *The Tenure of Kings and Magistrates*, in *The Prose Works of John Milton*, ed. J. Max Patrick, Doubleday, New York, 1967, p. 353; Rutherford, *Lex Rex*, e.g., questions 14–17; *The Westminster Confession*, ed. W. Carruthers, Presbyterian Church of England, London, 1903, chap. 23. This was a standard affirmation, possibly mediated via Althusius.

gations is assimilated to treason, the worst form of which is to country (which by implication seems to mean community), state, and *real* majesty. After that comes treason to *personal* majesty, 'in the general Representative of the whole Community' (*Pol.* 362) then treason to those who protect. Treason against laws, especially fundamental ones, is held to be worse than treason against persons. Or again, fidelity is above all to country, then to that under *any* form of *personal* majesty, then to the specific form of king, lords, and commons, and then 'to the person of the king which presupposes the former' (*Pol.* 369–70). It is a pattern of priority which could structure Leveller or Clubman allegiances.

As subjection and sovereignty are 'relates' (*Pol.* 50) defining the state (*Pol.* 336), the obligation of any subject, indeed subject status itself, ceases with the demise of sovereignty and thus obligation is dissolved in as many ways as sovereignty may be lost. The failure of sovereignty may occur through incapacity to protect, dissolution of a constitution or tyrannous behaviour (*Pol.* 366–7; *Exam.* 143–4). Here we have an intimation of what will receive far more attention in Atwood and in Locke – namely the notion that the conditions justifying resistance actually dissolve the relationship that makes resistance possible. It is an echo of the once clear and still discernible voices of medieval nominal definition. Thus John of Salisbury (*Policraticus*) defined a king in terms of his propensity to rule according to the law; as a corollary, Bartolus (*De tyrannia*, 2) had stated that kingdoms were forfeited through the sin of rulers; and Althusius, sounding as much like Lawson as Bartolus, argued that by going beyond their trust ephors *per se* simply became ordinary people who could be owed no obligation.

Lawson however, immediately continues in a way that seems designed to tone down the dramatic implications of this whole tradition of argument. If parliaments (being transformed into factions) move above their sphere, wronging kings or people, they cannot 'justly require or rationally expect subjection' (*Pol.* 367). And although private persons cannot call such bodies to account, 'yet the people by a latter and well ordered Parliament may both judge them and call the Exhorbitant Members to account' (*Pol.* 367). Here, confusingly, it seems a 'latter parliament' is seen as a representative of *real* majesty – the synecdoche by which the whole acts, whilst that which has moved above its sphere is a faction which, when operating within its sphere, was a part of *personal* majesty. If in general the fate and confusing status of English Parliaments are reflected here, those words immediately following seem to have a particular relevance to the wandering Charles: 'When a personal Sovereign cannot protect his Subjects because their Lives, persons and estates, are in the power of another, he cannot rationally require subjection, but for the time at least he should be willing to free them from

Allegiance' (*Pol.* 267).[7] This is no euphemism for resistance to the claims that such a 'sovereign' might theoretically have, for Lawson hurries on to remark that voluntary 'Revolt or Rebellion' cannot free subjects from lawful obligation (*Pol.* 367).

In his final discussion of resistance, Lawson seeks no middle ground in passive suffering, for, as he pointedly remarks in keeping with some earlier comments on neuters, positive action is not the only way to bring a regime to ruin (*Pol.* 370). As Arnisaeus puts it, can a subject resist or take up arms against a sovereign?[8] Expressed in this way, remarks Lawson, one has little difficulty in answering in the negative, but the question is inadequately put. It should be couched as follows: '*Whether he that is a sovereign may not in some cases be resisted by the people, and if he may, in what case a resistance is lawful and free from guilt of rebellion*' (*Pol.* 375). Again, as with the criticism of Bodin, it is a matter of not seeing the nicety of the problem if we do not have a sufficiently discriminate vocabulary.[9] As this exposition has shown, where Lawson wanted to defuse issues and subordinate problems, he minimised and blurred distinctions, but here we see the reverse process clearly and self-consciously. The crucial terminological distinctions are those between community and polity; subject and citizen; *real* and *personal* majesty; rebellion and resistance. The cumulative thrust of these is to leave Lawson in the position of being able to hold that the individual or people as subjects may never resist, might by definition only rebel; but a group or the people as *cives* may resist (*Pol.* 375), though such an issue can only be relevant within the context of political subjection. Yet rather than going on to choose between the rebellion of Arnisaeus on the one hand and the resistance of writers such as Buchanan on the other, or to provide criteria for any choice being made, he deploys his delineated vocabulary through a commentary on the Civil War, which he concludes was neither resistance nor rebellion.

The ecclesiological analogue of this circumscription of a vocabulary of understanding is to be found in Lawson's last discussion of separation. Again Lawson seems a good deal less cautious. Reasserting the distinction between officers and representatives, he states that officers must be obeyed no further

---

[7] Strictly speaking this does not cohere with the preceding argument, as such a *personal* sovereign nominally should cease to exist. I suspect that this is a late revision which presupposes a real definition of monarchy intended to help accommodate a settlement. It contrasts also with *Exam.* 143–4. See below of discussion for Lawson's equivocation between nominal and real definitions, (pp. 83–4).

[8] Arnisaeus, *Constit. Pol.*, chap. 12. The biblical locus is Judges 3.29–30. Peter Martyr Vermigli raises the issue in very similar terms in his commentary, as do the monarchomachs whom Lawson would have regarded as confused.

[9] It is indicative of significant changes in political perspective that we would probably see only a semantic difference here between Lawson and Arnisaeus, and would probably not regard the latter as posing a loaded question in the first place.

than the limits of power allowed them by church and biblical Word (*Pol.* 412); all particulars must submit to general representatives. But if representatives transgress their authority, they cannot justly expect submission. To avoid such problems leading to separation all churches should have fundamental constitutions, lest they themselves become potential causes of separation (*Pol.* 412–14). Membership of a church is from God's ordination, which does not require that we are all saints (*Pol.* 417–20). Prior membership is the condition for separation, which may be partial or complete and is now refined to encompass degrees of ejection (passive separation). All such voluntary acts may be just or unjust – the paradigm case of just and active separation being the incompleted English Reformation. The work must continue, though '[to] be hasty high and rigid in Reformation, is a cause of many and great Mischiefs' (*Pol.* 427).

The final sections of the book are devoted to a taxonomy of the classes to be subjected with random comments on their present states of health. Here we are told of the educational and moral decline of the nobility; the avarice of merchants (*Pol.* 409); of the wealth that Jesuit Spain devotes to scholarship;[10] of the necessary evil of war. It is a punishment for sins, a means of promoting virtue, and of making us appreciate peace – it is clearly nice when it stops.[11] Naturally most attention is given to the need to educate ministers, 'a spiritual militia for the defence of souls' (*Pol.* 408) and the need to promote love, understanding and peace. Book One ends abruptly, rehearsing the necessity of grasping that the rules of government are common to church and state, ignorance of which only fuels controversy (*Pol.* 452–3); and reminding the reader of the mortality of commonwealths, of the incipient constitutional and administrative corruption that brings 'woeful changes', 'subversion and ruine' through God's direction (*Pol.* 454). Such matters 'I shall speak more particularly and fully in the Second Book.' This, already roughly drafted will be easier to comprehend than the first more general part. It will, Lawson states, be printed if interest is sufficiently encouraging: 'I desire to know, what entertainment this first part may meet withal' (*Pol.* 454). The second volume however never appeared, and Lawson had been dead eleven years before the aging John Starkey once more before a breach of settlement salvaged a second edition of the *Politica*.

---

[10] Familiar greener grass mythology which must have irked given how evil the Jesuits were known to be, though Lawson does not show signs of Prynnish paranoia and sounds a little like sixteenth-century Jesuits.

[11] Cf. Milton, *Areopagitica*, in *Works*, on the necessity of sin in general; N. Machiavelli, *Il Principe e Discorsi*, Feltrinelli, Milan, 1973 edn, at length, on the ennobling qualities of warfare; Lawson cites Grotius, *De jure* for the notion of a just war, *Pol.* 407–8.

Part III

AN EXAMINATION OF THE *POLITICA*

INTRODUCTION

Having provided an interpretative exposition of the text, I want now to take up a number of issues arising from my reading, which are too complex to have been treated *en passant*. To begin with, a brief discussion of the providential frame informing the *Politica* leads to comment on the overall character of the work. In this context I then focus on the topic of corporate imagery with its cohering vocabulary of community, consent and representation. This is followed by a discussion of the resistance topos which is central to the *Politica* because of Lawson's emphasis on the nexus of community and political order. My purpose is designed to circumscribe the interpretative possibilities of this topic in Lawson's work, rather than to disclose his true position. Indeed, my argument is that any such revelation would be spurious. I turn finally to Lawson's understanding of his times and his explanation for the Civil Wars. Lawson's treatment of contemporary affairs has been largely ignored so far because it is an attempted vindication of his own precepts and an application of his nomenclature; a proper understanding of Lawson on the English Revolution requires first an awareness of his theories and their difficulties.

Each focus of my attention is intended not only to take up issues which so far have only been touched upon, but also it is intended to explicate the textual warrant for the use of the work during the seventeenth century. Part III is thus a pivot for the whole.

Providence and rhetoric

7

Lawson's world is providential; it is a world under the auspices of an all-powerful and, no doubt, ultimately rational God. It is also a world of the uncertain, unreliable and fortuitous, explicable in terms of the clash of human perceptions, fears and ambitions. The jostling shadows of Augustine and Guicciardini might seem to make for a particularly murky text, for modern scholars have taught us to treat the idioms of fortune and providence as sufficiently separate for them to be given discrete histories.[1] So the rise of an idiom of contingency is seen as a distinct and major factor in the beginning of modern political and historiographical sensibilities.[2] But Lawson was in fact in no way unusual in combining and deploying alternately what were for him only *distinguishable* modes of explanation. Indeed, in his world even a consistent emphasis on the contingent seems embedded in the providential. Such an idiomatic symbiosis is typical of *de facto* theory,[3] and is manifest in the histories of the English Revolution.[4] Even Machiavelli, whose thought might be seen plausibly as the apotheosis of the idiom of fortune, finds providence to hand when he needs it.[5] The self-conscious resolutions of potential tension between the claims of providence and fortune seem to have stopped well short of the obliteration of one by the other. Philippe de Commynes (1445–1509), an historian

[1] Keith Thomas, *Religion and the Decline of Magic*, Weidenfeld and Nicolson, London, 1971, sets an authoritative precedent.
[2] J. G. A. Pocock, *The Machiavellian Moment*, Princton University Press, 1975, for a masterly account of the idiom of contingency.
[3] John Wallace, 'The Engagement Controversy, 1649–52', *The Bulletin of the New York Public Library*, 68 (1964); J. G. A. Pocock, *Obligation and Authority in Two Civil Wars*, Victoria University of Wellington Press, 1973; Glen Burgess, 'Usurpation, Obligation and Obedience in the thought of the Engagement Controversy', *HJ*, 29, 4 (1984) pp. 515ff.
[4] M. Hartman, 'Contemporary Explanations of the English Civil War, 1640–1660', unpublished Ph.D. thesis, Cambridge, 1978, although clearly it seems providence should have little or no place in such literature, Leveller and Digger materials are excluded from consideration as too providential, pp. 5–6; writers like Thomas Ford, *Lusus fortunae*, 1649, are seen as incoherent in blending *separate* idioms of contingency and providence, e.g. pp. 61f., 57, 102–3.
[5] N. Machiavelli, *Il principe e Discorsi*, Feltrinelli, Milan, 1973 edn, 26 and 3.1.

admired by Lawson (*Exam.* 42), remarks that references to fortune could be little more than a poetic way of referring to God's providence.[6] This mode of assimilation was developed, via Calvin, in Thomas Ford (1598– 1674), but it did not prohibit discourse in the style of the fiction.[7] Conversely, the Venetian historian Paolo Sarpi (1552–1623) had elliptically, but penetratingly, explained the apparent tension between the claims of providence and contingency as being ultimately a matter of what we were in a position to explain. Providence was not so much absent from the world as it was inappropriate to the world of the historian.[8] Whatever mode of assimilation, we are left not simply with one authentic voice but a choice between idioms of persuasion. Logic and modern scholarship might not see this as good enough – in the last analysis either the world is controlled by providence or it is not. Perhaps, but in terms of sixteenth- and seventeenth-century sensibilities, more attuned than the twentieth century to the dictates of rhetoric, the separation of providence and contingency into opposing corners geared up for the cosmic fight over the rational faculties, rather lets the nuances of argument slip away.

A combination of faith in God and epistemological modesty (or indifference) enabled what we might see as the dictates of logic to be ignored; whilst the inherited canons of rhetoric emphasised the importance of finding the words appropriate to the subject matter. This was much more than a case of simply finding the right form of figurative speech to convey the things of the world; it was more largely a matter of finding the right language *per se* through which to present a persuasive structure of political possibility.[9]

As I have attempted to show in the exposition of Lawson's *Politica*, the shifts between providential and fortuitous idioms of discourse have a rhetorical rationale, even if they are logically arbitrary. The legitimising potential of providential control is kept well clear of the discussion of the papacy, which for so long had withstood the ravages of time; but it is introduced to explain the short-term misfortunes of English gathered flocks.

Turning to the field of abstract categories with which Lawson operates, one can see how the terms *power* and *force* are, for example, functions of the providential and fortuitous respectively. Power itself is good, coming

---

[6] Cited in A. Gilbert, *Machiavelli's Prince and its Forerunners*, Duke University, Durham, North Carolina, 1939.

[7] Ford, *Lusus fortunae*, pp. 8–12, discussed in Hartman, 'Contemporary Explanations', p. 102.

[8] Paolo Sarpi, *Pensieri*, ed. G. and L. Cozzi, Einaudi, Torin, 1976, on which see William J. Bowsma, *Venice and the Defence of Republican Liberty*, California University Press, 1968, p. 596. A similar position seems to have been adopted by the Muggletonians after 1681. I am indebted to discussions with Professor William Lamont for this point.

[9] For a pertinent discussion see Nancy Struever, *The Language of History in the Renaissance*, Princeton University Press, 1970.

from and ultimately being sanctioned by God. It is thus a term appropriate to the evocation of a providential idiom of argument. Force conversely, wrong, wayward, and unsanctioned by God, is found in the papacy. The crucial question with respect to both usurpation and conquest is, therefore, whether we can see power or only force at play; must we evoke a providential or merely fortuitous context of explanation and precept for action?

Lawson's text, perhaps like any, exists at the intersection of a rhetorical and logical plane of discourse. As we can see, although Lawson pays considerable attention to the logic of his own argument, and holds the logical sins of others to be significant, he seems also to have paid considerable attention to the demands of an effective rhetoric. The argument is most successful where one can hardly disentangle these discursive threads. Logic is best where most persuasive; rhetoric where it is least noticed. But because the rhetorical dimension of political discourse is apt to be discounted at the level of high theory, the interplay of logic and rhetoric should be considered further. It will help provide a context for the interpretative problems that coagulate around Lawson's treatment of representation and resistance, and for the use later made of his work. For example, logically speaking, Lawson's being a Protestant requires a theological hostility to the papacy, and that his attack on catholicism comes first in his discussion of the Keys is at least a gesture of identification with a Protestant audience. That this attack in general enables Lawson to cover crucial ground quickly, uncontentiously, suggests a flattering confidence in his audience's understanding of essentials. There is, he concludes, little need to repeat what so many learned men have said before (*Pol.* 203).[10] Having started with what he calls a monarchical claim to the Keys, however, it then seems logical that he moves to consider the claims of ever larger groups – though this is to move in accepted order through the conventional Aristotelian classifications of governmental form.

Again, in turning to Lawson's conceptual vocabulary, some terms are defined with particular and reciprocal intension, and are employed with logical precision. The notions of *real* and *personal* majesty, the distinctions between community and polity and, above all, the concomitant predications of the individual as *subditus* and *civis* are all cases in point. These are terms whose significance and currency Lawson wishes to promote in a noticeably controlled way. As we shall see, the significance of his logical refinement of the political lexicon was not lost on his contemporaries.

Conversely, other terms are handled with a broadening and accommodating tolerance. By giving them an amphibolous extension, he both co-opts

[10] Cf. also John Maxwell, *Sacro-Sancta Regnum majestas*, 1644, p. 65; Anon., *God and the King*, 1663, both of which attack the sort of position Lawson defends.

them and defuses their potential significance. Thus Lawson recasts and loosens the notion of a free state, which he assimilates to the general notion of mixed monarchy. In this way he can suggest a secular accommodation for Italianate republicanism and challenge an analogous ecclesiological co-option by Congregationalists, downplay the whole question of the form of settlement and expand the realm of ecclesiastical and secular indifference.

Sometimes, Wittgenstein remarked, the 'loose concept' is exactly what we need.[11] The point would not have been lost on Lawson, but one may say that the logical techniques of loosening or tightening are brought into play insofar as they serve a persuasive end of refining a body of precept for putative action. What this amounts to is a willingness to employ by turns both nominal and real definitions or, in Ramus's terms, both perfect and imperfect definitions, respectively. For Lawson it is the nominal *definiens* which is used to give terms intension; the real *definiens* which is used or assumed in order to give terms encompassing extension by allowing them to remain attached to phenomena despite empirical variation – it is a Ramist description. Lawson's understanding of governmental forms is drawn up in terms of real definitions giving ample scope for predicative variation; his understanding of subject and citizen is quintessentially nominal, affording little scope for such predication.

Some terms, however, operate in the context of both definitional forms. A monarch who has forfeited a throne is urged to be patient; his subjects are urged not to use what may only be temporary incapacity to rule as an excuse for changes of allegiance. Again, tyrants (kings or parliaments) may not rationally expect subjection. In arguing in this way Lawson presupposes real definitions of monarchy, forfeiture and tyranny. Conversely, however, forfeiture and tyranny are depicted not simply as plausible grounds for resistance but, presupposing nominal definition, are seen to be dissolutions of the governmental relationship on which the possibility of resistance is predicated. This sort of vacillation (it is to be found in Henry Stubbe and Philip Hunton as well) produces logical incoherence, but it also creates, intentionally or not, exploitable ambiguities in the terms existing at the nexus of real and nominal definition. These ambiguities facilitate a rhetorical room to manoeuvre, and a dual or two-stage defence of resistance against the accusation of rebellion. Thus tyranny (real) furnishes grounds

---

[1] L. Wittgenstein, *Philosophical Investigations*, trans. G. E. M. Anscombe, Blackwell, Oxford, 1968, pp. 66–7 on family resemblance; *The Blue and Brown Books*, Harper Row, New York, 1964, for the importance of the 'loose concept'. Understanding the plausibility and difficulties inherent in using loose concepts, dates from antiquity. Discussion of the *sorites* argument and Aristotle's *dicta* on the limits on precision when writing about the political attest to this.

for resistance; tyranny (nominal) itself destroys government, making resistance or rebellion redundant notions. As we shall see, these ambiguities
are not fully exploited by Lawson to defend resistance, but later in the
century they are fully capitalised upon by writers who cite Lawson and
by Locke and his friend James Tyrrell who do not cite him.

More immediately, one may say that Lawson's movement between different definitional modes raises the more general and difficult matter of the
relationship between our words and the world of action to which they are
addressed. Again, one may say that after Kant (who may perhaps be seen
as the great transitional figure) what has been firmly separated into opposing
epistemological camps were treated by Lawson and his world as distinguishable argumentative options to be appealed to in turn. On the one hand,
a complex physical or empirical reality could be used as a court of appeal
against which the use of words and the viability of whole conceptual vocabularies could be judged. Thus Lawson in discussing monarchy refers us to
the diversity of monarchical forms which can neither be captured in a single
word nor can be made to comply with an abstract nominal definition. Much
of his critique of Hobbes stems from this empiricist appeal, and the sardonic
reference to 'imperious dictators and masters of words' (*Pol.* 135) intimates
the failure of Hobbist conceptual and definitional simplifications to capture
the nature of the political world. On the other hand, Lawson was explicitly
aware of the sense-imposing and creative capacities of language. Without
an adequate battery of terms we cannot understand the world, to which
we have no access other than through our words. In some moods almost
everything depends on the *notions* (nominal definitions) through which we
can see things. This general direction of argument is seen in his criticisms
of Buchanan, Bodin and Arnisaeus.

The precedents for both propensities of argument were rich and deeply
entangled. What I have delineated as a broadly representative account of
the relationship between words and the world is intimated in Aristotelian
and Ockhamist appeals to 'experience' and the Baconian emphasis on 'induc-
tion'. It is also seen clearly in the rhetorical theories of Quintilian (35?–100),
where *verba* must be judged according to the fit with *res* – hence the long-
lived image of the appropriate clothing of words for the underlying body
of the things discussed, which encapsulates his notion of *decorum*.[12] Where
we have a clearly physical point of reference, such a model of the relationship
between words and the world seemed, and still seems, plausible; and so
understanding is a matter of hypotyposis. As Ian Maclean has pointed out,
it was precisely in domains such as medicine that appeal to the facts in

[12] Quintilian, *Institutio Oratia*, trans. H. E. Butler, Loeb Classical Library, Camb. Mass.,
1920–2, 8, pref. 21; 9.1.16.

order to monitor discourse seemed most effective;[13] and it is possible that Lawson, certainly familiar with Quintilian, was conversant with contemporary medical discourse.[14]

Conversely, what might be loosely called a linguistic idealism is expressed with varying degrees of confidence and extremity from Gorgias (483?–376 BC), via Aristotle, Cicero, the logic of Peter Abelard and the rhetorical theories of the Renaissance. It is evident, as Oakeshott has intimated, in the sceptical nominalism of Hobbes. He held that reason gives us truth only about names.[15] The view, broadly, that we are prisoners of our concepts and that understanding is both created and limited by their adequacy is to be found with respect to medicine in Julius Caesar Scaliger (1484–1588);[16] but paradigmatically it seemed most plausible where there was no physical referent to act as a putative court of appeal. Here the role of theology is crucial. The connection between the creative and controlling power of words and the initial creative act of God as *logos* was not lost on the poetry of Lawson's world; and with the intellectual burdens of the past being so formidable, and discursive delineation being so flexible, we cannot assume that the compass of Lawson's political theory was free from the resonant circles of metaphysical and devotional imagery.[17] Moreover, theology was a domain of largely nominal definition and it is when Lawson tackles the problems of predicating God that he most clearly espouses a theory of

---

[13] Ian Maclean, *The Renaissance Notion of Woman*, Cambridge University Press, 1980; and 'The Interpretation of Natural Signs: Cardano's *De Subtiltate* versus Scaliger's *Exercitationes*' in B. Vickers, ed., *Occult and Scientific Mentalities in the Renaissance*, Cambridge University Press, 1984, esp. pp. 240 and 242ff.

[14] Thomas More, kinsman of Richard More the younger, was a physician, his library was reabsorbed into the family possessions at his death. Richard More 'A Catalogue of my Books', SCRO, and on Lawson's encomiast see note 2, chapter 1.

[15] On Gorgias see, e.g., Struever, *Language of History*, chap. 1; W. C. K. Guthrie, *A History of Greek Philosophy, The Sophists*, Cambridge University Press, 1971. Aristotle has, ambivalently, a place in what ultimately became separate traditions. F. E. Cranz, 'Two Debates about the Intellect' (paper given to *The Society for Medieval Renaissance Philosophy*, December 1979) has suggested an explanation rooted in the notion of the conjoining of the interpreter and the world, which he argues was mistaken for a clear separation only after Anselm in the twelfth century. It was upon this separation that clearly opposing epistemological schools could develop. Whether Cranz is correct to posit a post-Anselmian watershed (and the twelfth century is presently a fashionable catchment area for such theories), the Aristotelian and neo-Aristotelian notion of 'intelligencing' as a conjoining of mental *forms* (*eide*) in matter, does help explain Aristotle's apparently contradictory appeal. Cicero's *De Oratore*, 3, at length, is also instructive on the relationship between *res* and *verba*. See also Peter Abelard, *Logica*, 'ingredientibus', ed. B. Geyer, Beiträge 21, 1–3, 7f., as discussed in Cranz, 'Two Debates'; M. Oakeshott, *Introduction to Leviathan*, Blackwell, Oxford, 1946, p. xxv.

[16] Maclean, 'The Interpretation of Natural Signs', pp. 244–5.

[17] Rosalie L. Colie, *Paradoxia Epidemica: The Renaissance Tradition of Paradox*, Princeton University Press, 1966; Archon, 1976, chap. 6 especially on George Herbert; Melissa Wanamaker, *Discordia Concors*, Kenniket Press, New York, 1975.

conceptual entrapment which makes it vital to have an adequate battery of nominal classifiers (see 'Amica diss.', at length).

Now what we may conclude from this is that in Lawson's world, and for Lawson in particular, the political and ethical domain occupied an uncertain and ambivalent status between, as it were, the discursive models of theology and anatomy. The political was in a sense physical, often violently so, and the facts of the English Revolution needed explanation – such a view is familiar enough for us who are the inheritors of the political as a firmly constituted domain constantly used as a court of appeal. Nevertheless the political was for Lawson, and most of his contemporaries, a branch of theology, and thus could easily be subject to some degree to the linguistic idealism of divine predication, loosing its uncertain status as a fully constituted domain of experience. The crucial point here is that the status of the political could shift, or be shifted, towards or away from the physical as one notion or the other of the relationship of concepts to physical reality came into play. Such movements were directly related to the employment of the idioms of providence and contingency. The *Politica* was written when such shifts through the process of discussion not only afforded a rhetorical flexibility but also a logical plausibility. The theological had not fallen away as an informing discursive context, and the political had not hardened into an autonomous domain, hence it was possible to cloak both understandings of the crucial relationship between the political and its vocabulary in a general pattern of precept enabling distinction but resisting separation. There may seem something logically arbitrary in appealing by turns to the facts of the political world and to the priority of adequately refined conceptualisation, just as there seems something arbitrary in appealing by turns to providence and mundane contingency, but our perception is a function of what we are *now* able to separate. Within the context of these general reflections we can turn specifically to some of the central items in Lawson's vocabulary.

8

Community, representation and consent

The notion of community is central both to Lawson's secular and ecclesiastical politics; but when taken in conjunction with the associated concepts of consent and representation it might seem to suggest some neo-democratic commitment on Lawson's part.[1] And certainly the inheritance of precept is similar, but Lawson is not Rousseau. Neither, despite a redolence of echoes from the 1640s, is Lawson's work at one with the 'radical' Levellers. He may as easily be seen in chorus with the 'conservative' Clubmen. If Lawson's apparent bringing together of those opposing wings of the English Revolution seems to be a dialectical *tour de force*, it is because we have become too confident in the classificatory power of the 'radical' and 'conservative' labels.[2]

As Tierney has demonstrated, Lawson's theory of community is a variation on medieval themes of Roman Law ideas of corporation. But Tierney has oversimplified its operation and its consequences for Lawson's notions of representation and consent.[3] Most generally, the notion of legal corporation can be seen as the answer to the problems of giving a diversity of individuals unequivocable status under the law. To see people as members of a defined corporation was to effect a legal economy of scale. Because of their common corporate status all were similarly answerable to and protected by the relevant pattern of laws; but there was a crucial difference between members as directly responsible for and active in the corporation, and members as subsumed appendages.

[1] Julian Franklin, *John Locke and the Theory of Sovereignty*, Cambridge University Press, 1978, pp. 125–6, suggests that Lawson had democratic tendencies, though admits they were not as advanced as those of the Levellers, which is sad, but apparently generous interpretation can rescue him.
[2] J. S. Morrill, *The Revolt of the Provinces: Conservatives and Radicals in the English Civil War, 1630–1650*, Allen and Unwin, London, 1976, stresses that there was common ground between the radical Levellers and the conservative Clubmen; Lawson provides perhaps the most articulate and theoretical evidence of what this ground was.
[3] See Brian Tierney, *Religion, Law and the Growth of Constitutional Thought, 1150–1650*, Cambridge University Press, 1982, at length, for a valuable account of Lawson's thought in a fitting theoretical context.

The former were a visible and manageable minority – in the medieval sense of the term majority, *maior pars*. The latter were a majority in the modern sense of the term, numerically dominant but submerged by their representatives. The corporation in law was predicated then on the rhetorical and logical notion of *pars pro toto*. Thus when the *maior pars* acted *qua* agents, the majority were fictively imagined to do so. In this way, the corporate persona of the few established and maintained a manageable legal body. So intimately related were the linguistic domains of law and politics in the Middle Ages that such a notion was easily transferred figuratively to structure perceptions of political relationships. As a metaphor, then, the notion of corporation insured a major role for irrevocable representation and, as a corollary, a negligible role for any notion of the prior consent of the subsumed members and accountability to them. If the corporation was legitimate, it was worthy of consent, or consent could be assumed, almost, because of the attribution of membership to a given individual or group. A theory of communal relationships such as this is clearly important in Lawson.[4] Looking at it, we may get some clues that help explain the shift in meaning of the word majority and its ramifications for much of our political vocabulary.

As I have shown, what legitimises the community for Lawson is its adherence to divine precept; thus he introduces a distinction between a proper community and an association, which parallels the distinction between power and force. To repeat, an association may be formed 'yea even by devils' out of rational consent, but that does not create a community (*Pol.* 17) which requires a just consent (*Pol.* 16); the 'firmness' of a community comes from agreement with divine precept (*Pol.* 34). Once formed, the community comprises members who act for the whole: on the one hand, *cives* and members *formalite et plene*; on the other hand, the extensive residue of virtual members. The *cives* too may themselves be subsumed by *eminenter cives*, a possibility which is later tied directly to Lawson's remarks on English socio-political structures, and is couched in his somewhat Marsilian terminology of a *sanior* and *valentior pars*.[5]

There is nothing eccentric or even un-English in any of this. As Tierney has clearly shown, a combined doctrine of agency and representation within the framework of corporation theory enjoyed almost unbroken political employment from the work of the thirteenth-century decretalists onwards in both secular and ecclesiastical spheres of argument. It was expressed

[4] *Ibid.*, on which I am drawing freely here.
[5] The process can be carried on with a pyramidic nicety of numerical relationship, see John Eliot, *The Christian Commonwealth*, 1659; and earlier, J. Althusius, *Politica methodice digesta*, 1614 edn, ed. C. J. Friedrich, Harvard University Press, Cambridge, Mass., 1932, for the elaboration of a federal theory through incorporation.

at the most sophisticated level of scholastic discourse;[6] was certainly important in the polemics of Marsilio of Padua and was adapted through the public law of Arnisaeus, Althusius and Besold. But such theories were by no means exclusively scholastic, a concept of agency and irrevocable representation seems clearly to underwrite the effective equation of the populus with the directing power of a regime to be found in the work of the Florentine humanist historiographer Leonardo Bruni (1370–1444). Similarly, in the *Vindiciae contra tyrannos*, it is a clearly presented theory of political corporation, agency and representation that is used to circumscribe the right to resist.[7] Neither were such theories freshly imported into the England of the sixteenth and seventeenth centuries. As Tierney points out, the articulate barons of the thirteenth century styled themselves a *universitas regni*.[8] A synthesis in microcosm of this whole broad inheritance is to be found in the translation of the *Defensor pacis* by William Marshall and sponsored by Thomas Cromwell in 1535. Explicitly, he associated Marsilio's concept of the *valentior pars* with the English Parliament and, whether in direct cognisance of Marshall's creative translation or no, such claims became the basis of parliamentarian apologetics during the 1640s[9] – claims to be challenged by Levellers and Clubman alike by stating that they instead represented the authentic community of England.

Lawson was very familiar with such a cluster of corporate writers as I have mentioned. Though he claims not to have known Jean Gerson (1363–1429) and the Sorbonne school whose importance Tierney underlines, he knew Besold, Arnisaeus, almost certainly Althusius, and above all, he knew Marsilio of Padua very well; but precisely because corporation imagery was so widely scattered it is not possible to specify any exclusive array of texts whose ideas Lawson adapted and transmitted. He was simply a legatee

---

[6] See Tierney, *Religion*, at length, who discusses the work of Hervaeus Natalis, also, Nicholas of Cusa and Gerson amongst others.

[7] Donald Wilcox, *The Development of Florentine Humanist Historiography*, Harvard University Press, 1969, Appendix C.; *Vindiciae contra tyrannos*, in J. Franklin, ed., *Constitutionalism and Resistance in the Sixteenth Century*, Pegasus, New York, 1969, question 2, pp. 149, 151, 154.

[8] Tierney, *Religion*, p. 11.

[9] William Marshall, *The Defence of Peace, Translated out of Latyn*, 1535; on which see G. Piaia, *Marsilio da Padova nella Riforma*, Antenore, Padua, 1977, pp. 145ff.; see also Thomas Smith, *Republica anglorum*, 2.1., where the consent of Parliament is taken to be the consent of all. Thus in this broad sharing of a community rhetoric, Lawson is quite at one with Hunton and Ball, as Tuck rightly suggests, *contra* Franklin, *John Locke*, pp. 125–6. Franklin's point, however, is that writers such as Ball, Parker, Rutherford, had little or no concept of a constituent authority and did not 'solve' the problem of resistance in a mixed constitution as Lawson, allegedly, did. This is taken up as a separate issue with respect to Lawson. Here one can only state baldly that Franklin is wrong on Rutherford and Hunton and helps ensure Lawson's originality by ignoring, e.g., Milton, to say nothing of more widespread 'Italianate' constitutional and legalistic inheritance which, flowed, as it were through English veins.

of a resonant repertoire of terms and arguments generated by the corporate image and its attendant notions of agency, representation and consent. His last parish entry as Mainstone Minister indicates how deeply corporate relationships penetrated to the most local levels of English society. As I have already cited, he records how 'it was not agreed amongst the parishioners that those that have purchased tenaments [and] have served the office of churchwarden must serve and beare that office not only for there owne selfs but also ... for there tennents'.[10] In the *Politica* it is precisely the corporate inheritance which defines the relationships between virtual members of the community, *cives* and *eminenter cives*. If we do wish to tie this down to a specific precedent, we can probably do no better than to turn to Marsilio of Padua's *Defensor pacis* (1324). Marsilio very largely defined political (secular) society in terms of a community of citizens called the *legislator humanus* and the various functional parts of society (the governing, priestly, agricultural, commercial, military and juristic). The *legislator*, however, could also be seen in terms of its weightier part, *valentior pars* which, as its agent, could be taken to be the same thing, *pro eodem de cetero supponatur*, as the *legislator* itself.[11] Similarly, for Lawson, a small numerical part of the community could act for the whole, effectively be the whole, as he makes clear at one point by citing the Paduan (*Pol.* 340). This conjunction of texts is further reinforced by Lawson's suggestion that the true heir of *real* majesty lies in the *sanior* or *valentior pars* of a community (*Pol.* 383), where he seems to be paraphrasing and partially quoting Marsilio.[12] Not surprisingly Lawson also affirms that *plebs* does not mean people (*Pol.* 62).

What should also be noted at this point is that the corporation metaphor from law is supported by a linguistic relationship drawn from rhetorical theory; and, as the corporation metaphor itself may be seen as an example of *pars pro toto*, such recourse to the nomenclature of rhetoric is hardly

---

[10] MPR, 1603–41, 10 April 1637, SCRO, 3277/1/2.

[11] *Defensor pacis*, 1.12.4; Condren, 'Democracy in the *Defensor pacis*: On the English Language Tradition of Marsilian Interpretation', *Il Pensiero Politico*, 13 (1980), pp. 304ff. See also *Vindiciae contra tyrannos*, trans. Franklin, *Constitutionalism and Resistance*, p. 151, 'And as the decisions of the majority of a corporation publically arrived at are taken as the decisions of the entire body, so the action of the majority of princes and notables is taken to be that of all of them, and what all of them have done is regarded as an act of the people as a whole.'

[12] This constitutes a shift away from the *Examination*, pp. 26–7, where Lawson refers to a more individualistic majority. The relationship between Marsilio and Lawson I have discussed in more detail in 'Resistance and Sovereignty in Lawson's *Politica*', *HJ*, 24, 3 (1981), pp. 673ff. and in 'George Lawson and the *Defensor pacis*', *Medioevo*, 5–6 (1980), pp. 595ff. These papers however do not make use of manuscript materials which further strengthen the relationship, and of the *Catalogus Librarum* which lists a Frankfurt edition of *Defensor pacis*, 1592. Given the diversity of citations from the Paduan in his work, this seems likely to have been Lawson's own copy.

strained – in some ways it might not even have been noticed. The domains of rhetoric and law provide fields of imagery of the most decorous sort for the political. As we have seen, Lawson refers to a rational minority representing the whole as a *synecdoche*, not properly the whole, 'an Instrument whereby the whole doth so act' (*Pol.* 340; cf. *Exam.* 37). If such a metaphor is taken seriously, questions concerning the accountability of representatives are doubly difficult to raise and consent as a criterion of legitimacy is even more tangential than it would be if expressed through an unadorned corporation image; for the synecdoche is the quintessential qualitative aspect of the whole without which the whole is useless or even non-existent.

Disengaging the *matter* of the community from the *form* of the polity we may say that images of corporation and rhetorical relationship conspire to make representation irrevocable and consent peripheral. But they conspire also to necessitate the distinction between express and tacit consent – the modes of consent being appropriate to one's communal status as representative or represented respectively. Remove the context of corporation theory assumed by writers such as Lawson and later Locke and the distinction, which has so exercised the energies of Locke critics since Hume, seems forced and difficult to sustain. Placed in proper context it becomes intelligible as a function of the theory of representation created by the metaphors.

In the totality of Lawson's theory, however, we cannot completely disengage the *matter* from the *form* of polity; and once the two are joined, Lawson introduces a supplementary vocabulary appropriate to political order. Overall it seems that communities have representatives, polities have officers. The important difference is that representatives are accountable only to later representatives because formally (nominally) the earlier representatives are no longer representatives. Conversely, officers have discernible spheres of operation and as such they are accountable to a wider or a different body (see also *Exam.* 79). The consequence is also that consent becomes a much more important criterion of legitimacy, and Tierney is thus wrong to draw no distinction between the role consent plays in Lawson's community and that which it plays in the polity.[13] Consent, Lawson tells us, is the very foundation of the polity, and is necessary even where government arises out of conquest; power is not fully held until it is accepted (*Pol.* 57–8, 82, 130). There is no inconsistency here, for polities arise from communities and the adherence of the community to divine precept elevates the consent such a community might give.

What immediately complicates matters is that the image of corporation is carried over to the discussion of governmental form as a means of ensuring

---

[13] Tierney, *Religion*, p. 98, 'In Lawson's work, both community and government were conceived of as corporate bodies deriving their respective authorities from consent.'

an indivisible sovereignty without necessarily having recourse to a monarchical or pure system of government. *Personal* majesty is a corporation imposed upon a corporation. All Lawson seems to want to extract from these Chinese boxes is the emphasis upon the mutual dependency of parts upon each other but, in making the metaphor of corporation less discriminate, he prepares for the erosion of the distinctions between officers and representatives in the later parts of the text, suggesting a Pandoric profusion of possibility.

Here the crucial point to note is that, in the context of the corporation metaphor, it was not so much that representatives might be accountable, but that they might cease properly to be representatives. This is a theme clearly visible, for example, in the Leveller manifestoes directed against parliament.[14] The distinction is easily overlooked now, or reduced to something trivially semantic, but it expressed both a doctrine of office and the importance of having an adequate battery of notions under which the phenomena of the world could be classified and reclassified. It also recognised a gap between precept and specific action. It was perhaps the failure to sustain the distinction between officers and representatives which is a large part of the 'development' of modern theories of accountable representation. Such an hypothesis is suggested by Lawson's ambiguous remarks which conclude his chapter on the acquisition of ecclesiastical power. Power may be lost 'When Representatives turn into a faction and betray their trust, they lose their power as Representatives' (*Pol.* 127–8). Are such men being reclassified so that accountability becomes a conceptual possibility, or are representatives beginning to be accountable, just like officers? Thereafter both possibilites seem suggested by the text, the former dominating only as the informing image of corporation is clear.

The ambiguities which emerge in Lawson's theory of representation may themselves be symptomatic of important modifications in political argument and suggest an hypothesis as to how such changes happened.[15] In miniature we may be witnessing, as it were, a shift from people singular to people plural, from *maior pars* to majority, an alteration in which men cease to be genuine representatives, at most accountable to later representatives, and become effectively officers answerable for their actions to a larger, normally passive, but scrutinising whole.

Lawson's text suggests that part of the answer may lie precisely in the

---

[14] *Leveller Manifestoes*, ed. Don Wolfe, Cass. New York, 1967 e.g. *The Argument of the People; An Appeal from the degenerate Representative Body*, 1647. But see also, e.g. Althusius, *Politica methodice digesta*, chap. 18, for ephors going beyond their trust and thereby ceasing to be anything but ordinary people. See also, Bartolus, *De tyrannia*, 2 on kingship dissolving through sin.

[15] Althusius, *Politica methodice digesta* seems marked by a similar ambiguity, as is indicated by the dual status of the ephors: they are representatives who may cease to represent, and accountable officers; participants in government, and watchers from without.

failure to sustain the felicitous conjunction of metaphors from rhetoric and corporate law which informed, structured and restricted the possibilities of a political vocabulary. Immediately, however, it takes us to the question of whether the people have (or has) any right to resist and bring to account those in authority who make government an intolerable burden to bear. This too, and its considerable interpretative difficulties, is partly a function of the control of metaphors – most notably those of *real* and *personal*, matter and form, and those arising directly from the analogical interplay of church and state. What follows is less the solution to the interpretative difficulties, in the sense of urging a choice between the specified options, than the exploration of two competing readings which I take to circumscribe the limits of plausibility; readings which are carried through into Lawson's account of the English Revolution, and which finish the process of making clear the textual warrant for the diversity of Lawson's later use.

9

Settlement and resistance

I COBWEB

Duncan Forbes has wittily remarked that political theories which make a
fetish of resistance are like theories of matrimony which emphasise a general
rule for divorce.[1] But as Lawson was concerned with subjection, its problematic limits are necessary preoccupations. To some extent, then, it is fitting
that critical attention has been directed to Lawson's alleged theory of resistance. As I have indicated through the preceding exposition, however, it
is only in the context of the ecclesiological analogue, separation, that we
might begin to see just what his theory might be and how close we come
to making a fetish of a ghost in the text: mistaking unwanted guests at
the wedding for bride and groom.

To repeat, Lawson's treatment of separation seems clear-cut. He is hostile
to the possibility of separation in the present, but in principle the possibility
may and has occurred justifiably. In the idiom of William Chillingworth,
for example, it is an option that must always be available to the believer
in fulfilment of theological duty. But despite the self-consciously analogical structure of the *Politica*, modern commentators have been unable
to agree on whether there even is a concomitant theory of secular resistance.[2]

Salmon's negative assessment may well have been coloured by allowing
specifically Huguenot and Calvinist resistance literature to loom too large.[3]
Although Lawson seems elusively to be descanting upon typically monarcho-
mach themes and/or their elaboration in England, judged by the general

[1] Duncan Forbes, *Hume's Philosophical Politics*, Cambridge University Press, 1975, p. 323.
[2] J. H. M. Salmon, *The French Wars of Religion in English Political Thought*, Oxford University Press, 1959, pp. 119–20; Julian Franklin, *John Locke and the Theory of Sovereignty*,
Cambridge University Press, 1978, chap. 3; C. Condren, 'Resistance and Sovereignty in
Lawson's *Politica*, *HJ*, 24, 3 (1981), pp. 673ff.
[3] The general characteristics are well summarised in Quentin Skinner, *The Foundations of
Modern Political Thought*, Cambridge University Press, 1978, 2, pp. 302ff.

characteristics of such literature the *Politica* leaves a good deal to be desired. There is no clarion call to resistance, either as a right or as a theological duty. There is virtually nothing of a theory of contract between people and government – single or double (a significant shift away from the explicitly contractual *Examination*). There is no emphasis on the potent parliamentarian tag describing the monarch as *singulis major universis minor* (cf. *Exam.* 41).[4] There is no special resistance role for the lesser magistrate.[5] There is no legitimating example of resistance; no sanction sought in biblical *loci*. As secular rulers are God's viceregents they have something of his power, and resistance against God is never a viable possibility. In contrast, of course, church rulers are not viceregents, and this alone makes separation a clearer option for the church member. Secular rulers, too, enjoy a dazzling and repetitively specified array of powers, the catalogue of which sits ill and humpishly on the back of resistance theory. George Buchanan, for example, is explicitly taken to task for avowing the rights of subjects to resist. These brief points pick out the strong threads in Lawson's constitutional thought which requires the simple subjection of subjects and seems to tie him closer to Hobbes, Hall and Filmer than to Franco-Calvinist resistance theory.

Conversely, however, there are grounds for Franklin's somewhat procrustean attribution of a theory of resistance to Lawson. If Lawson has moved away from a contract theory by the time he published the *Politica*, his writing is still suggestive of contract and he explicitly regards the government as a trust.[6] Further, just as a church exists prior to and independently of its political manifestation, so also a community is logically and temporally prior to a political form. The members of this community originally enjoy a state of liberty and equality which is not entirely lost on their becoming subjects.

That potent emblem of resistance scholarship, François Hotman (1524–90) is singled out as a great antiquary and lawyer and compared favourably with Jean Bodin (*Pol.* 103). In keeping with this intimated respect for resistance mythology, the coronation oath in England is held to bind the king to the fundamental laws of the country. More than this, however, Lawson

[4] The significance of this is stressed by C. C. Weston and J. R. Greenberg, *Subjects and Sovereigns*, Cambridge University Press, 1981, pp. 62, 64ff.; cf. Philip Hunton, *A Treatise of Monarchy*, 1643, p. 42.

[5] Cf. Beza, *Du doit des Magistrates*, 1574, 6; John Milton, *The Tenure of Kings and Magistrates*, in *The Prose Works of John Milton*, ed. J. Max Patrick, Doubleday, New York, 1967; J. Althusius, *Politica methodice digesta*, 1614 edn, ed. C. J. Friedrich, Harvard University Press, Cambridge, Mass., 1932, chap. 18, whom Milton seems to be following. For all three there is a positive ephoral duty to resist tyranny in word and deed.

[6] Cf. John Ponet, *A Short Treatise of Politick Power*, 1556? But for that matter so did Charles I, or his ghost, in the *Eikon Basilike*. The question is to whom is the trustee accountable? For all the answer was to God, for some also to an intermediate human agency.

generally subordinates history to matters of right. He suggests, for example, that the people retain rights and indirectly, that these may be defended (*Pol.* 93). Were there not some right of resistance in abstract, it is difficult to see why Lawson would agonise so much over the pragmatics of its exercise in the extremities of usurpation.

Even so, at this point a passing contrast with Grotius on usurpation is instructive. It became common in the seventeenth century for resistance theorists to cite Grotius, usually together with Barclay, as an emblem of monarchical or even absolutist theory, and thus with added force they were able to say that *even* he allows reserve powers to the people which may be exercised in the face of usurpation or the alienation of the kingdom.[7] There are two points of interest here. First, Lawson does not use this standard *topos* of resistance rhetoric. Secondly, he seems much less certain in his advice than Grotius. Where Grotius sees a right because of a pre-existing law, Lawson, who could consistently use such an argument, concentrates on what a usurper might rationally expect to happen to him. This somewhat obscures the acceptance of a right, but that a right exists is underlined by the fact that Lawson is as critical of Arnisaeus, who denies the rights of subjects to resist, as he is of Buchanan, who affirms them. Lawson, in fact, seems to be criticising the whole language of resistance theory, *pro* and *con.*, which he remarks has been 'too loosely handled' (*Pol.* 106). By discussing the rights of subjects neither side gets anywhere: Arnisaeus effectively tries to infer from a tautology; Buchanan is trapped by a contradiction. Neither has a sufficiently discriminate vocabulary with which to see the issues involved. Lawson's correction is to insist, from the outset, on a firm nominal distinction between subject and citizen. This seems to run against the dominant grain of English and much continental usage. With some degree of truth Pufendorf was later to remark that the usage of the term citizen was fluid.[8] Overwhelmingly, however, the standard pattern in English was for the word citizen to refer to urban dwellers as a socially defined class of subjects rather than to people as independent agents. This was understandable, after all England had no free cities, only privileged ones; but the conceptual corollary was that the term citizen lost most of its classical and Italianate associations with political equality, and indepen-

---

[7] But it was never necessary to read Barclay as well, for Grotius makes the same standard reference himself; *De jure belli ac pacis libri tres*, trans. F. W. Kelsey, Clarendon Press, Oxford, 1913, 1925, 1.3.17; 1.4.7–20.

[8] Pufendorf, *De jure*, trans. C. H. and W. A. Oldfather, Clarendon Press, Oxford, 1934, 7.2.20. He seems to have England in mind as he is criticising Hobbes, *De cive*, but his own usage varies between *De jure* and his earlier *De officiis*, 1660, see, e.g. 5.12; 2.5.4. Althusius, *Politica methodice digesta* also exhibits fluid usage. At different times citizens define the community and are members of cities, or commonwealths.

dent action.[9] Writers like Bishop Maxwell, Hobbes and later the Church of England polemicist Edward Stillingfleet (1635–99) effected a yet more drastic diminution of the term citizen by equating it with subject.[10] Even so, there were exceptions which retained a semantic independence for citizenship and thus kept alive classical and Italianate associations in England. Thomas More had gone so far as to suggest that the word subject was inappropriate to a political vocabulary (in Latin only one letter distinguished it from servitude). He preferred instead to write of people and citizens.[11] There is a varying proximity between *subdites* and *cives* in the writings of the Italian exile and sometime Regius Professor of Divinity at Oxford, Peter Martyr Vermigli (1500–62). Another Italian exile and Regius Professor, Alberigo Gentili (1552–1608), in his *De jure belli*, 1612 edition, had designated states as citizens precisely because of a legal equality between them and independence of action amongst them. At the beginning of the seventeenth century Henry Wright, in his little known *The First Part of the Disquisition of Truth* seems at least to shift between a Machiavellian notion of citizen as armed patriot and of citizen as city dweller, as he introduced Italian political learning to the city fathers of London.[12] Thomas May and James Harrington also do something to free the word from its subject moorings. For Harrington the word citizen makes sense in the context of his distinctly Machiavellian notions of virtue, corruption and independence of action; for Thomas May it is important in his attempt to assimilate the English Civil War to classical Roman historiographical models, which, given the status of any *rex* in Rome, was bound to result in a semantics of justification for the parliamentary cause.[13]

---

[9] Sir Thomas Smith, *De republica Anglorum*, 1.17.22, seems to be very representative; see also John Corbet, *A Discourse*, 1667, p. 47. Alexander Barclay, *The Citizen turned Uplandishman*; E. Ravenscroft, *The Citizen turned Gentleman*, 1672; see also dictionary definitions from John Minsheu, *Ductor in lingua*, 1617, who relates citizen etymologically to citadel, to Johnson, who suggests 'freeman of a city', 'trader', and 'inhabitant' are equivalent terms. Shakespeare's citizens, even in the Roman plays, are also subjects.

[10] J. Maxwell, *Sacro-Sancta Regnum majestas*, 1644, pp. 8, 14–15; Hobbes, *De cive*, at length, the most ambitious and sustained attempt, esp. pp. 93–4; Edward Stillingfleet, *Irenicum*, 1662 edn, p. 34; also Simon Lowth, *On the Subject of Church Power*, 1685, p. 65.

[11] This is true of the *Epigrammata* and *Utopia*, where the play on words is noted. For a pertinent discussion see D. Grace, 'Subjects or Citizens? *Populi* and *Cives* in More's *Epigrammata*', *Moreana*, 25 (1988), pp. 133–6.

[12] Peter Martyr Vermigli, *Political Thought*, ed. R. Kingdon, Droz, Geneva, 1980, for the variety of usage in his work; Alberigo Gentili, *De jure belli*, 1612, trans. J. C. Rolfe, Oxford, 1933, p. 263; and see Henry Wright, *Disquisition*, 1616, see pp. 25, 49, 67, 68, 83, 89.

[13] James Harrington, *Oceana* in *Works*, 1656, ed. J. G. A. Pocock, Cambridge University Press; on whom see the discussion by Pocock in *The Machiavellian Moment*, Princeton University Press, 1975; Thomas May, *A History of the Parliament of England*, 1647, on whom see M. Hartman, 'Contemporary Explanations of the English Civil War', unpublished Ph.D. thesis, Cambridge, 1978. I am also indebted here to an unpublished address given by John Pocock at the Folger Library, Washington, Oct. 1985.

Now, to some extent, as Lawson adjusts his abstract vocabulary to fit English circumstances, specifications of citizen status are made to fit subject status; but his central point is to maintain a rigid, almost antithetical, distinction between the citizen *per se* and the subject; the former definitionally free and equal, the later definitionally subjected. As political society is a matter of subjection, subject status is coextensive with political status. Civic status is that enjoyed before and beyond the reach of subjecting power, and it is assimilated to the notion of community. Fully worked out, Lawson's distinction between subject and citizen lies at the heart of his attack on Hobbesian politics with its drastic collapse of any effective distinction between subject and citizen. Hobbes and Lawson can be seen as representing the extremes between which floated the uncertain usage that the acute Pufendorf was to note, but with Hobbes being more attuned to the dominant drift of the political lexicon. For Lawson certainly, the failure to make a firm distinction between subject and citizen is to handle things too loosely, it is to oversimplify (one of the major themes of the *Examination*'s attack on Hobbes); it is to obscure political relationships, as he maintains Bodin obscures them (*Pol.* 356). It is also to misunderstand biblical imperative, for the distinction is not between public and private, let alone town and country, but between neighbourliness and hierarchy, between, that is, the New Testament injunction to love thy neighbour and the Old Testament Fifth Commandment to honour thy father and mother. To echo Aquinas, it formalises the notion that man is a social as well as a political animal.

The notions of *real* and *personal* majesty are introduced, apparently from the work of Christopher Besold, as adjuncts to and in order to maintain the integrity of Lawson's binary distinctions between citizenship and subjection, community and polity.[14] As *real* majesty is that which is housed in the community of citizens, *personal* that which is invested in the governing power, the right of resistance depends upon the balance of majestical power. As I have suggested, it is a balance that is much closer to equilibrium in a secular than in an ecclesiological context. How close to balance may seem to us simply a matter of ascertaining the extent to which Lawson adapted Besoldian terms (*pace* Franklin) and in understanding his assertion that *real* majesty is greater than *personal*, for Lawson explicitly declines to give us details (*Pol.* 72). Lawson however, having mentioned Besold in connection with the terms *real* and *personal* simply dismisses him as uninformative about *real* majesty (*Pol.* 54–5), as he had called him 'outlandish' with respect to the whole question of sovereignty in the *Examination* (42–3), so a brief indication of a broader context for his use of these terms seems required.

Real and *personal* were part of the complex and shifting relationships

---

[14] Christopher Besold, *De magistate in genere*, Strasburg, 1626, although Lawson at no point cites any text or quotes from Besold.

between the semantic domains of property and power relationships. The political conception of the state is perhaps the prime example, as it seems to arise from a felicitous conjunction of metaphors of status and estate. The medieval doctrine of *status regni* was an essentially casuistical attempt to place rulers beyond the reach of established laws and mores when acting in the interests of the realm. It was a doctrine of immunity analogous to that which might be claimed over unencumbered property, making the owner unaccountable to others with respect to the treatment of such property. Not unrelatedly, the propensity for rulers, certainly in fourteenth- and fifteenth-century Italy, to treat their areas of political control as personal estates, within which they had a uniquely unaccountable status, added plausibility to seeing the political in terms of status and estate, special rights and physical property. By the sixteenth century, in writers such as Machiavelli, the specification of political relationships through the vocabulary of physical property is fittingly encapsulated by the abstract noun state (*lo stato*) which, not surprisingly, facilitated edifice metaphors for political society, which Lawson was also to use.[15] Gradually over the early modern period there was a shift from the metaphor of state to the reified abstraction; and all along, there was a chance to capitalise decorously on a range of words found traditionally at the nexus of the political and proprietorial. Key terms such as *dominium, proprietas, possessio* were common to both political and property relationships, as were, more broadly, the notions of use, misuse, ownership and trust. In the thirteenth century the issues of literal ownership, use of and responsibility for goods had split the Franciscan Order and had escalated into a vitriolic controversy over power and sovereignty within the church.[16] The most important political treatise to emerge from this turmoil was Marsilio's *Defensor pacis* (1324). In this Marsilio had brilliantly, if selectively, exploited spiritual Franciscan arguments which relied upon a firm distinction between ownership and use of property,

---

[15] I am abstracting broadly here from Gaines Post's important work, in *Studies in Medieval Legal Thought*, Princeton University Press, 1964; and from J. H. Hexter's similarly valuable essays in *The Vision of Politics on the Eve of the Reformation*, Allen Lane, London, 1973. On edifice metaphors see especially Martyn P. Thompson, 'The History of Fundamental Law in Political Thought from the French Wars of Religion to the American Revolution', *American Historical Review*, 91, 5 (1986), pp. 1103ff.; and Harro Höpfl, 'Fundamental Law and the Constitution in Sixteenth-Century France', in *Die Rolle der Juristen bei der Entstehung des modernen Staates*, ed. R. Schnur, Duncker und Humblot (1986), pp. 327ff.

[16] C. Condren, 'Rhetoric, Historiography and Political Theory: Some Aspects of the Poverty Controversy Reconsidered', *The Journal of Religious History*, 13, 1 (1984), pp. 15ff.; the most stimulating study is Gordon Leff, *Heresy in the Late Middle Ages*, 2 vols., Manchester University Press, 1967. For further valuable discussion of property and power, Janet Coleman, 'Medieval Discussions of Property: *Ratio* and *Dominium* according to John of Paris and Marsilius of Padua', *History of Political Thought*, 4, 2 (1983).

both movable (*personalis*) and immovable (*realis*). Recognising that effective political power was dependent upon unrestricted possession of property, he urged that the spiritualist Franciscan standards of property apply to the whole of the priestly part of society; that it be allowed only use of goods; that ownership and ultimate power over them must lie not with a formal church structure of priests, but with the *legislator humanus fidelis* – the *legislator* acting in its sacred capacity; that this *legislator* should monitor use, judge misuse and withdraw privileges if necessary.[17] The position was just as clear with respect to power and property in secular society. The *pars principans*, governing part, he urged should enjoy the use of a range of governmental powers, but it must ultimately be controlled by the exterior, normally passive body of citizens, the *legislator humanus* or its weightier part.[18]

The poverty controversy, and Marsilio's work towards the end of it, can be seen as helping to refine and bequeath a complex vocabulary of sovereignty metaphorically entangled with the terminology of property relationships. This set a precedent and prepared the way for the transfer of the notions of *personal* and *real* to refer, respectively, to movable (removable) powers used by and entrusted to institutionalised rulers, and the underlying immovable powers of a restricting authority. Certainly one may say that by the time Lawson wrote, the evocative and fluid terms *real* and *personal* were already at home in a political context of discourse irrespective of Besold. Althusius in the *Politica methodice digesta* (11–13; 14) uses them in the context of powers of taxation at the interface of power and property relations; and later the Leveller tract *The Agreement of the People* (1647) deploys them in discussing rights of property confiscation. The terms were to limp on into the eighteenth century with Hume's distinction between *real* and *personal* political parties.[19]

What these terms do in Lawson's theory, drawing as it does on a specifically Marsilian inheritance, is to articulate a theory designed to control political powers, not in terms of sharing them (as for example to be found in the voguish mixed monarchy theory), but through their restriction by those not involved in the political process. Lawson may have been so dismissive of Besold because his use of *real* and *personal*, as Franklin notes, seems largely to refer to princely and popular participation *in* government.[20] But Besold, like many people, was apt to run sharing and restricting notions

---

[17] Marsilio, *Defensor pacis*, ed. H. Kutsch, Berlin, 1958, esp. 2.12–14; see Condren, 'Rhetoric', pp. 21–34; Kerry Spiers, 'The Ecclesiastical Poverty Theory of Marsilius of Padua: Sources and Significance', *Il Pensiero Politico*, 10 (1977), pp. 6f.

[18] *Defensor pacis*, 1.11–13.

[19] David Hume, *Political Essays*, 'Of Parties in General', ed. C. W. Hendel, Liberal Arts Press, New York, 1953, p. 78.

[20] Franklin, *John Locke*, pp. 66ff. esp. 67–8.

of governmental control together.[21] This too may have irritated Lawson. Thus on the authority of Cicero, Besold asserts through an unfortunate but well-worn metaphor, that *real* majesty consists in the fundamental laws of the political society and that *personal* is but the head of the body politic '*Caput est, non totum corpus*'.[22]

Despite Lawson's hostility to and probably his independence of Besold, the ground between them could easily be eroded as both theories were framed and penetrated by providence. Franklin notes of Besold that if there were a clash between the sharing parties in a mixed monarchy, the two sides had little option but an appeal to trial by war, to take their cases to the court of providence and fortune.[23] But it is no less a problem for Lawson – if such practical applications of so abstract a theory can be considered problems for it. For, as we have seen, the legitimate claims of *personal* majesty are sanctioned by God who may act, even in obscure ways, through it, just as the claims of *real* majesty are sanctioned by the community's adherence to divine law. Lawson provides no criterion by which the sanction of providence can be identified. Indeed, he seems to accept that *real* majesty's being greater does not mean more favoured in the eye of the Lord by his insistence that God does work in mysterious ways, even through tyrants and usurpers. As I have suggested the rhetoric of providence is capricious, and promiscuous; when *real* and *personal* majesty clash, they may be left as it were, with Besold, on the battle field. Franklin's attempt then to delineate Lawson's vocabulary of sovereignty largely in juxtaposition with Christopher Besold is unsatisfactory: his assertion that Lawson appreciated Besold is inexplicable; his claim that Lawson represents some strikingly original departure from Besold and conventional theories of sovereignty, untenable.[24] Summing up at this point, what we may say is that a nomenclature of dual sovereignty is required by Lawson's categorial distinctions between subject and citizen, community and polity. To an extent the choice of *real* and *personal* was particularly decorous. It drew on an evocative conceptual and metaphorical inheritance, encapsulating something of the movable, contingent nature of formalised political institutions as opposed to the relatively permanent nature of that which is diversely governed. That must have been encouraging and reassuring in 1660. In this way, to an extent, and again contrary to Franklin, on this reading the

---

[21] See, for example, Hunton, *A Treatise*. Franklin, *John Locke*, p. 66, suggests that Hunton might have been one of the few who knew Besold.
[22] *De magistate in genere*, 1.1.4. It is hardly conducive to the development of a restricting theory, nor to one which in any way diminishes governmental power unless one uses another locus of authority such as soul, which permeated John of Salisbury's organic specification of political society.
[23] Franklin, *John Locke*, p. 68.   [24] *Ibid.*, pp. 67, 86.

terminology fits well with the even older metaphor of form and matter on which Lawson also heavily relies.[25] Various political forms are impressed upon the malleable, flexible and lasting matter of the community. This immovable community, possessor of *real* majesty, is thus a little like the earth, which can be shaped, but like the earth too it has generative capacity. With such figuratively resonant concepts Lawson is himself able to generate a theory of settlement which has, as Franklin correctly stresses, clear advantages over its better known competitors. Mixed monarchy theory, though appropriate to an ethos of accommodation, had in fact led to conflict or failed to delineate sovereignty adequately; a sharing theory of government, it sat ill, as Lawson believed, with the indivisible nature of governmental majesty. Any theory which vested legitimacy in a single form of government was for Lawson theologically unacceptable, and by focussing attention on the issue of ideal form, any such theory was apt to present an uncompromising front to all who preferred other governmental forms; the result would be a narrow basis for settlement which threatened to escalate political into religious issues. *De facto* theory had the obvious advantage of being able to accommodate any arrangements that worked; but in the long term and in isolation it had the destabilising consequence of seeming to undermine the very sanctity of oath taking, for as soon as a government ran into trouble its legitimacy was in doubt. The Whigs were to realise the limitations of *de facto* theory later in the century, recognising that the provisional allegiance willingly given by the disaffected was itself destabilising.[26] As a short-term bandage it might be acceptable but more was needed for a permanent settlement.

If the shortcomings of these theories are all manifestly less obvious in Lawson's alternative solution comprising as it does the twin corporate identities of *real* and *personal* majesty, the problem still remained to control such residually metaphorical expressions in the interests of settlement. One general consequence of the ingrained habit of shifting terms between the semantic domains of power and property relationships was the pronounced tendency to reify power – a clear characteristic of Machiavelli's discussions of how to hold (*mantanere*) the state in *The Prince*. Reification is evident from the outset of the *Politica*. All power, Lawson maintains, is grounded in propriety and God is omnipotent, owning all and by degrees allowing rights of use in his powers (*Pol.* 1). With discursive practices such as this, it is easy to see how political sovereignty can virtually be seen as a physical

---

[25] *Ibid.*, p.71. The imagery is central to Aristotelian physics, biology and metaphysics, e.g. *De anima*, 412ª 16ff. it is found in Aquinas, Suarez, and Machiavelli, whose *Discorsi* are much concerned with *forma e materia*, and it is a preoccupation of alchemical writing.

[26] See Mark Goldie, 'The Revolution of 1689 and the Structure of Political Argument', *Bulletin of Research in the Humanities*, 1980, p.483, for the controversies surrounding a writer like Sherlock.

piece of property to be divided, unified, lost, mapped out, contained, entrusted and reclaimed. An inconvenient consequence of this sort of meta-phorically resonant language was that it gave rise to the question of how individuals could give power when, as individuals, they did not have it; just as on the other hand, it made the distinctions between *real* and *personal* seem plausible and important.

More immediately, despite Lawson's predominant emphasis on *real* maj-esty as a conceptual aid to settlement, it remains a moot point how sanguine he was about the more activist corollaries and looser associations arising from the suggestive field of terms in which both *real* and *personal* were situated (a field of terms already effectively exploited by the monarcho-machs);[27] or how far the resistance resonances of his vocabulary constituted a somewhat embarrassing family of metaphorical ghosts in the text. This question can most economically be elucidated first by comparing Lawson's *Politica* with Marsilio's *Defensor pacis* once more, not in order to suggest any exclusive derivation but to indicate the sort of activist inheritance he used and seems to be adjusting; and secondly by comparing briefly the *Poli-tica* with the earlier *Examination*, which relies on the same sort of inheritance and embraces its activism more openly. The point, overall, is to indicate the way in which Lawson seems to have tried to have his settlement cake without eating the resistance file he knew to be baked in the middle. One can certainly understand the sort of appeal that Marsilio might have had for Lawson. He attacked a common enemy in the papacy; and had developed a clear theory of an ecclesiastical and secular community. Moreover, his work had proved singularly adaptable to English circumstances during the sixteenth century.[28] Of most immediate relevance is the fact that like Lawson Marsilio had specified the citizenry both in the secular and ecclesiastical contexts as a clear constituent authority underlying the contingent human organisations of what Lawson would see as the analogues of church and state.

At this point, however, it is the differences that become interesting. Where Marsilio specifies an unequivocal hierarchical relationship between the citizen body (*legislator*) and the government, even outlining the extent to which the latter may be allowed to have physical force at its command, Lawson is unspecific or silent. Again, Marsilio emphasises the *legislator*'s capacity to discern what can be added, subtracted or changed in any law (though it is not a participant in diurnal government and lawmaking).

[27] Franklin, *John Locke*, pp. 64–5, notes the interplay of power and property in the monarcho-machs and in the *Vindiciae contra tyrannos*.

[28] G. Piaia, *Marsilio da Padova nella Riforma e nella Controriforma*, Antenore, Padua, 1977, chap. 3; H. S. Stout, 'Marsilius of Padua and the Henrician Reformation', *Church History*, 43, (1974), pp. 308–18.

104   *George Lawson's 'Politica' and the English Revolution*

Lawson, however, is oddly indeterminate. In the diagrammatic scheme which prefaces the first edition of the *Politica* Lawson, like Marsilio, lists a range of capacities which belong to the *real* majesty of the citizens; they can 'constitute, abolish, alter, reform' forms of government. These are repeated in the Latin diagram (*Pol.* 57).[29] The argument of the text, however, at no point converts these powers into the control of *personal* majesty operating within any established form, and much of the providential thrust warns against exercise of right if government moves beyond the form. The community's role in overseeing and even interfering in the centrally important legislative function of *personal* majesty is thus reduced to a willing consent when rightly informed (*Pol.* 383). Whether it is deliberate or not, the reification of the form of governmental power within which *personal* majesty operates seems to erect a semantic barrier against overt resistance to *personal* majesty. And, as Lawson forcibly reminds his readers, on more than one occasion, subjects may not rise up, yet it is definitionally where there is a form of government, and thus a *locus* of *personal* majesty, that people are subjects. On one occasion he even asserts that in a state 'none can be found but they are either Subjects or Sovereign' (*Pol.* 356). Although *real* majesty is held to be greater than *personal*, he even suggests on the weighty precedent of Apostolic patience (*Pol.* 360–1) that, despite everything entailed by his notion of citizenship, the only alternative to obedience is suffering. Even where resistance is not ruled out, and even where a clear hierarchy of loyalty is affirmed in which that owed to *personal* majesty is placed beneath that owed to the community (*Pol.* 369–70), activist rights are offset by prudential advice on the complexities of unintended political consequences, together with warnings about interfering with the play of providence in God's theatre of judgement.[30] One last negative point, Lawson illustrates his theoretical precepts with reference to historical examples where he has an interest in developing them. At no stage does he provide any illustrative backing to help justify or explicate a doctrine of resistance – indeed his excursus into the English Civil War is designed to show that something other than resistance took place.

Now, with respect to the *Politica* and the *Examination*, it should be reiterated that the works are largely at one with each other, but there are concep-

---

[29] Marsilio, *Defensor pacis*, 1.11–13. I am drawing freely here on arguments presented in more detail in Condren 'Resistance and Sovereignty'; and 'George Lawson and the *Defensor pacis*', *Medioevo*, 5–6 (1980). But see also, *The Foundations of Freedom*, 1648, in *Leveller Manifestoes*, ed. Don Wolfe, Cass, New York, 1967, p. 299, where the powers of the representatives of the people extend to the 'enacting, altering, repealing and declaring of Laws'.
[30] Cf. Hunton, *A Treatise*, who, despite repeated insistance on the necessity of non-violence, unequivocally affirms the right to resist; Henry Stubbe, *An Essay in Defence of the Good Old Cause*, London, 1659, pp. 4, 9, for the people as the only efficient cause of law, an authentically undiluted Italianate, even Marsilian voice, cf. *Defensor pacis*, 1. 10–12.

tual differences and a number of less tangible ones of tone and emphasis, some of which touch directly on the question of resistance. In the *Examination* we are told that the community has a veritable duty to reform, alter or improve the form in the name of reformation (*Exam.* 15). There is also held to be an unequivocable right of self-defence against tyranny, and that this can be laid aside is held to be 'ridiculous, absurd' (*Exam.* 116). Compare this with the statement that 'some tell us there is no Right that may not be defended' (*Pol.* 93). Private judgement on all such issues (not just ecclesiastical ones) is explicitly accepted to be, as with Chillingworth, a final court of appeal (*Exam.* 123). Moreover, Lawson suggests that the improper sequestration of property and the violation of natural law are sufficient criteria for defensive action against governments (*Exam.* 73) – although this is balanced by an insistence that there is a right to control property in the public interest and an enforceable duty to distribute to the poor. In contrast, on all three points, the *Politica* offers lacunae or passing asides balanced with a countervailing stress. Similarly, there is less emphasis in the *Examination* than in the *Politica* on the necessary subjection of subjects. The point is never denied, but rather Lawson's position is consistently that the subject status so insisted upon by Hobbes requires complementary notions under the auspices of which people may legitimately rise up, and it is these that are emphasised in the process of criticising *Leviathan*, and these that are far less evident where Hobbes is also virtually absent from Lawson's writing. In the *Examination* Lawson insists that Christians as Christians may not resist (*Exam.* 140) but that any resistance must be undertaken by them under another notion. It may be doubted if in Lawson's world any (classically derived) notion could take priority over Christian status; but the rider is nevertheless there. In the *Politica* a parallel passage offers only Apostolic suffering as an alternative to Christian obedience (*Pol.* 360–1).[31] As a corollary, the *Examination* plays down and leaves under-specified the powers of *personal* majesty, which, as Lawson objects (*Exam.* e.g. 4–11), Hobbes would make coextensive with society. The very balance of tone and scope of argument in the *Politica* seem to help create a relative air of equivocation; but in summary one may go further. The *Politica* resonates resistance possibilities appropriate to its theoretical inheritance and consistent with the attack on Hobbes, despite what seem to be constant attempts to offset, adjust and play them down; and despite its author's explicit disengagement from figures emblematic of resistance literature.

---

[31] In a different context of argument, however, Lawson does indicate what such another notion might be: 'The interest of *England* is twofold, Civil and Ecclesiastical: for we are English men and Christians' (*Pol.* 169). If men resisted under this notion of English men, as opposed to rising up as Christians, it is possible that they would sacrifice the legitimating force of community, which operates under divine sanction.

In which ways, then, might *real* be greater than *personal* majesty? On this reading, it is greater because it can establish and authorise a frame of government within which *personal* majesty operates; although malleable it is the lasting substratum upon which the negotiable species of *personal* majesty are erected, that lasting matter without which such forms cannot exist; it is the womb of a settlement. By implication it is greater also because it can change *personal* majesty, which seems hardly conceivable without exercising a right to resist, *in extremis*. Such intimations might have reconciled a few Miltonic souls to his argument but, if Lawson were to appeal to a sufficiently large audience to encourage both a settlement and establish his way of conceptualising it, such intimations are little more than necessary and unwanted evils in a naughty world, best left on the margins of political awareness. This explanation of the resistance *topos* sees Lawson then as trying to capture the elusive fly of settlement in a cobweb of activist and casuist language and, in adjusting this, being left with unwanted threads upon his fingers. The great dilemma seems to be that the sort of theory which might justify destruction is the only hope for reconstruction: it does not make for a sense of political permanence.

If this is so, one can see well enough why Lawson should want to circumnavigate resistance theory through the development of a theory of dissolution and the exploitation of nominal definitions – the dissolution of government rendered resistance (and rebellion) redundant terms and amongst the causes of dissolution, nominally speaking, were both tyranny and forfeiture. An ingenious line of argument, perhaps, but one perilously close to a euphemism for the very phenomenon that Lawson seems reluctant to entertain: if resistance is justified by tyranny (as it certainly was in the *Examination*) and tyranny dissolves government, we effectively abolish resistance – albeit in name only – and perhaps make the only real rebellions quelled ones. Lawson is not entirely consistent, at one point he indicates that rebellion can dissolve a government (*Pol.* 75). But the overall pattern of use is testimony enough to his desire to avoid or sabotage either specification of public turmoil.

Whether or not this first, cobweb, hypothesis is ultimately correct as it stands, it does not adequately pin-point the way in which Lawson argues, a mode of argumentation which itself may help explain the difficulties modern commentators have had with the text. So I shall suggest an alternative hypothesis and then see how far it is possible to move towards a resolution.

II   SEE-SAW

Now this whole preceding line of argument shares with the readings of Salmon and Franklin the assumption that Lawson's discussion of resistance is casuistical and should result in a clear commitment. If it does not, something has gone wrong. Such a reaction is not necessarily unreasonable. Resistance theory in general furnishes us with a clear example of a familiar species of *engagé* discourse designed to rationalise, justify and advance discriminate courses of action. In particular, Lawson furnishes us with such a theory through his injunctions to settle. But for Lawson, settlement and resistance were distinct issues, and to equate theory *of* with commitment *to* is potentially misleading because the *telos* of Lawson's discussion may be located in something other than clear justification.

Such an alternative to the cobweb thesis was suggested to me initially by a reading of Lawson's unpublished 'Amica dissertatio' (see also *Hebrewes*, pp. 152ff.; 230ff.), an extensive though very one-sided dialogue between Lawson and Baxter. A principal theme of the work is whether God is obliged to punish sin. This is standard theological fare. William Twiss (1578?–1646), moderator of the Westminster Assembly, for example, had developed an optional, or contingent punishment thesis.[32] Lawson, according to Baxter, advocated an inevitable punishment thesis, whilst Baxter himself wanted to negotiate a passage between the two, enunciated in terms of a flexible notion of divine judgement. To complicate matters, however, as Baxter seems aware (and as Lamont has noted with some puzzlement), Lawson's position is couched in such a way as to lead back repeatedly to the contingent thesis which, *per se*, he denied.[33] If we expect Lawson to be coming down on one side or the other of the issue, then this seems both confused and confusing. But Lawson's position on the divine punishment *topos* seems in fact to be as follows: if we ask whether God must punish us for our sins, then we presuppose a law defining sin and a judge to judge it. Nominally speaking, judges must judge and insofar as we sin they must punish us. If we then ask whether God is imprisoned in his law, that is, does he only have the attributes of a judge, then the answer is no. As lawmaker, nominally he is above and prior to the law; a maker can unmake. Thus he need not punish us, either because he can change the law, or because being above the law he can temper justice with mercy. In short, what really matters is the *notion* or nominal definition under which God is considered. To restrict the concept of God is to deny his illimitable power. The immediate point at issue with Baxter is that for Lawson there can be no passage between the binary classifications of contingency and necessity, which, as it were, define the issue absolutely; but underlying this is another more important point for Lawson, simply that each extreme

---

[32] According to Lawson or his scribe it is William Swiss. For Lawson's doubts about the conclusions of the Westminster Assembly, *Baxter Treatises*, DWL, 2, fos. 208–10, item 39(4) a lengthy series of indeterminate queries.

[33] William Lamont, *Richard Baxter and the Millennium*, Croom Helm, London, 1979, p. 144.

on its own results in an inadequate conception of God. The difficulty of
verbally capturing the concept of God was familiar from writers since
Augustine, and was being explored in Lawson's day by Descartes who had
taken up Scotus's thesis of omnipotence through the special case of logical
reflexivity – can we conceive of God being able to do the logically
impossible?[34]

Lawson's argument is at one with this general species of concern and
his sceptical and by no means idiosyncratic conclusion is that we cannot
literally conceive of God, but use our concepts as approximate metaphors
(cf. *Leviathan*, 31); and that to do even this properly we require compound
classifications. Notions requiring such pincer-like classificatory strategies
he calls 'duplex'.

There is here a strong structural parallel between Lawson's handling of
the punishment and resistance *topoi*, the full force of which may most readily
be disclosed by reducing the arguments to a common notational form. In
both cases the argument is not *a* entails *b* and *a* entails *non-b*. It is rather
a = *g* and *f*:*a* (as an *f*) entails *b* and *a* (as a *g*) implies the possibility of
non-b. The contingent *non-b* in both cases arises from the attribution of
power seen as an unrestricted freedom to act. God's freedom allows the
possibility of non-punishment; the citizen's freedom allows the possibility
of resistance. In both cases the necessary *b* is the result of obligation. The
obligation of the judge to execute the law or of a citizen to obey a higher
power, respectively. In each case also the possibility of *non-b* arises from
a duality of specific circumstances. With respect to sin, God might not punish
because of his mercy, or because of his capacity to remake the law (and
thus redefine sin). With respect to the possibility of resistance, the citizen
may act because of a prior commitment to community, or because of the
obligation to obey God.

The duplexity of God (judge/maker) and of man (subject/citizen) can
thus be expressed:

$$a = (g \cdot f) \equiv \left(\frac{(a \supset b)}{f} \cdot \frac{(a \supset \textit{non-b})}{g} \right)^{35}$$

Reduced in this way, the aporetic structures of God and political animal

[34] For a recent discussion see Richard Le Croix, 'Descartes on God's Ability to do the Logically
Impossible', *The Canadian Journal of Philosophy*, 3 (1984), pp. 455–75. Descartes' question
is an elegant version of that asked by the atheist lion in a den of Daniels, namely – whether
God could dig a hole so deep he could not reach the bottom.
[35] Adapted from David Wiggins's notation of his reformulation of Leibniz's Law of Identity,
Temporal and Spacio Continuity, Blackwell, Oxford, 1968.

seem sufficiently close for one to suggest that this is more than a matter of coincidence, rather that Lawson is re-employing a definitional strategy he had used before and that the problems of predicating divinity may have provided him with a model for dealing with the political when he came to elaborate a general thesis of politics.

In this light one can now emphasise a further departure from the *Examination*, perhaps a more rigorous development of its terms. In both the *Examination* and the *Politica* one finds the binary notions of subject and citizen, but in the earlier work the concomitant specifications of sovereignty are no more than empirical and prudential generalisations, or real definitions of a neo-Machiavellian nature.

(The) supreme power reserved to the whole community to be exercised as necessity or occasion shall require, might be called [*Realis majestas*] yet every Community is neither so wise nor so happy. For in most States we find only a personal Majesty, or supreme Power, and the same sometimes Despotical, and too absolute; yet in other Common-wealths, the supreme Governours are limited, and only trusted with the exercise of the power according to certain Rules and fundamental Laws (*Exam.* 10).

In contrast, the *Politica* not only lacks the sort of clear-cut commitment of the first sentence but also posits *real* and *personal*, subject and citizen, community and polity, all as categories *sub species aeternitatis*, the composite nominal *definiendum* of our condition (e.g. *Pol.* 50–5, 356). The insoluble tension of the duplex definition of the subject/citizen is the correlate of the conceptual balance of the universal species of sovereignty which had been unrealised in the *Examination*.

Now, in a different way, the universality of the *Politica*'s central terms has already been emphasised in developing the cobweb reading, but in the present context the interpretative consequences are significantly changed. If Lawson was employing a duplex nominal definitional model derived from, or authenticated by a process of theological definition, then we can explain the apparent pattern of equivocation in the *Politica* without hypothesising faint-heartedness or the inability to marshall a recalcitrant activist inheritance, as the cobweb thesis maintains. Indeed, equivocation, especially with its casuistical connotations, becomes a misleading description. Duplexity requires a sort of attributive oscillation contained within a text, precisely in order to avoid a simplex classification which is held to be too simple for the phenomena involved. So, rather than adjusting a cobweb to catch a fly of settlement, Lawson may have been trying to delineate something rather like a see-saw. In this way at least the *Politica* may be seen as closer to the 'Amica dissertatio' than to the *Examination*, and modern commentators have missed the whole point by seeking *simplex* conclusions to a *duplex* argument. Salmon, as it were, perceived only the resistance end of the see-saw when it was stuck in the mud, Franklin paid it attention when it was waving in the air, and I complained that neither end was really in the ascendency. Assuming that the point of Lawson's theory was either to justify or condemn resistance, I had remarked that it is unhelpful to be told that as citizens we may resist, as subjects we may not. We only require an answer when we are both. On this see-saw reading Lawson might well have replied that that is precisely the point; political being is a matter of *discordia concors*.[36] That is, if we were only citizens, resistance could not arise, there would only be *real* majesty and community, as there would be no order of political subjection. If we were only subjects (as Hobbes would have us be) resistance could not be justified, it would be but rebellion. In either case, there could be no political problem, no moral crux. The political and moral problem of our situation lies in the fact that we are duplex and the resistance *topos* lies, like the punishment *topos*, at the coincidence of two nominal definitions, the former being a consequence of God's being seen as the only absolute ruler; the latter a consequence of God's more general unrestricted freedom.

Further, Lawson's putatively duplex definitional strategy gives added point to his linguistically orientated criticisms of the whole issue of resistance, which he states has been so 'loosely handled' (*Pol.* 106). Those he dimisses are all taken to provide simplex classifications of the political animal just as Baxter and Twiss had earlier been taken to task for simplex definitions of God.

Rather than providing us, or failing to provide us, with a theory of, in the sense of a commitment to, resistance, there is textual evidence to suggest that Lawson was circumscribing a rhetoric, all aspects of which were needed for understanding, regardless of what one's commitments might be in different circumstances. The theory concerns not what we may do, but what we need in order to understand our political being – namely an adequate and stabilised battery of applicable 'notions' or classifiers. It needs little labouring that Lawson was surrounded by an abundance of pro- and anti-resistance literature of the most committed sort, which clearly reinforces contextually all previous readings of his arguments around the resistance *topos*.[37] But it should also be noted that a somewhat different intellectual inheritance gives plausibility to the see-saw hypothesis. To begin with there is at least a family resemblance between Lawson's tensile discussion and

---

[36] *Contra* C. Condren, 'Sacra *Before* Civilis', *The Journal of Religious History*, 11, 2 (1981). On *Discordia Concors*, see Melissa Wanamaker, *Discordia Concors*, Kenniket, New York, 1975.

[37] See Franklin, *John Locke*, esp. chaps. 1 and 2; Skinner, *The Foundations*, vol. 2, chaps. 7–9; Richard Tuck, *Natural Rights Theories: Their Origin and Development*, Cambridge University Press, 1979.

paradox literature. This is hardly clinching as paradoxicality covered a multitude of sins. It overlapped with dialectic, referred to technical *insolubilia*,
to views held to be against (*para*) common opinions (*doxai*) and to rhetorical
exercises of false praise.[38] The whole of this family of discursive phenomena
displayed a fascination with and, for very different purposes, a deliberate
development of contradiction and *discordia*. It joined with a widespread
persuasive preference for the open and protean palm of rhetoric as opposed
to the closed fist of logic.[39] Sometimes, certainly, contradictions were set
up in order to be resolved, paradox ends in a single-minded dialectical synthesis or the specification of a mean.[40] But tensions could be suggested and
left for the reader to overcome through a creative engagement with the
text – which is why Donne called his paradoxes 'swaggerers', like swaggering
youths, harmless if resisted.[41] Some, above all the *insolubilia* and paradoxical conceptions of God, seem set up to be contemplated as ineluctably aporetic. In some cases one cannot be sure what is going on and, not surprisingly,
inconclusiveness has been taken as a characteristic of much early modern
literature.[42] Indeed, it is against the background of the kudos widely enjoyed
by paradoxicality that one can understand, in part, why simplification

---

[38] On the more technical forms of paradox see Ashworth, *Language and Logic in the Post
Medieval Period*, Reidel, Dordrecht, 1974; F. Bottin, *Le antinomie semantiche nella logica
medievale*, Antenore, Padua, 1976; for the more extensive notions of paradox, Rosalie Colie,
Paradoxia Epidemica, The Renaissance Tradition of Paradox, Princeton University Press,
1966; M. T. Jones-Davies, ed., *Le paradoxe au temps de la Renaissance*, Touzot, Paris,
1982.

[39] On the importance and continuity of Zeno's image of the palm of rhetoric, see W. S. Howell,
Logic and Rhetoric in England, 1500–1700, Princeton University Press, 1978, p. 293. One
of its most articulate defenders was Lorenzo Valla, who according to L. Jardine was a
fashionable author at Emmanuel College about the time Lawson was there, 'Humanism
and Dialectic in Sixteenth-century Cambridge', in R. Bolgar, ed., *Classical Influences in
European Literature, 1500–1700*, Cambridge University Press, 1976.

[40] See for example the Aristotelian commentator Antonio Montecatini (1536?–99), *Politica
in progymnasmata* (1587) where the apparently contradictory virtues of father and citizen
are disclosed as being different species of a single genus. See Ian Maclean, *The Renaissance
Notion of Woman*, Cambridge University Press, 1980, p. 50; Althusius, *Politica methodice
digesta* arrives at the ideal size of a city (lamely like Aristotle) by locating it between the
extremes of too large and too small.

[41] John Donne, *Paradoxes and Problems*, c. 1590, ed. Helen Peters, Clarendon Press, 1980.
The more generally creative attitude to reading, an awareness of the author's inability to
control a public text, is explored intermittently in Montaigne's *Essays*.

[42] C. Condren, 'Cornwallis's Paradoxical Defence of Richard III: A Machiavellian Discourse
on Morean Mythology?', *Moreana*, 24 (1987), pp. 5ff., for an example of such interpretative
opacity. See also J. C. H. Aveling 'The English Clergy' in *Rome and the Anglicans*, Aveling
et al., Dr Gruyter, New York, 1982, p. 133, commenting on how equivocable much clerical
discourse seems to be; William Kennedy, *Rhetorical Norms in Renaissance Literature*, Yale
University Press, 1978, p. 124 on Commynes' tendency to undermine the logic of his own
position thus impelling the reader to critical scrutiny of what is going on.

became something of a term of abuse in Lawson's world.[43] Luther accused the Catholics of simplification by denying the paradox of God; Thomas Stapleton returned the compliment;[44] Lawson's 'Amica dissertatio' certainly understands God in terms of paradoxically conjoined notions, and in the *Examination* he accuses Hobbes of oversimplification. As we approach constitutional theory, it is also against a background of paradox that one can understand the appeal of the conjoined opposites that characterise doctrines of office. As these refer specifically to political role-playing, they provide us with a more refined context for understanding Lawson's aporetic subject/ citizen and what one might almost call the paradox of resistance in the *Politica*.

Ernst Kantorowicz has aptly styled the quintessential doctrine of office, the theory of the king's two bodies, as a fiction of legal theology.[45] It was also paradigmatically a duplex and paradoxical understanding of kingship. In one aspect, the king was pure office, immortal and divine, in another, as the office had always to be filled, the monarch was mortal and fallible. The crucial point was that it was a fiction – a nominal abstraction sustained by a conjunction of opposites; consequently, making the formal distinction between the defining aspects of monarchy was one thing, separating the aspects as discrete facts was quite another. As I do not think Kantorowicz makes clear, it was the confusion between the distinguishable and the separable that resulted in absurdity. When men tried to use one aspect of monarchy to justify a specific course of action or state of affairs, it became unworkably double-edged.[46]

The Leveller leader Overton seized devastatingly upon the dangers of applied doctrines of office when he reminded Parliament that its attempts to separate Charles Stuart from King Charles 'was the very Axeltree upon

[43] Sir Thomas Brown, *Religio Medici*, 1643, Scolar Press, Menston, 1970, negatively reflects on the common enjoyment of paradox, wishing that it could be kept out of theology, for it encouraged fragmentation and destruction of community – presumably because its indeterminacy allowed the reader room to manoeuvre. See M. Wilding, '*Religio Medici* in the English Revolution', in C. A. Patrides, ed., *Approaches to Sir Thomas Brown*, Michigan University Press, 1982, p. 103.

[44] A theme of Martin Luther, *Temporal Authority* trans. J. J. Schindel, Philadelphia, 1963; see also Jean Lebeau, 'Le paradoxe chez Erasmus, Luther et Sebastian Franck' in M. T. Jones-Davies, ed., *Le paradoxe*, pp. 143ff.; for Stapleton, see Aveling, in *Rome and The Anglicans*, p. 94.

[45] E. Kantorowicz, *The King's Two Bodies*, Princeton University Press, 1957, Introduction. Interestingly, Cleveland's 'Upon The Kings Return from Scotland', discusses the return of kingship through a series of paradoxes. See A. D. Cousins, 'The Cavalier World of John Cleveland', *Studies in Philology*, 78 (1981), p. 81.

[46] The difficulties assume a thematic importance in Malory's *Morte d'Arthur*; and they take on a tragic air of double-think in Charles I's final desertion of Strafford, as they do in Parliament's claim to be fighting for the King, the best ground on which Parker could justify the war.

which the equity of their proceedings were moved, and by which they still stand jústifiable in the eyes of reason and justice'. Moreover, he continued, if the king has two bodies, so does Parliament; the office and the men holding it are distinct.[47] A little later the Presbyterian Francis Rous (1579–1659), whose work helped trigger the Engagement Controversy, glided over any such distinction between power and those who usurped it.[48]

The line between distinction and separation was a thin one, but it was crucial to any employment of the doctrine of office to bolster political commitment; indeed, the handling of the difference between separation and distinction is an important clue to political manipulation of institutional bodies. Overton's insistence on *distinguishing* between office and men is a prelude to *separating* men from the authority of parliamentary office. Rous's refusal to distinguish was designed to help cement Oliver in office. Later the royalist Edward Bagshaw summed up the semantic crux neatly stating that the king's authority was inseparable from the rights of the king 'so that you must distinguish them but not divide them'.[49]

Lawson was directly familiar with this whole area of argument, and he was insistent upon the difference between the distinction and separation of the defining aspects of a complex unity. 'Matter and form are one in money, stamped. Not that matter is form or form matter, but because it cannot be money without being united together' ('Amica diss.'). *Aliud est distinctio, aliud separatio.* Form and matter, then, make money duplex, but this statement is particularly instructive precisely because the images of form and matter are used consistently by Lawson to elucidate the relationship between community and polity (*Pol.* 7, 8, 12, 13, 29, 35, 36, 39, 46, 50; cf. *Exam.*). Community is the matter impressed with the form of a particular polity. The consequence of this metaphor is that the head of the citizen is on the obverse; the emblem of *personal* majesty on the reverse; like God and money, the political individual is duplex.

In the light of the fictions of the king's and of Parliament's two bodies, and of Lawson's explicit understanding of duplex definition with its necessary conditions, he may have been suggesting then a nominal concept of the people's two bodies – their having *real* and being under *personal* majesty at the same time and from this duplex structure a simplex commitment could not consistently escape. That would require separation rather than purely elucidatory distinction. The priority of *real* majesty over *personal*, then, may reside in little more than the logical and theological prejudice that a cause is more important than an effect; it may stop well short of

[47] Overton, *Appeal*, 1647, *Leveller Manifestoes*, pp. 174–5.
[48] On Rous see in particular the discussion by Quentin Skinner, 'Conquest and Consent' in *The Interregnum*, ed. G. E. Aylmer, Macmillan, London, 1972.
[49] Bagshaw, *The Rights of the Crown*, 1660, p. 30.

the notion that *personal* majesty is in practice subordinated to *real* majesty, or that there is an unbalanced right for the citizen to resist. Our demand that Lawson establishes a clear pattern of priorities may be a little like insisting on the defacement of a coinage before it can be used.

In summary, the principal differences between the two readings of the resistance *topos* may be stated as follows. The cobweb thesis sees an implied, even intimated, but unwanted doctrine of resistance arising from Lawson's failure to orchestrate a discernably activist inheritance of political literature to the irenic interests of a settlement; in particular, this unwanted guest in the text is the result of a lack of figurative control over entrenched and resonant metaphors which in most respects were highly suitable to the rhetoric of peace and settlement. The see-saw thesis suggests that the apparent equivocations are part and parcel of a deliberate definitional strategy in which metaphors of theological discourse constitute a model for political understanding. For this one can construct an adjacent intellectual inheritance in which the paradoxical tensions of doctrines of office provide precedent for the subject/citizen aporia. The cobweb thesis locates Lawson's discussion within a context of practical political discourse; the tensions are failures to give clear doctrinal guidance for political action. The see-saw thesis argues that the discussion operates at the meta-level of the linguistic delineation of the political domain, offering a formal distinction and clarification of our discriminate options rather than any separable doctrine to be applied. If Lawson did not intend this, a further cluster of metaphors he employs stymie the escape of unambiguous commitment on the resistance question.[50] What distinguishes the two readings then is not the presence or absence of a conceptual tension, but the status, causes and elucidating contexts of the tension and its relationship to the author, whose intentions one can only hypothetically evoke. Insofar as we cannot choose between these two options, the resistance *topos* is marked by what I have elsewhere called coalescent ambiguity.[51]

To look ahead, either reading helps explain the *Politica*'s future exploitation. On the basis of the cobweb thesis one can see that there was room to manoeuvre between Lawson's own predominant point of emphasis on settlement, and its unwanted penumbra of resistance consequences which later commended the work. On the basis of the see-saw reading the use of the work was largely dependent upon its readers crossing the thin line between the distinction and separation of its propositional components.

It was a particularly thin line. Lawson was generally apt to stop theory

---

[50] In this context, Franklin would be correct to see Lawson's imagery of form and matter as inappropriate to a commitment to resistance, *John Locke*, p. 71.

[51] C. Condren, *The Status and Appraisal of Classic Texts*, Princeton University Press, 1985, chap. 7.

short of the point at which it might rigidify the prudential, by seeming to enable a digest of abstract principle to determine the details of concrete action. This was judicious, if self-sterilising, in a world demanding casuistical guidance on almost everything. But in such a world, any apposite theory was readily converted to such a rationalistic guide in the very process of application.

At this point, however, it may be argued that if Lawson does set up a tensile relationship between subject and citizen, the duty to obedience and the right to resist, then he resolves it in favour of the latter, and any ambiguities are merely elliptical. For he does set down a clear hierarchy of loyalty, placing that to community above that to *personal* majesty. If this is the case, then one can conclude that the aporia is set up to be resolved, a duplex understanding is a means to a simplex commitment *in extremis*. There is certainly precedent enough for such a hierarchical rearrangement of tensile concepts in order that straightforward priorities can be made clear, but I remain uncertain that in this case the work can be collapsed, its duplexity resolved.[52] Taken in isolation the hierarchy of loyalty (like any single component of an otherwise tensile whole) would seem to be crucial, precisely because of its unambivalence; but it occurs late in the argument in the possibly unpolished penultimate chapter. It is not tied in with the earlier discussions of usurpation and resistance where it could well have provided clarification; and above all, it occurs shortly after that equally unambivalent addition to the argument stating that Christians may not resist, only suffer (*Pol.* 360–1). This in its turn could be seen as undoing all the tentative work in favour of resistance, but, again, it is little more than a passing comment unrelated to previous discussions. At the level of proposition, resolution of tension is difficult to find and, at the level of informing metaphor, it is no easier. That of form and matter, to say nothing of the indirectly relevant imagery of money, and that of the duplex definitional model of God, all conspire to make resolution of tensile attributes of the subject/citizen difficult. What could be the resolution between form and matter; between God as judge and lawmaker; above all between the monarch as divine and perfect and as mortal and fallible?

For the moment one must forbear a firm choice between the see-saw and the cobweb. Restricted to the purely abstract plane of argument, Lawson's theory is neither simple nor clear-cut. Despite its difficulties, which were to prove fruitful later in the century, one can say this as a colophon abstracted from both readings; that in the first and last analysis only the community can settle or authorise the form of government within which

---

[52] Marsilio, *Defensor pacis*, is perfectly consistent, citizens may always be subjects but citizen status is the higher.

personal majesty operates. In this way, certainly, *real* majesty is greater than *personal*. But precisely because of this, without the authorisation of a polity the whole vocabulary of resistance and rebellion is irrelevant. It is only where there is a serious claim to *personal* majesty that such words carry force. Subjects may only be able to rebel but citizens can only resist a government. This reflects precisely the difficulties of resistance theory in Lawson's world which we have tended to overlook because we now habitually elide the rhetorical opposition between resistance and rebellion. Resistance might be justified in the seventeenth century, but rebellion was universally condemned (saving Algernon Sidney). Thus committed resistance theory always ran the danger of the odium of rebellion. It was, throughout the century, of great importance to those hostile to any right of resistance that they either elide the terms resistance and rebellion or explicitly deny any difference between them.[53]

Lawson provided not only a distinction between resistance and rebellion as adjuncts to his organising concepts of subject/citizen and community/polity; but also, through the deployment of nominal definitions, he argued in such a way as to enable both the notions of resistance and rebellion to be held in abeyance. This itself has an important place in his settlement strategy because both terms were inflammatory. It also adds a singular touch of irony to Lawson's rehabilitation as a political thinker, for his fugitive resistance theory is the only aspect of his thought that has been systematically discussed.

[53] *The Rebels Catechism*, 1643; Seth Ward, *Against Resistance to Lawful Power*, 1661, discussed below; Anon., *The Revolution No Rebellion*, London, 1709.

10

From Civil War to settlement

Reflection on the past constituted a powerful idiom of political theorising in early modern Europe but whether subsumed under the unstable notion of *historia*, chronicle, or restricted to more piecemeal reference and allusion, it was not an autonomous sphere of discourse. Rather, it was a subordinate means of illustrating general patterns of abstract moral, political and theological principle even when it acquired scientific associations. In the broadest terms, the place of history had been fixed by Cicero. The historian had an especial responsibility to be fair, and to get things right; but this, generally, was in order that a received and morally potent past could play its part in the more important realm of rhetoric.[1] In this respect the uplifting claims of rhetoric might be challenged by theology or philosophy but, regardless, hand-maiden Clio tagged along behind as, with more or less conviction, she has done in most people's eyes ever since. As Dionysius of Halicarnassus seems first to have put it: 'history is philosophy teaching by examples'.[2] Thus criticism and defence of historical writing were usually focussed on its efficacy in exemplifying the ethical and edifying. When examples were difficult to find, or to manipulate to one's ends, the authority of history could be rejected easily enough – for the time being.[3] Conversely, assumed precept might be barely visible on the surface of what looks, prima facie, to be an autonomous historical narrative; but in most political writing there is some blend of precept and illustration. 'Past relationships' permeated political awareness and did much to structure argument – their manipulation was rhetorically central.[4] As there was no shortage of abstract theory generated by the Civil War, so we might expect a preoccupation with explain-

---

[1] Cicero, *De Oratore*; also Aristotle, *Rhetoric*; see, G. Nadel, 'The Philosophy of History Before Historicism', *History and Theory*, 3, 3 (1964), p. 300.

[2] Cited in Nadel, 'The Philosophy of History', p. 301.

[3] Hobbes and Selden both denied the authority of the past but used it when they could tie it to favoured principles; or cf. Guicciardini's intermittent scepticism about being able to learn anything from the past (*Ricordi*) with its illustrative use in the *Storia d'Italia*.

[4] John Pocock, 'The Origins of the Study of the Past', *Comparative Studies in Society and History*, 5 (1962–3), at length.

ing the phenomenon, and using it to illustrate and defend commitment.
Hartman conservatively estimates that there were some 400 attempted explanations between 1642 and 1660, and he omits numerous works for being
too theological.[5]

Lawson's discussions of English history place him in the mainstream of
exemplum history and play an important role in his theory and strategy
of settlement. Appropriately, he rehearses the standard credentials of historical objectivity and accuracy and with similar decorum he reminds the reader
that examples only bind in virtue of good precept (*Pol.* 320). He persistently
ties his theories and vocabulary to English circumstances. The analogical
structure of the *Politica* counterpointing church and state allows him to
see his audience under the distinct but similarly analogical notions of English-
men and Christians (*Pol.* 169). As I have indicated, the abstract notion
of the *civis* is refined to take account of established class distinctions; and
the 40 counties are cautiously identified with the community – an equation
more confidently asserted in the *Examination* (15). The sporadic discussion
of the Civil War (the ostensible trigger for the *Politica*) is sufficiently sustained
for Lawson to be seen as taking on the persona of the historian.

A suitable starting place is Lawson's most extended passage devoted to
the events of the Civil War. It takes the form of a series of impressionistic
vignettes devoted in turn to the three nations, Parliment, the King, the constitutional changes, and the religious ones. It seems loosely modelled on Sir
Richard Baker's standard history, and is sufficiently interesting stylistically
for a good deal of it to be quoted at some length.[6]

The Royal Standard of *England* marcheth into *Scotland*, where an Army is ready
to oppose. Yet no blow given; no blood shed. After this, we see two potent Armies
in *England*, and only one little skirmish at the first, a pacification is made, the
National League concluded, both the Armies disbanded. But after this, no man
fearing it, a bloody massacre ... and ... begins the Tragedy in *Ireland*; Forces
are sent to revenge that blood, and thousands of the bloody *Irish* are sacrificed
to expiate former murthers. At length a Civil War is commenced in *England* ...
the Sword rageth in every corner, the cry goes up to Heaven. The Parliament desiring
not only to defend it self, but to relieve bleeding *Ireland*, is brought very low, is
ready to submit, calls in the Scot, recovers, prevails ... obtains total victory in
England, *Ireland* almost lost, is recovered again ... *Scotland* where the fire began
to smoke at first ... at last felt ... a bloody war ... They invade *England* Twice
and are twice scornfully foiled and shattered to pieces ... Never so many fearful
Judgements executed, never so many bloody Wars in so short a time ... (*Pol.* 183–4).

[5] M. Hartman, 'Contemporary Explanations of the English Civil War, 1640–1660', unpublished Ph.D. thesis, Cambridge University, 1978, pp. 5–6.
[6] Sir Richard Baker, *A Chronicle of the Kings of England*, with a Continuation to 1658 (1659),
but as Hartman, *ibid.*, p. 1, makes clear the terms of debate were set down by 1642.

As for Parliaments,

the great Bulwark of the kingdom when no man did expect, one is called, but suddenly dissolved. Yet the *Scots* entred with a puissant Army into the Kingdom, made a necessity of calling a second, which is summoned, confirmed by an act of continuance, acts high, makes great demands, continues long. Yet its deserted by the King and many of the Members, opposed by an Army defends it self ... This is that long sitting Parliament which some say might have been good Physic, but proved bad Diet. Never Parliament of *England* varied more, never any more opposed, never any suffered more, never any acted higher, never any effected greater things. It made an end of Kings and new model'd the Government.

The King deserting the Parliament set up his Royal Standard, and is opposed, fought, beaten ... is confined, secured as a guilty person, tried, judged, condemned to death, executed. His Family and Children banished, and disinherited of the Crown, wander in foreign Countries, and many Great ones suffered and fell with him ... from the height of his excellency laid in the dust and brought to nothing (*Pol.* 185–6).

Along with all these proceedings the civil government is much changed, though some maintained that they really had no intention of changing from the old form of kings, lords and commons, 'and perhaps (they) really intended what they spake; yet they could not perform: for that very frame was taken asunder and abolished. Upon which followed three several models one after another' (*Pol.* 186).

Lawson then lists the acts of alteration, the *New Instrument* and the *Humble Petition* stating that still we are not well settled. So difficult is it after a constitution is once dissolved to establish a new frame (*Pol.* 186–7). It is upon this negligible evidence, incidentally, that Franklin suggests that Lawson wanted Cromwell to become king and even dates the desire to around 1650 (*sic.*). Lawson concludes the section remarking on the diversity of suggested models – the last being the country being ruled by the 'General' and the 'godly party' '... a strange fancy and conceit' (*Pol.* 187). 'As for the Church,' he continues, many looked to Rome and became Papists:

Innovations were daily made in Doctrine and Discipline, and Prelacy seemed to advance with the Royal power. But this great Parliament puts a stay to all; begins to reform, and in reforming incline to an extream ... begin to settle a Presbyterian Discipline. Yet that in the very rise was opposed by the Dissenting Brethren, it could not be fully ... imposed, (and) contrary to promise, the Golden Reins of Discipline were loosed ... and swarms of Sects appear profess and Separate ... Never from the first receiving of Christianity in this Nation, was there so great a change in Religion known to be made in so short a time (187–8).

Here, I think, the drama, tension, and pace are finely sustained, and the impression of rapid and confused changes in fortune is conveyed by the intimacy of the dominant present tense, the disjunctive syntax and echoing phraseology which concludes each vignette. Overall, however, Lawson is concerned less with the drama than with the etiology and the precise predication of events. Etiology itself is a matter of the interplay of efficient causation and moral responsibility with providence continuing, selectively, to penetrate the account of human events.

In the idiom of providence the war was caused by sin (cf. *Exam.* 31–2). Peace and religion had been neglected (*Pol.* 8, 9, 19), hence the wrath of God (*Pol.* 83). With somewhat strained consistency he writes that the nation had been unthankful for its own peace and the gospel, and took no warning from Europe wallowing in blood (*Pol.* 167–8).[7] 'When God expected better fruits, our sins were ripe for vengeance' (*Pol.* 167). And (with a cosmic economy) Egyptians were set on Egyptians (*Pol.* 168). At this level, understanding the war is largely a matter of observing whom God punishes (*Pol.* 182).[8] In more mundane terms there are both civil and ecclesiastical causes, but, as Lawson's account is predicated upon providential punishment, patterns of efficient causation make sense, ultimately, as patterns of moral responsibility (*Pol.* 169–70).

With respect to ecclesiastical causes, most generally Lawson writes that the English Reformation had been an example of legitimate separation, but had failed to sustain the momentum towards a primitive episcopacy (*Pol.* 168, 45).[9] Instead, the corruption and innovations were such, when the Long Parliament reactivated reform, that many feared ruin more than they had hope of reformation (*Pol.* 168).[10] In the attempted reform, however, Parliament went to extremes, changing the liturgy under Scottish pressure and rooting out episcopacy (*Pol.* 187). In contrast, the King too was moving to extremes. Married to a 'popish lady' he had allowed the Irish rebels in his army and threatened the enlistment of French aid. With Parliament's failure to settle Presbytery on the country, discipline disintegrated (*Pol.* 187). To begin with, then, the issue was the maintenance of protestantism, not prelacy (*Pol.* 169–70).[11] But after the defeat of the King, Lawson argues, the causes were transformed by the clash between Independents

---

[7] Cf. Taylor, cited in Hartman, 'Contemporary Explanations', p. 94. These are standard themes, Clement Walker, *A Mysterie of the Two Juntoes*, 1647, see Hartman, 'Contemporary Explanations', p. 48ff.; R. MacGillivray, *Restoration Historians and the English Civil War*, Nijhoff, The Hague, 1974, pp. 19, 237ff. The element of surprise at the war which a few years ago might have been written off as widespread ignorance of the long-term causes, is now being taken seriously after long-term causes have themselves been questioned. C. Russell, ed., *The Causes of the English Revolution*, Macmillan, London, 1973; J. B. Morrill, ed., *The Causes of the English Civil War*, Introduction, Macmillan, London, 1982.

[8] These are standard themes to be found more stridently in *The Grand Remonstrance* and, on the royalist side, in *The Exact Collection*. See Hartman, 'Contemporary Explanations', chap. 1.

[9] Lawson seems to be at one here with Jos Hall, *A Modest Offer*, 1644 & 1660 or possibly Ussher's plans for the reduction of the episcopacy; but even here there is an ambivalence for reduced and primitive episcopacy were not necessarily identical.

[10] Standard mode of accusation, pre-dating Lawson and running through to Locke.

[11] Cf. Baker, *A Chronicle*, who saw the main causes of trouble in Charles's episcopal policy.

and Presbyterians – both better at destroying than at building. It is hardly wise, he remarks (*Pol.* 180), to pull down what might be repaired, before we have something better to put in its place (*ibid.*).

Nevertheless, writes Lawson, the model of Presbyterianism as established in England (not the Melvillian one the Scots had wanted) was an improvement; it had something of ancient discipline about it, and in many ways was in general agreement with Scripture. In the right hands it might have done some good (*Pol.* 254–5). It was, however, doomed to failure. It had too many enemies: episcopalians, because it abolished episcopacy; the dissenting brethren, because it remained parish based, was hierarchical and not pure enough in the qualifications it required of its officers; the profane and ignorant, because it was able to act against them. For some it was too close to Scotland; for others its lack of royal sanction was crucial; yet more objected to the participation of lay elders. It was tarred with a rebellious brush, yet was not a complete break with the past 'as the statutes of the former Discipline' remained intact (*Pol.* 255). On top of this, there were technical problems: Parliament required the prior adherence of ministers to the Solemn League and Covenant, yet expected the system to be set up universally (*Pol.* 256); it was an incomplete compromise between different ideals of reform and, Parliament having set the system up trusting neither elders nor priests, 'reserved the chiefest power unto it self' (*ibid.*).

Lawson's succinct account seems to have the marks of one who struggled with the system from the inside – and it is interesting to see how close it lies to Yule's recent explanation of the failure of Presbyterianism in England.[12] With this failure went the rise of the Independents under the protection of the powerful (*Pol.* 349). These were no better than the rest, few really seeking a genuine reformation (*Pol.* 349), and with them we have seen the greatest changes in the shortest time (*Pol.* 187–8) – 'swarms of Sects ... Errors, Heresies, Blasphemies'. Yet some, as I have quoted him before, were good men whom Lawson would willingly have embraced in a national church (*Pol.* 309).

Lawson's emphasis on religion as a cause of war is at first sight at odds with the elliptical statement in the *Examination* that 'every man liked that opinion best, which was most suitable to his own interest. Our several opinions in Religion have heightened our differences, and hindered our settlement; yet Religion is but pretended; for every party aims at civil power, not spiritual liberty from sin' (*Exam.* 32). This apparently secular explanation had at one time appealed to Baxter but Lawson may have been referring to the insincerity of political motive as Selden had seemed to admit rather than asserting the irrelevance of religious issues. It is also possible that

---

[12] George Yule, *Puritans in Politics: The Religious Legislation of the Long Parliament*, Sutton Courtney, Oxford, 1982, Appendix B.

between the *Examination* and the publication of the *Politica* Lawson changed his mind, and that there is a genuine sense of discovery behind the remark (*Pol.* Epist.) that as he searched for the causes he discovered the importance of religion amongst them.

Be this as it may, in the context of the work a theme of religious causation is important, complexly entangled, and it shows faults and virtues on all sides. Where there has been punishment, there is yet hope, and responsibility is shared. Secular causation is distributed between the responsibilities of king and Parliament and Lawson's first approach to the problem is uncharacteristically one-sided. The King was to blame for unsettling the constitution; Parliament justified in its judgement upon him. The judgement of providence has been disinheritance and a family suffering which suggested considerable guilt (*Pol.* 95–6). This passage, better than any he actually cites, supports Franklin's claim that Lawson 'looked to' the exclusion of the Stuarts. But the Miltonic mood does not last and is gradually balanced by a cumulative emphasis on the difficulties of establishing responsibility.

The revolution cannot be judged by the quality of persons involved. There were good and bad on both sides (*Pol.* 169–70) and both sides acted wrongly (see also *Exam.* 31–2). Moreover, wickedness in a good cause is no excuse, for dubious means erase just ends (*Pol.* 171).[13] Knowledge of even the recent past can be faulty, and judgement of motive very difficult (*Pol.* 181, 171). Thus the question of responsibility is blurred in principle at all levels of analysis and the question in practice becomes which of the two sides was nearer to the genuine interests of England. It is a question Lawson is reluctant to answer, and his discussions of the Isle of Wight Treaty and the Exclusion of Charles II confirm his reluctance to provide simple answers – even when the technicalities of initial responsibility seem clear.

Parliament split over the question of coming to terms with Charles through the Isle of Wight Treaty. Whilst some thought it a genuine hope of settlement, Lawson argues that others thought any agreement with the King was treacherous (*Pol.* 180). That the proposed treaty did not take effect he thought a blessing. Indeed, he suggests that if the King were as guilty as the uncompromising party (and the Scots) believed, agreement with him would spell the undoing of the English interest. However, from the King's alleged guilt 'some would dare conclude, that they who attempted to make an agreement with the enemy so guilty could not be so faithful as those who refused all such reconciliation' (*Pol.* 181). This unbending party, he remarks, having destroyed one arbitrary power 'a malignant party as they called them' put another in its place; and the protection of sectaries and the erection of

---

[13] Cf. the discussion of Clarendon's attitude to the relationship of means and ends, in I. Coltman, *Private Men and Public Causes*, Faber, London, 1962.

'new models of their own brain' can, writes Lawson, be no act of fidelity (*Pol.* 181). The point, however, is not mainly to express approval of any party, let alone to stipulate who were the real traitors to the English interest, but to stress the difficulty of ascertaining fidelity once motive, action and consequent conduct are considered. It seems best not to apportion blame but to pray for all who seek peace and just government; to try to learn from error rather than to specify the faithful (*Pol.* 181–2).[14]

Charles I's being initially responsible for the outbreak of war and Parliament's being justified in punishing him raises the question of whether the family of a defeated monarch can be excluded from power. In England's case this seems to be so but, says Lawson, such matters in general must be known by the laws of God and the constitution of the state in which such happenings take place. And, in any case, it is difficult to know if justice was done in England, with the Parliament on the one hand claiming to be fighting for the King, and on the other executing him. Such matters are 'difficult points' on which 'its not possible to have true and perfect information ... or to meet with an impartial Judge' (*Pol.* 93–4). The issue is then left in the air until much later when Lawson hints that dispossessed monarchs should be patient, and be prepared to release their subjects from obligation *pro tem* (*Pol.* 367).[15]

Whoever was responsible, the years of war ushered in an Interregnum under which, he remarks, England is still living (*Pol.* 386). Scattered through the text are the remnants of Lawson's unknown Engagement tract, the lines of which (if his thought remains relatively unchanged) emerge reasonably clearly.

Peoples may be punished for their sins by the visitation of calamities. Amongst these are usurpation and conquest (*Pol.* 83), which may achieve full legitimacy only by the regime's duration, which is dependent upon providence and consent (*Pol.* 364).

The claims of what Marvell called 'helpless right' were important, but, Lawson urges, one must not forget the principal protective purpose of government. The point is put succinctly in the *Examination*, manifestly in agreement with Hobbes,

---

[14] Again and quite obviously, Professor Franklin has misread the passage and conjured a simple commitment from a very different point. There is little clear hostility to those who would have (mistakenly) effected the Isle of Wight Treaty; and what little there is, is balanced by hostility to the very group whom Franklin thinks that Lawson is praising, Julian Franklin, *John Locke and the Theory of Sovereignty*, Cambridge University Press, 1978, pp. 87ff.

[15] Again (monotonous word) Franklin notes that Lawson 'looked to' the exclusion of the Stuarts. At best such a reading is distortion by omission. Looks *at* would be a less misleading phrase, as Lawson backs off from the possibility and later seems to be holding out a restoration palm. And, again, the point of Lawson's comments can hardly have been to affirm party commitments.

For whatsoever (the King's) title may be, and how unjustly soever it may be taken away, and howsoever his subjects may stand well affected towards him, yet seeing there can be no protection from wrong within, nor from invasion of enemies without, nor administration of justice, without which any people return unto the condition of Anarchy, except there be actual possession of power; therefore Obligation for the present must cease, or at least be suspended (*Exam.* 74–5).

At their inception new regimes nearly always pose a moral problem created by the play of old habits, loyalties, oaths and established right on the one hand, and perceptions of prudence and putative providence on the other (*Pol.* 87, 9, 362).

It was probably in this context of concern that Lawson's hierarchy of fidelity originated. Clearly designed in general terms to underplay allegiance to specific persons and contingent governmental forms, it may specifically have been intended to assuage the doubts of those committed either to Charles I personally, or to the destroyed form of government which had included him. It fitted well with the intimated advice to Charles II to suspend his claims on his subjects (*Pol.* 367). Above such loyalties, suggests Lawson, must come loyalty to country regardless of the type of government form, and loyalty to country, that is community itself. Such a taxonomy was well suited to the Engagement Controversy and could certainly play its part in Lawson's ameliorating plea for a settlement, irrespective of its activist implications which were to be drawn out later in the century.

We must remember too, writes Lawson, that there is a difference between the origins and the exercise of power: Richard III and Henry VII were both adjudged usurpers, but their laws were good (*Pol.* 88).[16] Since the execution of Charles and the total destruction of the old frame of government a *de facto* regime has been established in order to resettle.[17] For this such governments need obedience, and, for a time, extraordinary powers (*Pol.* 75). Lawson's remarks are thus at one with much of the Engagement literature of 1649–51; an obvious difference, however, is that after a number of years the promise of settlement is still unfulfilled (*Pol.* 386), and there is a greater emphasis on the difficulties of re-establishing a permanent political order than in the early literature. Despite the insecurity, and in a sense the failure of the Republic, yet

the Universities stand, Schools remain, Learning flourisheth ... never better Sermons, never better Books ... Matters in Religion are not so much taken on trust and tradition as formally. Arts and languages advance, the light of the Gospel shines. The Laws abide in force, Justice is administered, peace enjoyed, the Protestant

---

[16] Cf. Baker, *A Chronicle*, pp. 242ff. Richard, however, cannot win. Because he was bad the good things of his reign have to be considered under another monarch.

[17] The references to the destruction of the frame of government were an important motif in royalist literature, see Hartman, 'Contemporary Explanations', pp. 22f.

Interest in foreign parts Maintained ... and if we could agree amongst ourselves, it is a happy Nation (*Pol.* 188).[18]

In this, which reads almost like a syntactic and thematic parody of *Leviathan*, 1.13, it becomes quite clear that despite the sectaries, the 'General' and the threatened rule of a 'godly party', the Interregnum itself has not been an unmitigated disaster. There is much of the peace and prosperity of the years before wars began. As John Donne had written, 'Disorder is never so barren that it affords no fruit ...'[19]

The problem then is not settlement on any terms, but the course towards settlement which is not alien and arbitrary, which truly accommodates without undoing all good (*Pol.* 189–91). A settlement, like any new regime, will need time, it must begin in generals and gradually move to particulars (*Pol.* 190). The ancient constitution could provide the right model, but understanding it and recovering it are no easy matters (*Pol.* 148–9). Lawson defers to more expert judgement, but in any case states that specific form is a secondary matter: 'when we cannot do what we will, we must be willing to do what we can' (*Pol.* 385). Other things being equal, some element of hereditary government is to be preferred (*Pol.* 191), but even this, if at odds with the public interest, as it may prove, is 'not so much to be regarded' (*Pol.* 191). The religious dimension of the settlement requires the biblically permissible establishment of a national church according to a brief general rule based on plain Scripture (*Pol.* 193), as close to ancient confessions as possible, but with 'nothing being imposed upon all, which any rational Christian, as such may not receive without scruple' (*ibid.*). In both dimensions then, Lawson offers somewhat nebulous formulae of a genuinely latitudinarian nature, which could encompass most differences, given good will and the alleviation of ignorance (*Pol.* 189–90). But good will was made difficult, as Lawson must have been aware, in an atmosphere of uncertainty, poisonous political accusation, embarrassed defensiveness and tenacious wartime memories. Ignorance he stated was chiefly of the rules of government and, he argues, of its requisite terms and notions and how all these applied to English circumstances and recent English history.

Overall, Lawson read the whole Civil War and its aftermath in such a way as to undermine its status as a divisive symbol and a barrier to settlement. It is in this light that his evenhandedness in apportioning blame, his stress on the difficulties of interpretation should be seen – for on the

---

[18] The royalist, John Davies, *The Civil Warres of Great Britain and Ireland*, 1661, p. 362, gives credit to Cromwell for re-establishing Britain's overseas greatness, as Hartman notes. Lawson's happily optimistic account of the general state of the nation in 1660 was not universally shared, but his persuasive point is clear enough. *Contra*, Anon., *A Coffin for the Good Old Cause*, 1659, pp. 6–7; Anon., *No Droll but Rational account*, 1659, p. 6.

[19] John Donne, *Paradox* 9, 15–16, of which Lawson's account is reminiscent. See Donne, *Paradoxes and Problems*, ed. Helen Peters, Clarendon Press, 1980.

surface they suggest a balanced historiographical sophistication appropriate to the more sober forms of Whig constitutional history.

Certainly, Lawson's sympathies remain with the Parliament which originally tried to set things to right; but manifestly this does not convert into a commitment to the Protector, either as king, or as *gonfaloniere a vita* in a republican free state. On the contrary, I would suggest that Lawson's account of the war and Interregnum was designed to undermine commitment by rendering it negotiable. I am, he assured the reader at the outset, of no party, as party (*Pol.* Epist.). Indeed, if Hartman is correct to see the hard lines of early royalist and parliamentarian apologetics circumscribing the terms of debate over the revolution,[20] it is notable just how much of the parliamentarian case and its hallowed symbols of oppression are missing or but lightly touched upon; how even royalist critique is given credence; and how many of Lawson's reflections are couched in such a way as to suggest common ground. The King's lack of command over the purse is mentioned to indicate that Parliament traditionally had a voice in government (*Pol.* 76–7), but ship money passes silently in the night.[21] The widespread fear of Romanism is voiced but there is no mention of conspiracy. Innovations there may have been but, in matters of religion, innovation was a universal idiom of accusation, and Lawson does not dwell on detail. Laud does not become a scapegoat.[22] The very causes of corruption which brought down the wrath of God are dissipated by reference to their long-standing and well ingrained nature and are not exclusively or explicitly linked to the Stuart dynasty. Under Charles, prelacy grew, but that was not the real issue.[23] And if Lawson echoes 'The Grand Remonstrance' and touches on points discussed at length by May, he empties these of much force by evaporating specific responsibility or by finding a formulation too general for party affiliation to exploit. Parliamentarians had gradually moved from blaming the King's advisers, to blaming the King (as even royalists did), then to making the general point that kingship *per se* was prone to tyranny.[24] Lawson's point is that all governments tend to move beyond

---

[20] Hartman, 'Contemporary Explanations', p. 1.

[21] Lack of money is not mentioned explicitly as a cause of the War (though see *Exam.* 142) but Lawson's account of sovereignty clearly encompasses a command of purse and patronage as it did for Hobbes, and as it had for Fortescue before him, *The Governance of England.*

[22] Cf. E. W., *The Life and Death of William Laud*, 1645; Baker, *A Chronicle* calls Laud 'a busie man and one violent in his wais', p. 492. It is true that earlier Laud had tried to promote Lawson's career, but his scapegoatly absence from the *Politica* is more than a residue of old loyalty. Strafford's trial is mentioned but he too is no scapegoat.

[23] Thus Elizabeth does not represent a symbolic golden age as she often did in implicit counterpoint to that of the Stuarts.

[24] John Milton, *The Tenure of Kings and Magistrates*, in *The Prose Works of John Milton*, ed. J. Max Patrick, Doubleday, New York, 1967, is the apotheosis of this.

their sphere and, further, that this should elicit some understanding as governance is so difficult a business (*Pol.* 189).

Lawson shares with May, Baker and later Clarendon a conventional enough tendency to protest an even-handed fairness;[25] but unlike them he does not dwell on divisive events and colourful reportage, which render other protestations excessive. In part this may be a function simply of the fact that he is not attempting a full history and more detail may have dredged up more commitment. But that is not all. May, Baker and Clarendon differ from Lawson in claiming authority for their moral judgements. May and Clarendon claim the authority of insiders, like good retired generals they write to set the record straight. Baker claims the authority of having read all the best histories and of having a new method. In contrast, Lawson exploits his position as an outsider at one with his audience. This enables him to avoid both detail and final judgement; and in the one passage where there are the marks of inside expertise (the failure of Presbyterianism) the question of responsibility gives way to the terms of efficient causation. The effect, then, is not with an air of authority to vindicate a party, but to illustrate how difficult such enterprises are.

In one way, Lawson is asserting the importance of prudence – that realm of political judgement that can neither be reduced to predetermined rules, nor be directed by those excluded from the intricacies of practice. Also, however, Lawson's account as a whole has the force of undermining what, in John Pocock's expression, was a potent set of past relationships.[26] The reader confronted with a difficult and imperfectly understood past must doubt more and judge less. Models drawn from the past should not be seen as authoritative, but as providing guidance in the light of precept. In this way, then, Lamont's assessment is not quite right in claiming that Lawson's understanding of the Civil War stood for that sort of sober analysis that missed the whole emotional point and force of a civil war. The point was not so much missed as sabotaged; in asserting the significance of the war, he undermined its emotional meaning: he is offering as it were an act of oblivion. In this context, Cousins's judgement on Marvell might do nearly as well for Lawson, 'a critical intelligence deliberately isolated, almost keeping its judgements, resolved or not, silent.'[27] The *Politica* was a plea for others to do likewise. Lawson's treatment of the period is thus

---

[25] No doubt they were all aware of Cicero on the responsibilities of the historian – quite appropriately too, for they did not overlook that, for Cicero, history was subordinate to rhetoric.

[26] Pocock, 'The Origins of the Study of the Past', pp. 209–46.

[27] William Lamont, *Richard Baxter and the Millenium*, Croom Helm, London, 1979, p. 118; cf. Cousins, 'The Cavalier World of John Cleveland', *Studies in Philology*, 78 (1981), p. 70; and 'The Idea of a Restoration and the Verse Satires of Butler and Marvell', *Southern Review*, 14 (1981), pp. 138–40. But there is also a strong reminder of Hooker in this.

an historiographical analogue of his more abstract attempts to demote the significance of certain words and concepts for which people had been prepared to fight. Historiography is part of a sceptical rhetoric of healing. As a corollary, his own body of precept and conceptual priority is designed to rescue the wreckage of the past by redefining and imposing a new conceptual shape on what had really happened.

The apportionment of guilt for the war and the establishment of an authoritative right to reorganise the country after it, were vitally if not logically engangled problems. Any perceived difference between authoritative right and political action resulted in the accusation of rebellion or of arbitrariness and tyranny, depending on the status of the accused. The distribution of this abusive vocabulary had therefore been and remained central to political argument concerned with the Civil War and the settlement. A large part of the political literature of 1659–60 shows this clearly enough: increasingly ascendant royalists creeping out of the woodwork, waving brushes dipped in tar and vitriol; and large numbers of 'moderate' parliamentarians and Presbyterians covering their tracks and ducking away from the tar brush of rebellion. Increasingly, Cromwell not Charles becomes the tyrannical scapegoat,[28] and supporters of the 'Good Old Cause' – parodied with a quasi-theological lewdness as rumpers – are painted more and more into an isolated corner.[29] Lawson's precepts fit this general ambience in part, as a means of easing the atmosphere, by subverting the abusive lexicon surrounding rebellion and tyranny. As his treatment of the whole issue of responsibility muddies the waters of guilt, so his body of theory restructures the past.

On the surface this is disarmingly simple. *Personal* sovereignty is indivisible, in England this had been in the shape of a polyarchical trinity, no part of which could act, nominally speaking, as sovereign without the other (*Pol.* 170). Thus whichever part acted in constitutional isolation first did not so much justify actions taken against it as simply dissolve the whole of *personal* majesty. In this way, Lawson is at one with Harrington, dissolution preceded the war. The King initiated the dissolution but, from Lawson's

---

[28] Cf. Abraham Nelson, *A Perfect Description of Antichrist*, 1660; Anon., *A Speech tending to the Settlement of Kingly Government*, 1660 – a particularly ingenious blend of backsliding and the stealing of parliamentarian rhetoric.

[29] *Fanatique queries Proposed to the Present Asserters of the Good Old Cause*, 1659; *The Qualifications of Persons Declared Capable by the Rump Parliament*, 1659; *A Mirror*, 1660; *Bum-Fodder and Wastepaper . . .*, 1660; *Arsey-Versy: Or the Second Martyrdom of the Rump*, 1660; *A New Map of England*, 1659; *Free Parliament*, 1660; *A Word for All*, 1660; *The Rump Held Forth Last Feast Day*, 1660, all Anon. All are patchy but cutting in parts. The last starts as a fine parody of a Quaker sermon as well. *Rump Enough*, 1659, had made the elementary blunder of trying to deal with this sort of literature seriously on its own terms. Stephen Greenblatt has drawn attention to the proximity of scatology and eschatology, hence my tentative suggestion that theology might help control the imagery arising from the Rump. See his interesting 'Filthy Rites', *Daedalus*, 3 (1982), pp. 1ff.

point of view, had Parliament acted first, the result would have been theoretically the same: the collapse of *personal* majesty. Thus Lawson is able to define the whole traumatic period as an example of the failure of succession (*Pol.* 90). This has several important consequences for him. First, the Civil War, as just one of several potential forms of failure of succession, suggests a de-escalation of the crisis. Lamont has captured something of the force of this by stating that Baxter transformed Lawson's understanding of the Civil War into a constitutional 'hiccough'.[30] If Baxter had the *Politica* in mind, this was not so much of a transformation. Secondly, as subjection and *personal* majesty are co-relative terms, a failure of sovereignty automatically and by definition means that subjection ceases. The question as to whether people following the dictates of Parliament, or the King, were rebellious has been put in many ways, writes Lawson, but

the Truth is, that if the Fundamental Government be by King, Peers and Commons joyntly, and that [acting alone no part] could alter this Constitution, nor lawfully act any thing contrary unto it, then so soon as the Commission of Array on one side, and of the Militia on the other were issued out ... the Subjects in strict sense were freed from their Allegiance. And if they acted upon either side, their actings were just or unjust, as they were agreeable or disagreeable to the Fundamental Laws, and the general and principal end of Government (*Pol.* 378).

Thirdly, the explicit corollary is that the very issue of resistance or rebellion evaporates and such a vocabulary of accusation and justification is beside the point. Attempts to employ it, as he illustrates, have proved self-defeating (*Pol.* 372–3). The people remained throughout obliged to the laws of God and the peace and recovery of the community (*Pol.*378–9). This Clubmanish notion not only produces an ameliorating and conscience-salving rabbit from the steeple hat of turmoil, it emphasises also that the good of the community must be the end sought by the well affected on all sides. For clearly, though it bleeds, the community, sanctioned by God, survives and in many respects does quite nicely thank you. Concomitantly, the fourth major consequence for Lawson is that once *personal* majesty had dissolved, its powers reverted to the locus of *real* majesty, which has the capacity to reinvest or reform *personal* majesty. The people, then, for Lawson had been in effect a third party, damaged between the warring claimants to *personal* majesty – a point too that Clubmen would certainly have appreciated – and loyalty to community must remain intact. It is the rational part, or weightier part (*valentior pars*), of the people which is the true heir to *real* majesty; and this, as a representative of the whole must re-establish a form upon the matter of the nation (*Pol.* 382–3). As the community endures so there is and always has been a residual constituent authority (Franklin's felicitous expression) to cope with failures of succession. If Lawson's precepts and

---

[30] Lamont, *Richard Baxter*, p. 118.

their application be accepted, then, there is not only a practical but authoritative way of settling the nation, independent of the claims of and commitments to *personal* majesty, no part of which, precisely because it is (or was once) *personal* majesty, can resettle the system in toto:

> The form of Government was first constituted by the Community of *England*, not by the Parliament. For the Community and people of *England* gave both King and Parliament their being: and if they meddle with the Constitution to alter it, they destroy themselves, because they destroy that whereby they subsist. The Community indeed may give Parliament this power, to take away the former Constitution, and to frame and model another, but they cannot do this as a Parliament, but as trusted by the people for such a business and work (*Pol.* 162–3).

And again, the Parliament presupposes a structure of *personal* majesty, so if that is dissolved, a parliament cannot reconstitute anything as a parliament but only 'considered under another Notion, as an immediate Representative of a Community not a Commonwealth' (*Pol.* 59).[31]

In these words, then, Lawson is able to provide a powerful conceptual rationale for the eventual settlement of 1660; the actions of General Monck and his associates could well be considered under the notion of a *valentior pars* of the people; the Convention Parliament, not as a parliament but under that other 'Notion, as a Representative of the Community' in moot to re-establish the frame for *personal* majesty.

Lawson's precepts however are not without their difficulties and application does not resolve interpretative antinomies. I have suggested that it is not always clear whether Lawson's conception of representatives involves any notion of accountability to the represented and this uncertainty is not solved by Lawson's references to Parliament as a representative body. The corporate notion of representation (irrevocable, synecdochical), seems clearly uppermost when Lawson is referring, for example, to the early church meeting virtually through its representatives (*Pol.* 315–6); or to the extraordinary role of a 'Convention' parliament (*Pol.* 162–3); and again he refers to *personal majesty* (kings and or parliaments) as representatives. But by acting above their spheres they cease to be representatives. Here it is not clear if we are dealing with accountability or a matter of definition, that is, with the notions under which phenomena may be considered. Lawson (who has no high opinion of the quality of men in Parliament) also refers to Parliament as the general representative of the nation needing more regular and orderly elections (*Pol.* 192). He seems here to imply that Parliament

---

[31] *Contra, A Word of Settlement*, 1659; *Parliament's Plea*, 1659; *The Grand Concernments of England Ensured*, 1659; W.C. *A Discourse for a King and Parliament*, 1660, all Anon. All of these run Parliament and the representation of the people together, reflecting and reiterating Parliament's earlier claims. Such notions are hinted at in Hunton, *A Treatise*, pp. 17–18, 42, but are not so clearly articulated – and Lawson would never have given 'subjects' a role in government.

should be a good deal more accountable than it is. These different possibilities seem to be run together where Lawson remarks that in Parliament many are officers, but as a whole do not act as officers, but as representatives of the whole (*Pol.* 246–7).

I have suggested elsewhere that Lawson's references to Parliament in this context may reflect more than a century of uncertain and changing status, which is to suggest that Lawson, drawing on a mixture of materials from different periods of English history, may encapsulate different theories of Parliament's status.[32] It remains the context of his own arguments however, that creates or sustains any difficulties that might seep into the text from a wider discursive context. Here what seems significant is the presence or absence of an image of corporation, of *virtuality* and a purist doctrine of office.

Just as the uncertainties surrounding representation are sustained by Lawson's application of precept to English history, so too the ambiguities of his discussion of resistance remain unresolved in the shift from theory to concrete illustration. To the question did Parliament rebel or justifiably resist (*Pol.* 376–7), Lawson's final answer is that because Parliament was a part of *personal majesty*, the issue does not arise. That much is clear and consistent with both readings of the resistance *topos* that I have suggested.[33] However, his handling of the doctrine of office in the context of the Civil War is another matter.

Irrespective of other arguments that resistance theorists might use, the clear separation of 'man' from 'office' was important. In the context of the English Civil War, it was (as Overton remarked) the *Axeltree* of Parliament's proceedings against the King; it was similarly central to his own resistance to the dictates of Parliament. For, by such a separation, he was able to hold the office itself in continued respect, use that respect to deflect accusations of rebellion, and at the same time resist the commands of the officeholders.

By contrast, a refusal to separate office from office-holder gave no grounds (as Rous had been reminded) for withstanding even the most appalling tyranny. And a willingness to distinguish but not separate office from holder could always be an effective conceptual barrier against resistance. If the distinction be granted but the separation be disallowed, then a resistance theory had to stand upon the more exposed ground which required an attack on the office *per se*. It was this escalation which rendered it particularly vulnerable to the curse of Meroz, that is the rebounding

---

[32] C. Condren, 'Resistance and Sovereignty in Lawson's *Politica*', *HJ*, 24, 3 (1981), pp. 667–8.

[33] But Lawson's terminology is not always consistent – he does in passing refer to Parliament's resistance to the King (*Pol.* 363), although, when he does, it is in the process of setting up the issues to be refined and answered.

accusation of rebellion. It is little wonder that a royalist like Edward Bagshaw should thus assert only a distinction not a separation could be made between king and office.

Now, insofar as resistance theory hovers in the *Politica* as a necessary but quite unwanted guest at a settlement wedding, it is not surprising that we find Lawson dissecting the King's two bodies: Charles could not command his subjects through his person, but only through his lawful office (*Pol.* 176). Again, more clearly, many had been of the mistaken belief that Charles was an absolute ruler, but they should have realised that in obeying his personal commands, they disobeyed him as King (*Pol.* 174).

Here I think we have as authentic a shoot from Overton's *Axeltree* as we might wish for. Moreover, it flourishes in direct opposition to the see-saw reading of Lawson's discussion of resistance, which explicitly requires his unwillingness to separate only formally distinguishable duplex bodies. Had Lawson nothing else to say on the matter of *Charles Stuart* and King Charles, we would, I think, have to give cobweb precedence over see-saw.

In fact, however, Lawson alludes to the very pattern of parliamentary casuistry he is to use (*Pol.* 174–6) as being at least perplexing (*Pol.* 94) and then goes on later to claim that it is quite unsatisfactory. In the confusions of the war, he writes, whilst the King was fighting a Parliament he had not deemed rebellious, the Parliament claimed to be fighting for the King. Hopelessly entangled in their own 'curious distinctions' (*Pol.* 373), it seems

they found differences between the King and himself, and the Parliament and itself. These distinctions were not altogether false: yet though *Charles Stewart* and the King, and so the Parliament and a party in the Parliament might be distinguished, yet they could not be separated. And woe unto a people that is brought into such straights and perplexities. For if they kill *Charles Stewart*, they kill the King; and if the King destroy that party in the Parliament, he destroy the Parliament (*Pol.* 373).

Leaving aside what might be called the balance of conceptual confusion which Lawson sees between both sides and which is at one with his handling of the revolution in general, it is clear that there is a direct contradiction between his main statements on the King's two bodies in the English Civil War.

In the first of these he is deploying part of a casuistic rhetoric of resistance against the claims of absolutism made on behalf of Charles. In the second, however, he is criticising as invalid such arbitrary attempts to exploit insolubly duplex notions of understanding.

Taken together, his differing reactions to the two bodies may thus be located in the contexts of differing theoretical possibilities suggested by the text; so a coalescent ambiguity sustained in a body of theory, is brought down to lie on the revolution's polished grass.

Part IV

THE FATE OF THE *POLITICA* FROM THE SETTLEMENT TO THE GLORIOUS REVOLUTION

INTRODUCTION

The diffident conclusion to the *Politica* did not augur well for a spectacular reception and initially the work sank from view. The simplest reason may be that once a settlement had been achieved, Lawson's work no longer touched on burning issues. But so much appeared around 1660 that almost everything was lost under a floating tide of paper. The *Politica* is unusual in surviving at all and one can only speculate on the fate of *Leviathan* had it appeared in that monstrous year of the word. However, there may be a serious discrepancy between significance and citation. In a way we are quite properly restricted by the latter, but we should not on this basis assume that the only importance a writer might have had is to be found on the page. Caution is needed here to avoid the phantom world of hidden influence, but Maclean has pointed out that Lawson's works were widely distributed in the libraries of the English gentry; they found their way to America; and the *Politica* was still being read during the Napoleonic Wars.[1] Both the auctioneer's and Baxter's paeans of praise seem to reflect a recognised importance which belies the paucity of textual citation.

Further, if one looks at the pattern of citation in the seventeenth century, this may not be unduly surprising. References to the works of others fall roughly into the following main categories. First, much political argument was subsumed under the established authorities of the past, biblical, ancient and (to a lesser extent) medieval. And the manipulation of potent names might have but a strained or tangential relationship to their original texts, or any formative influence they had upon the user. Secondly, writers get frequent citation as emblems of opposing political and religious groupings, either in order that the assumed authorities of one's opponents might be turned against them, or so that the user may establish his credentials amongst them.[2] Thirdly, contemporaries, perhaps otherwise insignificant, are used as ammunition to be fired at unnamed adversaries, or phenomena more significant than the authors themselves. It is hardly surprising in a world of eristics if writers choose those they take to be their weakest opponents and by suggestion and association seem to refute more than in fact they do. To justify such manoeuvres might even require the exaggeration of

---

[1] A. H. Maclean, 'George Lawson and John Locke', *Cambridge Historical Journal*, 9, 1 (1947), pp. 72f.; John Dunn, 'The Politics of Locke in England and America in the Eighteenth Century', in Yolton, *John Locke, Problems and Perspectives,* Cambridge University Press, 1969, p. 69. The University of New South Wales's copy of the *Politica* is annotated with reference to Napoleon.
[2] C. Condren, 'Authorities, Emblems and Sources' *Philosophy and Rhetoric*, 15 (1982); for further elaboration of a hierarchy of authority see Grotius, *De jure belli ac pacis libri tres*, trans. F. W. Kelsey, Clarendon Press, Oxford, 1913, 1925, Prolegomena.

the significance of the victim. The catalogue of debts and the revelation of the intellectual origins of one's own arguments was only a small and unreliable part of this wider pattern of combative citation. So correlating rhetorical usage and formative significance is naïve; usage is hard evidence, but too seldom for the things we now want to know.[3] The relationships between Lawson's *Politica* and its principal carriers reinforce this general scepticism about the charting of intellectual relationships to such an extent that the stuff of intellectual history seems to mock Ranke's famous aphorism of historical ambition.

Before coming to the harder evidence of usage in the form of men like Baxter and Humfrey, I have found only a few suggestive straws. *The English Episcopacy and Liturgy Asserted* (July 1660) and Bagshaw's *The Rights of the Crown* (1660) may be attacking Lawson, and certainly do attack the ground on which he stood with others, but there is nothing specific. In the following year, Bishop Seth Ward (1617–89) produced a sermonical blunderbuss designed to scatter quickly on a wide front called *Against Resistance of Lawfull Power*. It defines *the* Christian theory of politics as simple subjection to monarchy, equates resistance with rebellion (a new doctrine preached by that familiar alliance of Catholics and Puritans), the final 'pretence' of which seems to echo Lawsonian terminology.[4] The notions that there is a reserve power in the 'diffused multitude or the people's Representative' and that there can be a 'failure of duty' and a 'forfeiture of power' are all destructive of peace, making human artifice of what is really the work of God.[5] Tantalizingly, Ward seems to assume familiarity with an unnamed body of recent literature, and if the *Politica* came within the range afforded by his pulpit, it may already have been quite widely read.[6] It might not have been a simple lack of interest but hostility of reaction that permanently forestalled Lawson's second volume. Indirectly some support for this hypothesis comes from the fact that the clearest evidence of Lawson's being taken seriously is to be found not amongst his fellow conforming clerics, but those reluctant non-conformists, Baxter and Humfrey.

[3] One of the most frequent references to Grotius is to the effect that even he allows resistance *in extremis*. Grotius makes the same point about Barclay, thereafter the two names usually appear together as if on a ritual tandem.
[4] Seth Ward, *Against Resistance*, 1661, p. 7.   [5] *Ibid.*, pp. 31–2.
[6] Between the publication of his *Elementum jurisprudentiae universalis*, 1660 and his *De jure naturae*, Pufendorf clearly had to come to grips with the distinction between *real* and *personal* majesty. His criticism of the distinction, *De jure*, 7.6.4, could reflect a direct familiarity with Lawson, for he is attacking a restricting more than a sharing use of the distinction; but he is both elliptical and non-specific, and at 7.6.10 seems to be accepting a position at one with Lawson's.

11

Lawson and Baxter

At the end of his life Baxter, like Cephalus paying his debts, lavished extravagant and lengthy praise on Lawson, 'the ablest man of almost any I know in England ... a man of great skill in politics, wherein he is most exact'.[1] Indeed, Baxter maintained that Lawson was one of the greatest influences on his life and political judgements. Such praise takes us back to before the publication of the *Politica*, and to an extent to one side of it, for despite criticisms (*A Treatise of Episcopacy*) it was the *Theo-Politica* Baxter most admired, and in *A Holy Commonwealth*, Lawson's *Examination* is taken as a sufficient argument against Hobbes.[2] With respect to the *Politica*, however, I suspect that Baxter's attitude was a good deal more ambivalent; indeed that Lawson may even have been a nameless target in the *Commonwealth*. Looking at these two works will reveal the full force and the partial disingenuousness of Baxter's remarkable valedictory tribute to George Lawson.

On the surface my thesis here looks perverse, for there has certainly been no reason to regard the *Politica* as a context for the *Commonwealth*; after all, the chronology of publication is simply wrong. But when Underhill, who had printed Lawson's *Examination*, printed *Commonwealth* in 1659, Lawson and Baxter had known each other for a number of years. They had enjoyed a friendship, beginning around the time Baxter printed his *Aphorisms of Justification* (1649), and it seems to have been strong enough to survive their turgid and often tetchy theological animadversions.[3] Baxter's familiarity with Lawson's political thought was certainly not

---

[1] Baxter, *Relig. Baxt.*, 1.1. p. 108, elsewhere he refers to Lawson as 'my highly valued friend ... (a most judicious politician)', cited in William Lamont, *Richard Baxter and the Millennium*, Croom Helm, London, 1979, p. 118.

[2] Baxter, *A Treatise of Episcopacy*, chap. 2; *A Holy Commonwealth*, 1659, Thesis 79; his admiration is also clear from *The Christian Directory*, 1673.

[3] Baxter, *Relig. Baxt.*, 1.1.108, when (if) they first met is unknown. Baxter, reviewing some discussions with Lawson *c.* 1654 ends with a statement that might indicate they were yet to meet 'Pardon my mistake at not knowing you', *Baxter Treatises*, DWL, 7, fos. 327–35, item 274.

restricted to the *Examination*, for it is Baxter who tells us of the unpublished Engagement tract. As the *Politica* was long in gestation it is possible that Baxter was familiar with a version of the work, or even the manuscript much as it came to be published. The absence of a published text to comment on would itself explain why the *Politica* is unmentioned and yet seems to loom behind *Commonwealth*.

Both works share a range of explicit affirmations common to much seventeenth-century discourse. Like Lawson, Baxter affirms that God is a universal sovereign in a providential universe; the papacy and democracy are bad things; state and church are distinct and the magistrate and pastor must not be confused. Sovereignty and subjection are co-relative terms.[4] The ruler (*pars imperians*) must be obeyed by the subject (*pars subdita*); government is divided into administration and constitution.[5] The consent of the people is needed for a change in government – even conquest requires that they yield.[6] England traditionally has been governed by a mixed monarchy, by which initially Baxter means what Lawson means, a civil person or corporation; and he suggests also that a cause of the late wars lay in misunderstanding the nature of this system. He also nicely captures the ambivalence of Parliament's status as it is understood in the *Politica* (more so than in the *Examination*) when he refers to it as the representative of a free people and considers it as a part of the sovereign power.[7] There are, however, a number of differences of emphasis. First, Baxter explicitly embraces the 'Good Old Cause'. He measured his world against an ideal and consequently there is more stress on the best and worst forms of government.[8] For Baxter democracy is a genuine evil, Harrington and the Levellers are to be feared. His ideal is less an amphibolous formulation of a free state cum mixed monarchy, than a magisterially guided and holy enterprise – which conspires to make Baxter look more Erastian than Lawson.[9] Secondly, for Baxter the consent of the people is only *normally* required for government and the people are only *usually* a prior community.[10] Indeed, the aggregate of men who contract to form a polity are far closer to Hobbes's naked individuals than Lawson's *cives*.[11]

---

[4] *Commonwealth*, e.g. Theses 28, 52, 82.
[5] *Ibid.*, Theses 51, 66, 65. The phrasing is sometimes very similar to that found in the *Examination*; cf. Theses 95–8 with *Exam.* p. 72.
[6] *Commonwealth*, Theses 374, 143.   [7] *Ibid.*, Theses 79, 69.
[8] *Ibid.*, Preface but in more precise terms the nature of Baxter's commitment has been disputed; cf. Richard B. Schlatter, *Richard Baxter and Puritan Politics*, Rutgers, New Brunswick, 1957, with Lamont, *Richard Baxter.*
[9] *Commonwealth*, Theses 232, 240–4. This is well in keeping with the peculiarities of the English Reformation; Yule, *Puritans in Politics*, at length, esp. Introduction.
[10] *Commonwealth*, Theses, 374, 143, 68.   [11] *Ibid.*, Thesis 51.

These differences of emphasis lead to more serious conceptual contrasts, which seem, *in toto*, hardly coincidental. In many important respects where Lawson had insisted on precise conceptual delineation, Baxter's terminology is more fluid. Baxter's use of conquest covers the territory divided by Lawson into conquest and usurpation; Baxter runs together consent and yielding; and his magistrate is not clearly the sovereign in the indivisible sense, regardless of governmental form. Most importantly, there is little notion of the binary oppositions of community and polity, citizen and subject, which, underlying the *Examination*, emerge as central to the *Politica*. Indeed, in Thesis 51 Baxter explicitly attacks the distinction between *real* and *personal* majesty as Lawson's *Politica* uses it.

Baxter calls it the result of an unholy alliance between papists and Protestants (who else?), and, as Seth Ward was shortly to, he asserts that the people can have no power, no *real* majesty. Citizen was a difficult word for Baxter anyway, as he was writing with one eye on Harrington but, in this context, it is little wonder that he runs together citizen and subject so that they are conceptually indistinguishable as subject members of a commonwealth.[12] Instead of the community/polity distinction Baxter relies on a social contract before which each individual is judge in his own cause, having a propriety in himself.[13] The contract establishes a range of rights and it is this range of rights *given* by government which some have mistaken for *real* majesty.[14] But Baxter is not entirely happy with the absolutism this would seem to suggest; the theological principles he shares with Lawson would explain this easily enough. So, in a more Lawsonian, if apparently muddled, vein we are also told that the people do not *give up* all rights; they may restrain the sovereign from taking some rights from them without consent; and even that constitutional form which gives them their rights cannot be changed without their consent.[15] Yet, even if this makes government look like a trust the government may break that trust *in extremis* and still require obedience.[16] On this basis there is, as one might expect, a bewildering range of injunctions to the people concerning resistance. They may not resist; they must obey infidels, but not the pope; they may resist lesser magistrates.[17] They may resist a prince if he acts *ultra vires*, but elsewhere this is not resistance.[18] Individuals may not decide, yet they must

---

[12] *Ibid.*, Theses 179, 220, 349 for citizens as subjects. See also *The Christian Directory*, 1673, part 4, chap. 3 answer to objection 12.
[13] *Commonwealth*, Theses 51–2.   [14] *Ibid.*, Theses 51–2.   [15] *Ibid.*, Theses 378, 114, 374.
[16] *Ibid.*, Thesis 115.   [17] *Ibid.*, Theses 317, 332, 336.
[18] *Ibid.*, cf. Theses 340, 333, and chap. 12 *passim*.

obey the laws of God first.[19] Not all of these statements are irreconcilable, but, after all this and much more, it does come as a relief to be told that one may flee the country.[20] With respect to the Civil War, although the matter was primarily constitutional, there was no dissolution of the constitution. Rather the people remained throughout the subjects of the Parliament. Here Baxter also departs of necessity from the initially Lawsonian specifications of mixed monarchy – for a part of sovereignty clearly remains intact. The people are always subjects, there is conceptually nothing else for them to be.[21]

It is ironic that Baxter had a reputation for making overly nice distinctions. But for the somewhat antinomian example of the people not choosing but only being the effective cause of a particular sovereign, what is most noticeable at the level of abstract conception and individuation is Baxter's lack of discrimination.[22] The whole aura of confusion as to what the subject might do arises from the paucity of his vocabulary and his apparent refusal to discriminate between injunctions appropriate to different classifications. There is no difference between subject and citizen, between *real* and *personal* majesty. In this way one cannot hypothesise that the *Commonwealth* provides a deliberately aporetic structure of argument, as the *Politica* may, for Baxter's concepts are *simplex*. Again there is a striking parallel with the 'Amica dissertatio'. Where Lawson regarded a single predication of God as inadequate to express the diversity of God's options with respect to sin; Baxter wanted all options encompassed by the simplex heading of God's judgement. The cumulative differences between the *Commonwealth* and the *Politica* and *Examination* make Baxter's reference to the latter a shade disingenuous. For the very grounds on which Lawson attacked Hobbes are denied in Baxter's work.[23] Yet had Lawson been confronted directly, it would have been more difficult for Baxter to wave the *Examination* in the general direction of Malmesbury and leave it at that. The differences between Lawson's *Politica* and Baxter's *Commonwealth*, then, may not be piecemeal but neither may they be the result of accidental confusion. Lawson and Baxter seem to be involved in the same species of verbal manipulation though with respect to complementary sectors of the political lexicon.

Overall, as I have suggested, one can see Lawson refining and intensifying some areas of his political vocabulary at the expense of others whose significance he wished to undermine. Baxter may have adopted the same argumentative strategy, but he wanted to emphasise the nomenclature of

---

[19] *Ibid.*, Theses 332, 328.   [20] *Ibid.*, Thesis 345.   [21] *Ibid.*, chap. 14.   [22] *Ibid.*, Thesis 182.
[23] For Baxter's more detailed, unpublished reflections on Hobbes, *The Baxter Treatises, Reliq., Baxt.*, part 3, DWL, MSS 349.

governmental form as he was concerned with England's approximation to an ideal. It is here that we find Lawson loose to the point of being offhand. Baxter's apparent conceptual insouciance may have been an attempt to sabotage the abstract vocabulary surrounding the notion of citizenship, for there is no doubt he saw it as dangerous. That this putative strategy was directed partially at Lawson seems further indicated by Baxter's final reflections on George Lawson. In the *Political Catechise* Baxter rehearses again his respect for Lawson, but precisely draws the line at Lawson's conceptual distinction between citizen and subject. Such a distinction opened the way for rebellion.[24] It is, in short, the corollary of the distinction between *real* and *personal* majesty which Baxter attacked in 1659, and it is difficult to imagine that Baxter failed to see the connection then. His occasional use of the term citizen to mean subject, like Hobbes's consistent equation in *De cive*, can be seen then as an attempt to forestall the augmentation of the political lexicon, the price for which was paid in the currency of conceptual confusion. The price may have been high, but perhaps it was paid throughout his life in order to make the world safe for the non-conformist—never the citizen, always the good subject. Lawson however was a conformist, a theorist before an activist, so he could afford either an hypothetical embrace of resistance in the interests of theological consistency; or he could engage in a theory to one side of, and as a precondition for, any range of activist injunctions. *Prima facie* it seems supremely ironic, that the apparently quiet conforming cleric should be seen to aid rebellion; the outspoken and principled man of action, who wore the stigma of imprisonment, should be the one who could find only a shifting and uncertain image of himself. Theoretical courage is a luxury that the committed can rarely afford.

Whatever the soundness of this hypothetical reconstruction of a putative relationship between two very adjacent texts, the publication of *Commonwealth* before the *Politica* obscures any clear pattern of usage thereafter, and serves to indicate how tricky charting intellectual traditions can be. Just as we cannot tie the *Politica* itself down to an exclusive and formative array of texts, so too we cannot be sure how, when, and to what extent it was used; we know only that some *claimed* it to be important. But if much that looks like Locke might well be Lawson, much that looks like Lawson might be Baxter. Similarly, the *Politica* itself and certainly the ideas it shares in the *Examination* may be seen as an important part of the context for the *Commonwealth*. If Baxter thought in 1659 that he had the answer for the settlement, the questions were provided not only by Vane, Harrington

---

[24] *Political Catechise, Baxter Treatises,* 6, fos. 284–95, item 205, DWL, the residual authority is called a 'dangerous error'.

and to a lesser extent Hobbes, but also by Lawson. The *Commonwealth* was perhaps both a statement of indebtedness and of freedom by a man who was, as the *Political Catechise* suggests, to remain politically haunted by Lawson for the rest of his life. As in so many other ways, the *Reliquiae Baxterianae* was an act of exorcism.

12

Lawson and Humfrey

'I will go with the wickedest man alive to the church, but I must leave him at the ale house . . .' So wrote John Humfrey in an early piece of sacral theology.[1] Even if the ellipsis unintentionally suggests the concept of a gathered pub, it is quite clear that for Humfrey (1621–1719) the church must be inclusive. The Keys belong to the church as a whole, but internal matters are the preserve of Christ.[2] This is commonplace enough but, more important, it is very much at one with Lawson's church beneath the sign of the wheat and tares. So whenever Humfrey first came across Lawson's *Politica*, it would not have shed a Damascan light, or formed a pothole, on his long and troubled ministerial journey. It did become, I suspect, a staff on which he increasingly relied and which, in the end, he began to wave about publicly.

Initially, then, the *Politica* is just one of a series of texts from which Humfrey could have selected formulations of general points, but texts and their general principles could divide men on the nicety of conduct, and be torn between differing camps more hostile in practice than in theory. This is illustrated by the interesting controversy that played its part in Humfrey's defection from the re-established Church of England in 1662.

He had been ordained during the Commonwealth by a presbyter, but the re-established church, amongst other things, required that all such priests be episcopally reordained. This made the issue of priestly equality a difficult sticking point.[3] Humfrey initially accepted reordination on the grounds that given the equality of priests, reordination was a matter of indifference.[4] Sacramental form, not mediating priest, was what counted. Lawson might

---

[1] *A Vindication of a Free Admission to the Lord's Supper*, 1653, p. 38.
[2] *Ibid.*, p. 40. For the background to Humfrey's sacral theology, E. Brooks Holifield, *The Convenant Sealed*, Yale University Press, 1974, pp. 118ff.
[3] But cf. Hooker, *Laws*, 5.77.3, though it was not such a pressing issue when he wrote; Ian Green, *The Re-Establishment of the Church of England, 1660–63*, Oxford University Press, 1978, for further discussion of the issues.
[4] Details of Humfrey's life I have taken from the *DNB* entry; and A. G. Matthews, *Calamy Revised*, Oxford, 1934.

143

have accepted this; but in a cogent and incisive tract, *A Letter to a Friend*, R.A. appealed to a shared range of authorities and principles in order to persuade Humfrey he was in error. It is, the author argued, precisely because priests are equal (on the authority of Andrewes and Marsilio) that the reordination of validly ordained priests is wrong.[5] In the present case it implies the *jure divino* superiority of bishops. Humfrey replied in *A Second Discourse* (1662) defending his position in terms of biblical indifference, and a somewhat Lawsonian reason of church. He brought a battery of familiar established church authorities to his aid, and tore up his ordination papers. This was perhaps not such a Chillingworthian *volte face* as it seems, ripped from context, and Humfrey's defection, like that of many others, was not complete.[6] Even though he set up his own congregation, he continued to take the sacraments at his parish church.[7] He had effected what Lawson would have called a 'positive partial separation' (*Pol.* 421–2). The points relevant to Lawson here are that, from Humfrey's perspective, a settlement that did not include him was still incomplete; and that the texts which surface in the dispute are at one with the *Politica* and those works cited in it. Possibly sick and certainly shaky in 1662, Lawson probably had to smuggle a fair bit under his own notion of reason of church to keep his living, and was probably glad to be so old that he did not personally have to cash precept of priestly equality into the coinage of reordination. On the evidence of the *Politica*, his justification might have been R.A.'s or Humfrey's. Lawson's ecclesiological identity then lies at the uncertain nexus of settlement conformity and non-conformity.

By 1668 Humfrey might well have known Lawson's work; if not, the intellectual proximity of the two men is reinforced with reference to the former's *Defence of the Proposition*. Magisterial power is only external; there is a difference between political form and matter, as there is between constitution and administration over a body of 'free subjects'.[8] The old Bartolan/Salutatian distinction between tyrannical origins and actions is maintained and the inclusive nature of the church is reiterated.[9] The texts referred to are a part of Lawson's own armoury – Arnisaeus, Spelman, Grotius and Barclay. Excluding the antiquary Sir Henry Spelman (1564–1641), however, Humfrey accords these more respect than does Lawson.

---

[5] Marsilio on ordination is quoted extensively, R.A., *A Letter to a Friend*, 1661, p. 55.
[6] Retrospectively, more political issues surrounding the extent of obedience and the implied termination of the Reformation assumed greater significance for Humfrey. This may indicate a gradual and more obvious political involvement as he grew older. See, at length, *A Plain Honest Determination*; and *The Free State of People Maintained*, 1702, pp. 6ff. contrasting the oaths of allegiance required under the Stuarts and William.
[7] D. Lacey, *Dissent and Parliamentary Politics*, Rutgers University Press, 1969, pp. 23–4. Humfrey, *Healing Spirit*, 1678, e.g. p. 17, reiterates this partial conformity.
[8] *Defence*, pp. 20, 19, 26.   [9] *Ibid.*, pp. 30f.

Always with one eye on an inclusive ecclesiastical settlement, Humfrey was, perhaps, apt to underline texts that might establish credentials. But the expression 'free subject' suggests that Baxter might be closer than Lawson here. The arguably loose use of subject may be an accommodating manipulation of the notion of subjection, to which Humfrey was always so sensitive.[10]

From around 1670 Humfrey's attempts to plead for comprehension take on a more overtly secular dimension. These times were of increasing difficulty even for the most reluctant and partial of non-conformists. Only agonising arguments in the Lords had stopped conventicles being defined as riots, and as a consequence, any degree of non-conformity becoming virtually rebellious. Then, lurching to another extreme Charles II's carrot of indulgence had confronted non-conformists with the choice between unpalatable but certain laws, or tempting but unreliable prerogative. Either option kept them exposed and vulnerable while the latter (horror) might accommodate Catholics as well.[11] As Humfrey's arguments take more explicit cognisance of the secular ramifications of ecclesiology, the Lawsonian mnemonics become, overall, more striking and begin to seem more discriminate. 1662 had been a long year for Humfrey: there was still no settlement, there were instead danger for and a distrust of non-conformity, which was insufficiently distinguished from willing sectarianism. Calming and diffusing strategies of argument were all the more important when accusation of rebellious intent could so easily be made. Sectarian extremity had to be abjured and credentials of loyalty to be reaffirmed – and all without compromising on a narrow front of principle. Few writers would have fitted the exigencies of political argument more effectively than Lawson.

In an acrimonious argument with the Bishop of Oxford, Samuel Parker (1640–88), Humfrey affirms his argument that the higher powers must be obeyed, though absolute obedience must be given only to God.[12] The present government to be obeyed is a corporation and, as with Baxter, the people are equated with their subject status;[13] but two years later there is change of emphasis. The mixed corporate government of England is a settled order of inferiority and superiority (the tautologous phrase much liked by Lawson); the church is directly parallel to the state, being a virtual

[10] See also on the point: Humfrey, *The Peaceable Design*, 1675, p. 34; *A Case of Conscience*, 1669, pp. 4–5; *Healing Spirit*, 1678; *The Two Steps*, 1684, pp. 26–8; good subjects obey, hide, or run away: they do not resist.

[11] Lacey, *Dissent and Parliamentary Politics*, pp. 60ff. for a succinct account of the difficulties and politicisation of non-conformity. The fear of catholicism is a theme of many of Humfrey's works providing the opening or closing of the following: *The Healing Attempt*, 1689; *A Modest Enquiry*, 1681; *A Draft*, 1705.

[12] *The Obligation to Human Laws Discussed*, 1670–1, pp. 62, 67, 132.

[13] *Ibid.*, p. 46; but Baxter had already expressed concern that Humfrey's political involvement was taking him too close to an acceptance of resistance, see William Lamont, *Richard Baxter and the Millennium*, Croom Helm, London, 1979, p. 93.

association of parishes and congregations.[14] Lawson is not mentioned, but these are points Humfrey was one day to rehearse against Baxter citing Lawson's authority.[15] In the meantime, Humfrey, still explicitly hostile to resistance, suggests a more Lawsonian notion of the *pars subdita* than Baxter would have been happy with. Although people are subjects, if government should fail through dissolution then power is returned to them.[16] Humfrey, I suspect, was beginning to search for a Lawsonian passage between outright subjection and resistance which, perhaps to show his seriousness, he equates with rebellion.[17] This may have been some solace for the edgy Baxter. The full irony of textual identity and disentanglement is captured, representatively, in Humfrey's *An Answer to Dr. Stillingfleet's Book* (1680), in which he sets out to defend Baxter in now strikingly Lawsonian terms and the defence is, still, obliquely a plea for adjustment and comprehension. The very notion of a church as a species of political organisation is vital here. Humfrey insists that the Church of England is a political church: in other words, it is a particular visible form of the universal church. The establishment and maintenance of this form involves human legislation and it has a political head (the king). If it were not a political church, it could only be a community of Christians, amongst whom (Humfrey supposes) there is no government yet introduced. Even the syntax seems Lawsonian.[18] Consent makes a church or a society – if Lawsonian, this is a simplification of his position – and the community, in either case, becomes political by the introduction of an order of superiority and inferiority.[19] The foundation of either species of government is a human (and implicitly contingent) constitution; the church is 'an organical body'.[20] Church and society must both further be supposed to be prior to a rule, and it is the rule not just the consent that makes a national church. By implication, what is humanly set up can be amended: hence the question – why aren't we yet comprehended? Baxter certainly needed no crutches to his own writing – but without citing chapter and verse, it is difficult to imagine a more Lawsonian notion of a national church.

Humfrey's most instructive text, however, was the *Peaceable Resolution of Conscience*, 1680. This does provide the chapter and verse as well as revealing a well-rounded image of Lawson's *Politica*. The *Peace-*

[14] *The Authority of the Magistrate About Religion Discussed*, 1672, pp. 28, 130, 37–8.
[15] *Union Pursued*, 1691, on which see below, p. 159.
[16] *The Authority of the Magistrate*, pp. 28–9.   [17] *Ibid.*, p. 35.
[18] *An Answer to Dr. Stillingfleet's Book*, 1680, p. 15; see also *A Reply to The Defence*, 1681, written with Stephen Lobb.
[19] *An Answer*, pp. 19–20.   [20] *Ibid.*, pp. 20–1.

able Resolution was written not as a specific polemic, but as a general treatise on politics from the text of Romans 13. It was directed explicitly and disarmingly to young university minds, which, unlike those of his own generation, he hoped were still unprejudiced and flexible.[21]

Throughout Humfrey argues for comprehension, and that the loyalty of dissenters is not to be doubted. The first two chapters deal respectively with the origin of civil power and the legitimate grounds for seeking political change. The remainder of the work deals with the proper responses to irregular magisterial behaviour, with a final chapter on how magistrates should treat their subjects in return. The opening chapters, then, seek to circumscribe the terms of debate and they do so in increasingly clear Lawsonian terms: power is from God, governmental form is contingent 'humane every jot' and, although monarchy is to be preferred, form is unimportant to those who are merely subjects.[22] Power, that 'ray of divine majesty', must not be resisted; if, in a personal capacity, magistrates require evil of us, we can only avoid them or suffer.[23] The original of power is from God via the people as a community who freely choose subjection. 'Majestas is duplex, *realis* and *personalis*';[24] and although sovereignty is radically in the people, only a *personal* sovereign may exercise it.[25] Occasionally Humfrey intimates that the power might be removed, but overwhelmingly he suggests the opposite. Thus, for example, we are told that a polity is not like a marriage (certainly when it is absolute); a breach of contract does not free the innocent party from obligation.[26] These principles, he claims, are universal, applicable to the full honour of kingship and even to absolute government.[27]

I am therefore very little offended with the *Politica* of Mr. *Lawson*, that dextrous person in this sort of Learning, whose book considering the time it came out, both for its Light into Civil Government, and his peculiar notion of Ecclesiastical, as Nationally Independent, whereby in his capacity he strewed the way in that season, for return of King and Bishop, is not to be envied its due praise and cautious use to be made of it.[28]

Due praise and cautious use indeed, for Lawson is not only extolled as a conceptual architect of the Restoration, but is almost shackled to monarchy

---

[21] *Peaceable Resolution, Epistle.*   [22] *Peaceable Resolution*, p. 8.
[23] *Ibid.*, pp. 16, 20–24.   [24] *Ibid.*, p. 29.
[25] *Ibid.*, pp. 31, 41–43, 70.   [26] *Ibid.*, pp. 44–45, 65; cf. p. 38.
[27] *Ibid.*, p. 47; *real* majesty is no threat to annointed kings, p. 44.   [28] *Ibid.*, p. 47.

in its most potent guise; for the chapter concludes, if the people irrevocably give power to the monarch, 'who can have a word to say for Resistance, Non-Subjection or Rebellion?'[29] Humfrey seems to be strewing the way for a rehabilitation of Lawson amongst the pantheon of establishment divines.

Humfrey proceeds to renegotiate the question of whether the people, generally speaking, can take power away from *personal* majesty. Power, he concedes, may be forfeit, but this is moral forfeiture not political and 'subjects as subjects' cannot call majesty to account. This is clearly half Lawsonian, but significantly there is no mention of the community as a citizen body, or even a mention of the term citizen. The community may take power, but this does not mean taking up arms against the king. Calling *personal* sovereignty to account, Humfrey assures us, is in any case something that never need be done, but one wonders, in the absence of a clear vocabulary of community action, how it can be done.[30] The terminological gap in what is both a redaction and application of Lawson's nomenclature is telling. It is the price of rehabilitation through cautious use. Yet, government may be dissolved. Citing Lawson again, Humfrey refers to England as a mixed monarchy or free state, whose *personal* sovereign is a tripartite moral person. If the king and the two houses give up their power, the government is dissolved and then 'the people are turned into a community'.[31] Manifestly this is not a theory of resistance and the little Humfrey says on the topic is kept clear of dissolution and is associated not with Lawson but with the established authority of Bishop Bilson and Richard Hooker. Resistance is reduced almost to a form of petitioning. Thus, in extremity, the people 'may plead their right against the Prince and not be charged with rebellion'. And, he remarks with a deft inversion of the vocabulary, in renouncing resistance, one does not renounce subjection to the ordinance of God.[32]

In all of this, we can see an explicit Lawsonian thesis and nomenclature being etched to map a narrow path between obedience to God and to man. To some extent Humfrey does retain some of the *Politica*'s ambivalence, but, on the whole, he manages to fashion a more passive and exclusively settlement Lawson than will later appear, a Lawson whose respectability does seem to need establishing. The adaptation is effected in two ways.

---

[29] *Ibid.*, p. 53.

[30] *Ibid.*, p. 59. The reading is like Ashcraft's dismissive reduction of Lawson, *Revolutionary Politics and Locke's Two Treatises of Government*, Princeton University Press, 1986, pp. 310–11. This is ironic as Humfrey was promoting Lawson and Humfrey himself is pantheonised by Ashcraft as a 'radical'.

[31] *Peaceable Resolution*, pp. 75, 79, reiterating that this notion does the King no harm.

[32] *Ibid.*, pp. 111, 136.

First, but for a single passing mention of *eminenter cives*, the word citizen disappears under the less discriminate notion of the 'people', who are almost always seen as subjects, a terminological compression of the sort that we will find Locke employing when the *Two Treatises* are finally published, though exploited to a very different end. Secondly, the people *qua* community ceases to be coextensive with the polity. The shift is, as it were, from a layered notion of community and polity in the *Politica*, to a linear projection, which greatly eases the tensions created by Lawson's text. So a question of loyalty is converted into an assurance. This is a distortion, a creative adaptation, but it is a subtle one, and it is no more distorting than the appropriation of Lawson to the cause of resistance.

Pausing before the Allegiance Controversy and its aftermath, one may hypothesise, tentatively, that Lawson's ecclesiology maintained a relevance for a man such as Humfrey who widened his arguments to embrace and confront the more secular context of church government so that a reading of Lawson's theory of sovereignty became important. But, to repeat, the appeal to the Lawsonian community as prior to political form and as a receptacle for dissolved political power is distinct from any appeal to a right to settlement. Humfrey's pre-Revolution Lawson was a Restoration man. Indeed, insofar as Humfrey relied on Lawson's *Politica*, it may well have been precisely because it facilitated an avoidance of the touchy subject of resistance without falling into the embrace of absolute subjection. The most trivial flirtation with resistance could be read as part of a Machiavellian, and/or Jesuitical preparation for rebellion, as Humfrey well knew; and theological qualms about absolute subjection were flirtatious enough.[33]

Yet if Humfrey found the *Politica* so useful, why is he so coy in citation? The reason may lie in the standard strategy of authority citation mentioned earlier; that is, in the citation of authors assumed emblematic of one's opponents' position in order to placate or establish credentials. If this is so, it might indicate that Lawson was regarded with suspicion within his own church. This seems borne out by the *Peaceable Resolution of Conscience*, dedicated to young and open minds, associating Lawson with the Restoration and suggesting a cautious use of him. Later Baxter was to reveal important grounds for suspicion of Lawson's *Politica* when he remembered the conceptual consequences of Lawson's distinction between subject and citizen, a distinction which Humfrey so noticeably avoids. Moreover, if Ward's early sermon is indicative, the insecure enthusiasm of the new *status quo* might well have smelt a euphemistic rat in the notions of dissolution

---

[33] John Nalson, *The Countermine*, 1677, at length and p. 313; and *The Common Interest of the King and the People*, 1678, chaps. 8–10; Edward Stillingfleet, *The Mischief of Separation*, 1681.

and failure of government and of the capacity of the community or its *valentior pars* to resettle, a fear of which Humfrey, too, seems well aware.[34]

That one might use such terms only hypothetically, or use them to provide an *ex post facto* account of events rather than as justifications for future action, would hardly be safe enough; their very currency could destabilise a fiduciary issue allegedly dependent upon the standard of the king. Once a settlement had been achieved, the stress on contingency and negotiability of political form, far from being encouraging, could begin to take on an ominous tone, especially with a notion of community integral to the vocabulary of explanation. So ideas can change even in reiteration, and regardless of an original author's intentions. It is this that has been overlooked, or simplified in the reification of ideas and dispositions in intellectual history. Lawson's materials may have been 'radical', his use of them to answer the problems of 1659–60 was not. It is this which we see Humfrey so deftly exploiting in 1680. But Lawson's precepts retained a 'radical' potential when placed in a different political climate; and in another context as we shall see they could be used again to avoid the seventeenth-century equivalents of that now edifying label. Thus in arguing that the church was political, a human form imposed upon the matter of a Christian community, Humfrey (like Lawson) was making a point about adaptability and human ingenuity which might lead to substantial comprehension; but it may have seemed discreet largely to leave out Lawson's name or simply unnecessary to include it.[35] But after 1689, when a new edition of the *Politica* was a new statement of political relevance, Humfrey, operating in a more open and creative environment, begins to deploy the name more fully where he believes it to be worthy of respect. Others use Lawson's categories to redefine past events and it is not until quite late that the *Politica* is made to offer 'radical' solutions to future possibilities.

[34] This of course is a very hypothetical argument from silence, or indolent inductivism. I have not found reference to Lawson in the high church and absolutist materials I have read for the period. See, e.g., the otherwise compendious Nathaniel Johnstone, *The Excellency of Monarchical Government*, 1686, and the intelligent Sir George Mackenzie, *Ius regium*, who systematically attacks much under the heading of resistance theory in terms similar to those Lawson uses against the same range of thinkers, p. 79; but he shows no awareness of Lawson's alternative to absolutist conclusions, except to say that forfeiture of power is its evaporation, pp. 80–3.

[35] This is not to imply that Lawson would have been congenial only to non-conformists. The thrust of Humfrey's arguments directed towards comprehension was in principle much at one with the latitudinarians with whom he fought and who certainly sound, in their later phases, like Lawson. See e.g. John Gascoigne, 'Anglican Latitudinarianism and Political Radicalism in the Late Eighteenth Century', *History*, 71 (1986), pp. 22ff.; John Marshall, 'The Ecclesiology of the Latitude Men, 1660–1689: Stillingfleet, Tillotson and Hobbism', *Journal of Ecclesiastical History*, 36, 3 (1985), pp. 407ff., who might well have discussed Lawson in this context. By the period of latitudinarian ascendancy Lawson's views seem to be too widely disseminated and alternatively encapsulated. Even Hoadly provides nothing more than a general blurred echo of what might have been Lawson.

13

The 'Politica' and the Allegiance Controversy

In 1689 some nineteen works were reprinted from earlier times. Buchanan's *De iure* and the *Vindiciae contra tyranos* reappeared from the sixteenth century; five works originally printed in the period of the Monmouth Rebellion set a precedent for Locke's *Two Treatises*; Hunton's *Treatise of Monarchy* was reprinted twice; works by Ascham and Milton from 1649 reappeared together with ones by Sancroft, Sexby and Hammond from 1657. But from the largest print year of them all, only Lawson's *Politica* reappeared in a new quarto format.[1]

All these works had a role somewhat different from the bulk of materials directly generated by the controversy. Obviously the most immediate question of the controversy concerned allegiance to the new regime. Answering this, however, depended largely on the prior characterisation of the various royal comings and goings; and indeed even on the question of who had acted, with God always lurking off-stage left or right (delete according to political prejudice). Any specification of events more informative than exit pursued by an Orange carried with it a range of ethical and political injunctions and pre-empted answers to those immediate questions of allegiance, legitimacy and settlement, which have attracted so much attention.[2] It was largely the predication of events that divides the literature of allegiance, and the older, republished works are important because they helped provide conceptual frameworks through which the very recent past could be assimilated in a way appropriate to one's cause.

---

[1] See Mark Goldie's invaluable study, 'The Revolution of 1689 and the Structure of Political Argument', *Bulletin of Research in the Humanities*, 83 (1980), table 6, pp. 522–3.

[2] This frivolous description would no doubt have been deemed atheistic. A marginal gloss to Tyrrell's *Patriarcha non Monarcha*, 1681 (Folger Library) by Francis Gibbon (?) makes the point that should James return, 1688 as well as 1642 and 1649 will be redefined as rebellions, p. 197. See Stephan Zwicker, *Politics and Language in the Age of Dryden*, Princeton University Press, 1984, chap. 3 for some perceptive emphasis on the sensitivity in language choice by contemporaries, but also for the belief that there was a real character of events that could be established independently of words, p. 31. See also R. J. Smith, *The Gothic Bequest*, Cambridge University Press, 1987, p. 14.

In an important political sense, then, the events of the Glorious Revolution as significant happenings were only fully created through the language of predicative apologetics. They were problematic insofar as the language used was unable to accommodate the happenings in an intelligible and uniformly acceptable manner, an obvious point perhaps; but putting it in this way enables us to see more clearly that if the grounds and extent of allegiance were as diverse as the descriptions of events, then these too were as diverse as the structure of language allowed. What the language allowed however was a moot point; the inherited fields of terms and their patterns of articulation were neither entirely stable or controllable. What is fixed in print now is but the residue of active manipulation. Any predication of events might be to some extent satisfactory; but it might also carry unwanted connotations, inconvenient echoes and associations, unpalatable consequences. Determining what had happened was vital for contemporaries, but it does not directly help us understand the surviving political literature, all of which was a partial prisoner of the cracked and straining currency of previous dispute, to which the nineteen reprinted works testify.

In a very general way there is much in the Allegiance Controversy literature that might have come from Lawson, or for which he could have provided corroboration and precedent. Theories of abstract right which have been associated with the 'radical' Whigs, and arguments from history associated with the more 'moderate' ones, are both found in Lawson. It is possible, too, as Goldie suggests, that the terminology of trust is Lawsonian in origin.[3]

More specifically, however, the *Politica* helped to add to what Goldie, following Hickes, has specified as the six or seven hypotheses around which controversy was organised.[4] Amongst these are two main resistance variants, one wedded to contract, the other to emergency. These cohabited well, for breach of contract could easily have been subsumed under extremity. Together these must have had considerable initial appeal. If resistance was legitimate, it was easy to specify recent upheavals accordingly. Perhaps to the modern mind the notion that resistance *in extremis* had taken place may well seem to be the most natural specification of events. But although Goldie estimates that about half the number of pamphlets accepted in principle a right to resist, yet of these 'little more than half conceded that resistance had actually occurred'. This 'backsliding' towards 'moderation' and the generally poor representation of 'radical' accounts of the Revolution is strik-

---

[3] Goldie, 'The Revolution of 1689', p. 486; but see also Ponet, *A Short Treatise of Politick Power*, *A Declaration of the General Council of the Officers of the Army*, 1659; Henry Stubbe, *A Letter to an Officer in the Army*, London, 1659; Anon., *Parliament's Plea*, 1659. All these predate the *Politica* and refer to trust without contract.

[4] Goldie, 'The Revolution of 1689', p. 486, citing George Hickes, *An Apology for the New Separation*, 1691, pp. 12–13.

ing, and Goldie is right to emphasise it.[5] Modern dispositional labels, however, may get in the way of an explanation here.

What we do see is a sense of rhetorical vulnerability. As I have indicated, the concept of resistance was difficult to disengage from that of rebellion. In the seventeenth century almost no-one attempted to justify rebellion, hence the staple elision of royalist polemics. The two terms constituted what I have elsewhere called a rhetorical compound,[6] and what Lawson provided was a circumnavigation of this dangerous dyad.

To repeat, as subjection and sovereignty are 'relates', if there is no sovereign there can be no subject status. Rebellion and resistance are both terms whose meaning is predicated on prior subjection. Thus if the whole form of government is dissolved, or more generally has failed, then this sub-set of the political vocabulary has to be placed on one side until it is resettled.[7] Expressed in these broad terms, Lawson was not alone in providing avoidance of the resistance *topos*.[8] But whether the specification of events in terms of dissolution avoided or became a refinement of resistance or even, through a domino effect, a euphemism for it depended greatly on the dissolutionary trigger. Manifestly, if it takes a rising to dissolve a government, dissolution entails resistance and so a notion of dissolution may do little to dispel the odium of rebellion. Revolution could be, in Tyrrell's expression (*Biblioteca Politica*), 'a softly worded rebellion'. However, such efficient causes of dissolution are hardly touched on by Lawson, they are mentioned only in passing or are dematerialised through the consequences of definitional exactitude; and they are beyond the purview of the overtly Lawsonian Humfrey of 1680. The *Politica* was well suited to act as a wedge between dissolution and resistance. The corporate nature both of personal majesty and the community meant that his notion of dissolution, or the more encompassing failure, did not mean also the complete collapse of society and its traumatic reconstruction *de novo* – an important point precisely because nothing like that had happened in 1688. Neither in Lawson's eyes did dissolution require any formal 'resistance' first. It could occur through technical blunder within the realm of *personal* majesty, and had some of its traumatic force diminished by being one of many forms of govern-

---

[5] Goldie, 'The Revolution of 1689', p. 489.
[6] 'The Quest for a Concept of "Needs"', in *Human Needs and Politics*, ed. Ross Fitzgerald, Pergamon, Oxford and Sydney, 1977, pp. 244ff.
[7] Thus Goldie misreads the relationship between dissolution and resistance by seeing them as logical adjuncts, 'The Roots of True Whiggism', *History of Political Thought*, 1 (1980), p. 211, such a reading would have pleased a non-juror such as Hickes, whose *Apology* does not specify a distinctive dissolution hypothesis. The absence of such an hypothesis makes the assimilation of rebellion and resistance that much easier.
[8] See e.g. H. Grotius, *De jure belli ac pacis libri tres*, trans. F. W. Kelsey, Clarendon Press, Oxford, 1913, 1925, 1.4.9 and especially Pufendorf, *De jure*, trans. C. H. and W. A. Oldfather, Clarendon Press, Oxford, 1934, 7.8.4.

mental failure. This Lawson had illustrated with reference to English circumstances: Charles I had technically dissolved the constitution by acting as if he were an independent part, or the totality of a corporate *personal* majesty. As such, *personal* majesty had to act as one civil person and was, by being made up of many men, somewhat vulnerable to dissolution. Thereafter, subject status itself and thus rebellion and resistance as possible descriptive terms were alike irrelevant. Community and fidelity to it was the only thing to hold to. This compression of Lawson's argument indicates how close he was to the circular evaporation of the very possibility of resistance. As I have suggested, such a nominal vaporising is, on occasion, intimated and, ironically, could read as a mere euphemism for resistance.

The possibility of a purely verbal avoidance of resistance, and hence the collapse of a distinctive dissolution hypothesis, was to be more fully realised in the course of the work of the constitutional historian William Atwood (d. 1705?), *The Fundamental Constitution*, in Tyrrell's *Brief Enquiry*, and in the second of Locke's *Two Treatises*. Politically we know where we stand with these men, but Lawson's *Politica* remains a different and protean matter, for there is a good deal in the text that, in addition to offering a distinct dissolution theory, stands in the way of any simple appropriation to a resistance cause, not least the balance of citizen's rights with subject's duties. Creative interpretations were needed in 1689, as they had been for Humfrey in 1680, if Lawson were to be neatly tied to a cause. The second edition is revealed as part of such a process of indenture through one crucial departure from the original text. Appended to a passage discussing the rights of the people as citizens a marginal gloss provides the abridgement 'subjects may defend their rights' (*Pol.* 93). It is both a blatant contradiction of everything Lawson says about subjects and a brute contraction of his fastidiously maintained conceptual vocabulary. Lawson's *Politica*, then, carries an explicit dissolution theory appropriate to 1689, but its publication – with a one-word marginal amendment – helps prepare the ground for Lawson's assimilation to a resistance cause, or for use in an ambivalent and obfuscating mix of resistance and dissolution arguments.

The events of 1688–9 had provided in Sir Bartholemew Shower's expression an 'agony of Wonder'.[9] Whatever else could be said of them, the ease, speed and bloodless nature of the changes instigated by a minority claiming to act for a larger whole must have given a tempting plausibility to the somewhat Lawsonian theory of dissolution and settlement. Here at last, Humfrey, a Presbyterian and thus by definition a rebel in the eyes of men like Nalson, becomes helpfully specific. The *Politica* surfaces and, by a twist of textual fate, Humfrey's own identity is run together with others.

[9] Sir Bartholemew Shower, *Reasons for a New Bill of Rights*, 1692.

Lawson is the flux. Using Humfrey's works as far as possible as a thread and using Lawson to help identify them, we pass into a labyrinth of anonymous tracts of similar titles and often interchangeable arguments.

Good Advice Before It Is Too Late has been attributed both to Humfrey and to that remarkably fly politician John Wildman (1621–93).[10] The Lawsonian theme running through the tract would seem strongly to support the attribution to Humfrey. In now standard fashion the author distinguishes subject from sovereign, and administration from constitution, and asserts that prior to the introduction of an administrative form there is only a community in which there is no order of superiority and inferiority. Only with the introduction of a rule is a notion of ruler and ruled also introduced; and whatever powers the people reserve to themselves are their rights. England had a mixed government in a corporate form which is now dissolved.[11] Under these circumstances, then, the author concludes, we have the greatest chance to settle the religion of the nation to ensure there is no popery. A convention must therefore be called for a parliament *per se* cannot settle the nation, for it represents the people only where there is a commonwealth, not as members of a community. If the people do not take the opportunity before them, they will deserve the opprobrium of later ages.[12] Much of this argument and its phrases, the hortatory tone, and the specification of the present open-ended situation in terms of the dissolution of government, is to be found in *Proposals to the Present Convention*, which I also take to be by Humfrey; both tracts are consistent with works appearing under his name once the new regime was fully established.[13]

In *Good Advice*, however, Humfrey at least appears to be flirting with the possibility of a republic (hence the Wildman entanglement), whereas in later works he has fully accepted the Williamite regime. Moreover, in them he writes of forfeiture rather than dissolution and of the more archaic and ambiguous escheatment, and of *personal* majesty ceasing and descending 'into that our politics call *real*'.[14]

These differences do not I think undermine the case for Humfrey's authorship of *Good Advice* and *Proposals to the Present Convention*. They may

---

[10] *Good Advice Before It Is Too Late*, *Somers Tracts*, 8, 1688. For the controversies concerning authorship see Goldie, 'The Roots of True Whiggism', pp. 212–13 and n. 62.

[11] *Good Advice*, esp. pp. 21–3.

[12] *Ibid.*, p. 24. J. W. Gough, *The Fundamental Law in English Constitutional Thought*, Oxford University Press, 1955, p. 121, notes Lawson's remarkable anticipation of the Revolution's Convention Parliament. It might be nearer the truth to say that the use of his theories helped shape its significance.

[13] *Proposals to the Present Convention for the Perpetual Security of the Protestant Religion ...*, *Somers tracts*, 8, 1689, pp. 33ff; *The Free State of the People Maintained*, 1702; *A Plain ... Determination of the Late Controversy*.

[14] *A Plain ... Determination*, p. 4; *The Free State*, p. 10; the quotation is from *A Plain ... Determination*, p. 10.

reflect only changed circumstances, flexible though associated terminology, and the introduction of more than seems Lawsonian. The linking text may be another hitherto not associated with Humfrey, printed about the same time as the above, and which provides some of the best evidence of Lawson's significance in the later seventeenth century.

Proposals Humbly Offered to the Lords[15] stylistically sounds like Humfrey and parades in the same order and argumentative context writers associated with his opponents in *The Free State of The People Maintained*. In both texts it is noted that even Barclay, Grotius and Arnisaeus, amongst the most eminent who have argued against resistance, accept it in extremity, and these are names to which Humfrey had earlier appealed in just this way in his *Peaceable Design*.[16]

Proposals has rightly been called a précis of the *Politica* by one who knew the work well:[17] all power is from God directly or indirectly via the community. There is no orderly government without express or tacit consent. Even conquest makes way for government by consent. The supreme power in every community is inseparable from it and this can form any mode of government, supply any defects and reform abuses. This power is called *real*, that of administration is *personal*. In England the latter is by king, lords, and commons and there are three ways in which it might fail: dissolution, forfeiture (through alienation) or desertion. Those communities are best which bring themselves back to first principles (alluding to Machiavelli)[18] and this self-evident truth implies the right to renew '... and the most ingenious Mr. Lawson observes in his *Politica* that the community of England in the late times, had the greatest advantage that they or their ancestors had had for many ages, for this purpose; though God hid it from their eyes'.[19] The phrasing is strikingly similar to that found in the peroration to *Good Advice*.[20] Immediately, however, the author continues, other ways of settling the nation have too many disadvantages. What in fact he lists are other ways of *describing* what has happened.

Thus, he writes, we cannot say that the king is dead. Instead we must conclude that the community alone has the right to take advantage of governmental failure, the Houses of Parliament *per se* being unable to 'justify

---

[15] *Proposals Humbly Offered*, Somers Tracts, 8, 1688; cf. *Some Short Considerations Humbly Offered*, State Tracts, 1, 1705, pp. 175–8.
[16] *The Free State*, p. 5; *Proposals*, p. 3; *The Peaceable Design*, pp. 44ff.
[17] Julian Franklin, *John Locke and the Theory of Sovereignty*, Cambridge University Press, 1978, pp. 100–1.
[18] *Proposals*, pp. 2–4.   [19] *Ibid.*, p. 4 – he observes nothing of the sort.
[20] *Good Advice*, pp. 23–4.

themselves'. We must act to exclude popish successors, and, as the world agrees William is a great King, let us acclaim him.[21]

Despite the strong family resemblance this work has to others putatively or certainly by Humfrey, it has been put to one side by modern scholars who have found no clear place for it in the allegiance literature. It provides a fairly activist reading of Lawson, but it seems it is not sufficiently 'radical' to be associated with Humfrey, or Wildman, or perhaps to be Lawsonian; and Goldie seems to distance himself from Franklin's claim that the tract really is Lawsonian.[22]

Again, however, the notion of 'radical' may be getting in the way. There is no reason why Humfrey, never one to leave a good furrow untrodden, should not have adjusted the bite of his plough as circumstances and/or perhaps audience demanded. The important point about this tract is that the specific thesis of dissolution as a descriptive option or a 'technical' possibility[23] has been subsumed under the more general Lawsonian conceptual framework of governmental failure, merged into dissolution in a broad sense. The author places before us a range of alternative routes to the one conclusion that there is now no *personal* majesty, only a residual communal power to settle form once again. Any route to this conclusion (dissolution, forfeiture, alienation, demise, desertion, act of God) would have the same effect of rendering subjection beside the immediate point and of giving authority to extraordinary proceedings. This underlines the close connection between the specification of the past and overt political injunction. If we persist with the terminology of radical and moderate, we cannot simply count 'radicals' as a stable group identified by levelling proposals, republicanism and the right to resist. Some clearly saw the dissolution hypothesis as euphemistically disguising resistance, that is (as they saw it) rebellion.

As one author was shortly to argue, if we remember the maxim that the king never dies, dissolution does not fit the recent facts; and if there has been no dissolution, then the people still owe James allegiance as his subjects. It is, moreover, under the cloak of dissolution that some have tried to foist their own new models of governmental form upon us.[24] Another writer calls the dissolution thesis ridiculous and dangerous; but for the physical absence of the king, things go on as before. If there has been a dissolution, then we are back in a state of nature and this raises

---

[21] *Proposals*, pp. 4–5; *Contra* e.g. Anon., *A Word to the Wise*, which argues that power has reverted to Lords and Commons.

[22] Franklin, *John Locke*, p. 101; Goldie, 'The Roots', p. 215.

[23] Franklin, *John Locke*, p. 100.

[24] *Reflections on our Late and Present Proceedings in England*, Somers Tracts, 10, 1689, pp. 7–9.

the spectre of levelling.[25] Instructively, the immediate answers to these anti-dissolution tracts change the terms of debate.[26]

Humfrey was always sensitive to the possible accusation of rebellion, and true to his early writings had not been an advocate of resistance theory; but he had embraced a dissolution theory, and may have felt at some stage exposed and forced to the more thoroughly abstract and Lawsonian position articulated in *Proposals Humbly Offered*. Certainly the spectre of a Hobbesian state of nature is irrelevant if one postulates a Lawsonian community, in which there is equally no hint of levelling. The notion of a failure of *personal* majesty encompasses a range of more specific and immediately vulnerable descriptions of past events in a way that seems intended to bring together a diversity of people sharing a hostility to a Catholic succession. 'Radical' or not, the force of the *Proposals* is at one with the *Politica* itself and with the cause for which Humfrey fought. We can see further signs of this generally amphibolous and accommodating strategy in Humfrey's *Plain ... Determination* and his *Letter to a Parliament Man*. In these he uses the same elision as Lawson does in the *Politica* between free state and mixed monarchy, and I suspect it is to the same end of adjusting quasi-republican emblems to the realities of a new monarchy.[27]

At the risk of undue repetition, and in order to keep some bearings, it is possible to draw the following interim and tentative conclusions. Humfrey, for a good while familiar with Lawson, found his secular as well as his ecclesiological arguments valuable after 1688. Initially he used a specific formulation of a dissolution of government and the reversion of power to the community in order to avoid resistance arguments. He moved, however, to a more abstract and all-encompassing formulation, possibly in response to the sort of attack that could associate dissolution theory with resistance and levelling. In making the move he evoked Lawson systematically as one who provided a specification of recent changes acceptable to all who opposed catholicism. The chronology is very cramped, so there may be no linear direction of movement. Men writing quickly under the pressure of events may easily shift between variants of a more general position. But in either case, we can also say that Humfrey was much more active and sensitive to changing circumstances than has previously been thought and that he was largely responsible for the immediate promotion of Lawson's name and conceptual armoury. After the *Proposals Humbly Offered*, no one needed to have read Lawson to sound like him. As a postscript to Humfrey's efforts, one can note that once secular settlement had been achieved, he returned to his concern with the establishment of a suf-

---

[25] *A Letter to a Member of the Convention*, *Somers Tracts*, 7, pp. 21, 26.
[26] *Ibid.*, pp. 27–9.   [27] *A Plain ... Determination*, pp. 4–5; *A Letter*, p. 12.

ficiently comprehensive ecclesiastical one. In doing so, the man who had
used Lawson to defend Baxter, now used him to attack Baxter's late conception of a national church. In *Union Pursued* he presents a very Lawsonian
vision of a national church, seeming to digest and take phrases directly
from the *Politica*. Thus, 'a community is but the matter disposed for the
receiving of a form of government' and the power of a church is of 'a narrow
scantling'.[28] The conceptual parallels are direct and persistent, whilst the
names he cites could come directly from the *Politica*. It is recommended
that Baxter read Lawson on the notion of a national church, 'he hath many
clear things to say upon it, as a man of exceeding skill in that study'.[29]
Baxter hardly needed an introduction to Lawson, and it is unlikely that
Humfrey is under any illusions; but that is often the point of citation. The
names cited are those an author expects the audience to respect. As Lawson
was a common bond he emerges in *Union Pursued* as something of a non-
conformist authority.

Whether or not I have attributed too busy a pen to Humfrey in these
years and rationalised a fugitive chronology, the vital point is that someone
disseminated and simplified Lawson's *Politica* and Humfrey does cite him
and rely on him after 1689 in a way he did not before. The very circulation
of Lawson's views and precepts, however, makes the use of him in any
clinching sense more difficult to detect: and the rationalised vision of the
Politica merges it with its activist inheritance. Lack of clear evidence may
be a sign of widespread and adaptive familiarity. Leaving aside Humfrey,
there is a good deal to suggest the *Politica*'s importance before it fades
in the shadows of Defoe and Locke.

Goldie suggests that tracts by Wildman and Edward Stephens adopted
a Lawsonian line which was also at one with the arguments of Locke. Convincingly he attributes *Some Remarks Upon Government* to Wildman.[30]
This does have some Lawsonian touches and one or two phrases reminiscent
of him, but these are neither telling nor significant in the overall structure
of the work.[31] As Goldie emphasises, the work is above all a striking blend
of contract theory and well digested Harrington. It focuses clearly on institutional arrangements, most notably the need for parliamentary reform and

---

[28] *Union Pursued*, 1691, in *Ecclesiastical Tracts*, 1691, pp. 2, 35; see also *A Draft*, 1705,
though it is not as explicit.

[29] *Ibid.*, p. 25; see also *Of Subjection to King George*, 1714, a valedictory echo and resumé
of *A Peaceable Resolution*.

[30] Goldie, 'The Roots', pp. 212–14; *Some Remarks Upon Government*, *State Tracts*, 1,
pp. 149ff.

[31] For example, that property is founded on dominion, p. 155, cf. *Pol.* 1; that on the dissolution
of governmental power there is a reversion to the people, p. 161. But see also Grotius,
De jure, 1.3; the striking similarity of phrasing with *Good Advice*, p. 25; that the people
are not made for kings, was a well-known tag, used by Sidney and by Pufendorf, *De jure*,
7.6.6.

the political role of judges. It rehearses Harringtonian notions of causation and climatic theories of government, all of which seem to be attached to a Leveller inheritance. This all sounds most unlike Humfrey, so to confirm Goldie's identification, if Wildman wrote *Some Remarks* it is unlikely that he wrote *Good Advice* or any of the more Lawsonian tracts I have associated with Humfrey. With respect to *A Letter to a Friend*, Goldie's Scottish verdict should also be entered. It shares with *Some Remarks* an emphasis on institutional reform and the importance of the judiciary.[32] It uses 'property' for the older 'propriety' which Humfrey characteristically favoured. On the other hand, the overall theoretical shape is Lawsonian rather than Harringtonian. The principal task of the great men of the Convention we are told, is the protection of liberties and property; without due care, the crown could end up in the hands of Catholics yet. The great question for all to consider is whether there has been a dissolution of governmental form.[33] If so, then the power is with the people, who can set up any form they wish. The distinction between administration and constitution is made, and after claiming ignorance of politics, the author reasserts that power must have reverted to the people, now that the corporate form of the old government is broken. The people must therefore set up a convention, not a parliament, which must be seen as accountable only to God – a somewhat extreme formulation of Lawson's notion of the relationship between God and community.[34] In several respects, then, this too could be an early allegiance tract by Humfrey, but one cannot discount either that it is the result of the compromises of collaboration, or that it is the handywork of an unknown party.

Stephens's *Four Questions Debated* arrives at a broadly Lawsonian conclusion through an argument that James had subverted the constitution – a shepherd turned wolf. With proper government thus destroyed, the power of settling the government must have reverted to the people who can choose representatives to settle the exercise of government.[35] If this is dependent upon Lawson, it is perhaps reminiscent of the more activist *Examination* rather than the *Politica*. Another putatively Lawsonian piece may also have relied on the *Examination*, or wedded contract theory to the *Politica*.[36]

---

[32] *A Letter to a Friend*, Somers Tracts, 6, 1688–9, p. 15; Goldie, 'The Roots', p. 212 for a possible attribution to Wildman.

[33] *Letter*, pp. 13–14.

[34] *Ibid.*, p. 15.

[35] John Stephens, *Four Questions Debated*, State Tracts, 1, 1705, p. 155, 6; Pufendorf, *De jure*, 7.8.4, for another working of the shepherd/wolf *topos*, presumably out of Plato, *Republic*, Bk. 1 and for a definitional manoeuvre similar to that in *Four Questions*.

[36] *A Discourse Concerning the Nature Power and Proper Effects of the Present Convention*, State Tracts, 1705, 1.

There are two contracts, one in which a people become a community and another in which they agree to become subjects. The second (rectoral) contract does not invalidate the first, thus subjects remain in some degree citizens, who retain a *share* in the government.[37] The present Convention Parliament, it is argued, consists of representatives of the community prior to the rectoral contract, thus they must be seen as citizens not subjects. Although in some respects the terminology is not Lawsonian, conceptually there remains a family resemblance, and indeed it focuses as other tracts have not on the bifold nature of Lawson's subject/citizen.[38] In this respect the work finishes on a strongly Lawsonian note. Given that we can be seen as subjects or as citizens, then the crucial thing is to know under which conception the Convention is meeting. It is an appeal to classify discriminately and think clearly.[39] A similar dichotomy is set up in *A Word to the Approaching Parliament*. What happens, it is asked, if a monarch goes beyond the laws of monarchy? If persuasion fails, should there be submission or resistance – should the people cease to act as subjects when sovereigns cease to act as sovereigns?[40] The quandary arising from an awareness of such duplexity, however, is resolved in a simple way uncharacteristic of Lawson and indicative of a shift away from nominal definitions. The answer is to obey. The question as raised could however have been resolved in favour of resistance and it would have been no more or less Lawsonian for that. Perhaps the resolution in either way is the really non-Lawsonian move. This indicates just how easy it would have been to have used Lawson as an authority for resistance; the lines between dissolution, governmental failure, settlement, and resistance remain thin.

That dissolution and failure theories could run into the dangerous embrace of resistance theory and carry Lawson with them is well illustrated by two of the most interesting and substantial tracts of the time. In *A Friendly Debate*, Dr. Kingsman, a dissatisfied clergyman, questions the very idea of giving thanks for the descent of William into England. His neighbour, Gratianus Trimmer, is compensatingly delighted.[41] The two men share common ground in condemning rebellion and disliking catholicism. Kingsman, however, holds that there is still strict allegiance due to James and that

---

[37] *Ibid.*, pp. 218–9.

[38] *Ibid.*, p. 220; *A Discourse*, however, has 'commonwealth' for the Lawsonian community and it *shares* in government.

[39] *Ibid.*, p. 224. See also, *The Late Honourable Convention Proved a Parliament*, State Tracts, 1692, p. 457, which, but for the equation of Parliament and Convention, also seems like Lawson in its use of the vocabulary of failure and corporate governmental form.

[40] *A Word to the Approaching Parliament*, Somers Tracts, 1689, pp. 4–5.

[41] *A Friendly Debate Between Dr. Kingsman and . . . A Neighbouring Minister*, 1689.

those who think otherwise are disloyal and rebellious. Subject status is irrevocable so there is no difference between rebellion and resistance.[42] Trimmer holds that there is no allegiance due to James and the grounds for the thanksgiving are proper. Trimmer dominates the debate producing an array of arguments and authorities to confront Kingsman's bedrock and reiterated case that the Christian duty even in the face of a monarch like James is to obey or suffer – the only recourse being 'petitions, Prayers, Patience, Tears'.[43] Lawson emerges as a major spokesman in Trimmer's case being cited as 'judicious', 'learned', 'a good Civilian and politician', his arguments being called 'concise' and 'rational'.[44] The *Politica* underlies much of the text and it is quoted on four occasions,[45] it is acknowledged and summarised, and its terminology variously alluded to.[46]

The themes most explicitly formulated with reference to Lawson's work concern loyalty, community, *real* and *personal* majesty, and the relationship between subject and sovereign. Lawson's hierarchy of loyalty is quoted to support the notion that loyalty to James was less important than that owed to God and to community.[47] Lawson's conception of community is summarised to affirm that communities as such are not subjects; later to suggest that the community houses *real* majesty and that only a convention of the representatives of the community can properly settle the governmental form.[48] *Real* majesty is seen as a framing authority for the operation of *personal* majesty; in the case of England, *personal* majesty is held to be a corporation. Mixed monarchy is agreed by both men to be 'absurd'.[49] Subject and sovereign are seen as relational terms: 'If one term of the relation be changed or ceased, the obligation of the other relate and Correlate ceaseth'.[50]

These Lawsonian materials are used to organise a picture of recent events which is turned against the hapless Kingsman in two ways. For the most part Lawson is made to play his part in a theory which justifies resistance *in extremis*. James had flouted the fundamental laws of the constitution and the religion of the people; tears and petitions had got nowhere, resistance was a final recourse in order that higher loyalties might be maintained. But in the face of Kingsman's dogged insistence that there is no justifi-

---

[42] *A Friendly Debate*, e.g. p. 6. It is characteristic of Dr Kingsman to elide rebellion, resistance and rising up against a sovereign.
[43] *Ibid.*, p. 8.   [44] *Ibid.*, pp. 25, 16, 24–6.
[45] *Ibid.*, pp. 16, 27, 69, 73.   [46] *Ibid.*, e.g., pp. 38, 62, 70, 72.
[47] *Ibid.*, pp. 24–5, cf. pp. 2–3.   [48] *Ibid.*, pp. 38, 39, 72.
[49] *Ibid.*, pp. 23.   [50] *Ibid.*, p. 21, cf. pp. 6–7.

cation for subjects rising up against their sovereigns, Trimmer also uses a dissolution argument. He applies a doctrine of office reliant upon a very clear separation between James Stuart and King James, which is used in conjunction with Lawson's definitional fastidiousness to bypass resistance rather than (as with Overton) to justify it. If subject and sovereign are relates, then the dissolution of one concept destroys the other. James 'altered the government in his own personal Dignity, so he manifestly destroyes the other part of the Constitution'. The subject is thus discharged from subject status for, 'I am subject to the King and not to him who is no King.'[51] And again, subjects do not break the bounds of subjection when acting for their preservation.[52] In this deployment of themes from Lawson, Trimmer enlarges on the shepherd-turned-wolf image of the king's two bodies in a way that capitalises on dissolution to deflect the charge of rebellion. Overall, this conjures up from Lawson's words a more uniformly activist *Politica* than Lawson wrote; for another strand of Lawson might have regarded Trimmer's doctrine of office being a case of men being entrapped 'in their own curious distinctions' (*Pol.* 373). The wavering line between resistance and dissolution results in an air of uncertainty in a text that backs off from the embrace of resistance despite its obvious appeal.

A little after the *Friendly Debate*, William Atwood's *The Fundamental Constitution of the English Government* appeared.[53] It argues both from the abstract political principles of natural law and from the details of English history. The conclusions drawn are that legitimate government is bounded by fundamental laws and a breach of these laws by a monarch means the cessation of the subject's obligation. Government in general, and in England in particular, is a trust based upon contract. Drawing loosely on continental public and international law theorists Grotius, Coringius and Pufendorf, Atwood suggests, in terms directly at one with Lawson, that citizens form a society through consent, some virtually giving their suffrage to those (representatives) who conclude arrangements on behalf of all.[54] The acquisition of subject status does not, however, eradicate the prior status of the citizen. If the trust is broken, then resistance *in extremis* is allowed. Indeed, with respect to James, resistance was a duty. Barclay's notion that the alienation of a kingdom provided grounds for resistance and Bilson's that a Catholic monarch must alienate the kingdom, lie directly behind Atwood's duty to

---

[51] *Ibid.*, pp. 6–7.
[52] *Ibid.*, p. 42, cf. Tyrrell, *A Brief Enquiry into the Ancient Constitution*, 1695, pp. 36–48.
[53] William Atwood, *The Fundamental Constitution of the English Government*, 1690, reprinted, Scholarly Resources, 1973.
[54] *Ibid.*, p. 9.

resist.[55] Throughout, his discussion also presupposes, like Lawson, that resistance itself is predicated on the claims to rule which are the result of having a settled political order. For the most part he goes even further, suggesting that the English Constitution allows the right to resist and is able to conclude that resistance had taken place in 1688. Yet, on two occasions, even Atwood seems verbally to back away from the potentially exposed ground of resistance. In what seems like a conceptual insurance policy of the same kind taken out by Trimmer, he suggests that James simply deserted the kingdom and thereby ceased to be a reigning sovereign.[56] Even more gymnastically he suggests that the very actions which justified resistance against James automatically divested James of his sovereign status. This, if taken seriously, would make any doctrine of resistance technically impossible.[57]

Now Atwood argues largely and self-consciously through the citation of authorities and it may be that his authorities pulled his specification and justification of events in 1688 in differing directions. We may also be witnessing the results of a confused compression of different modes of definition. Be this as it may, it is in such a context of citation that the 'judicious Mr Lawson' is quoted.[58] Although on the side of the angels, it is not directly as a resistance theorist that Lawson is exploited. Mistaking the first for the second edition, Atwood uses several lines from Lawson's hierarchy of loyalty, pushing it, like Gratianus Trimmer, in a resistance direction. Lawson's emphasis on the sacrosanctity of fundamental law is backed up by Bilson, and Plato. But from what has been said so far, although Lawson is not as evident in Atwood as he is in the *Friendly Debate*, his arguments underlie or are at one with a good deal of the text. Later in the work, Atwood returns to James II and again begins to sound strongly Lawsonian. He suggests that after James's departure, power returned to those accounted constitutionally to be the people or their representatives, and these have a right to reform the government and the succession.[59] He then cites Pufendorf and significantly turns to the 'author of the best treatises of civil polity which I have met with in the English tongue', who shows that government is founded upon the choice of the people, in whom (as a prior community) 'there is a power to provide for the necessities of

[55] *Ibid.*, pp. 3–4, 26, 10, 12; Baxter's *Holy Commonwealth*, had also exploited Bilson's association of alienation and catholicism in *Christian Subjection*, see Lamont, *Richard Baxter*, esp. chap. 2, but for neither Bilson nor Baxter was resistance *per se* justified by the alienation, Bilson's alienation theory was yet another way of avoiding an affirmation of the right to resist; cf. Tyrrell, *A Brief Enquiry*, p. 36.
[56] *Fundamental Constitution*, pp. 85–6.   [57] *Ibid.*, p.21.
[58] *Ibid.*, p. 26.   [59] *Ibid.*, p. 98.

the Public.'[60] According to Goldie this is one of only two citations of Locke's *Treatises* in the whole Allegiance Controversy.[61] It is, however, only in the continuation of Atwood's discussion that one can disengage Locke from Lawson. With a somewhat abrupt abridgement, Atwood states that the monarch's violations of the constitution returned the people to the state of nature 'there being no common judge in that state of war'.[62] He then goes on to supplement this rather Hobbist Locke with a quotation from the most Lawsonian passage in Wildman's(?) *A Letter to a Friend*. This concerns the corporate nature of the government, the breaking of a part of which means the dissolution of the whole, and thus the return of power to the people so that they may form a new government through a representative convention rather than a parliament.[63]

All this is curious and instructive. It is Atwood's understandable willingness to argue through authority which brings intimated textual identities to the surface of his work. As a corollary one can see, too, how cited works could by compression be made, as it were, to squeeze up to each other, and how differing theses about the events of 1688 could be orchestrated to give, if not the sound of one voice, some sort of polyphonic support. This returns us by another route to the difficulty of finding an exclusive and formative set of texts behind another. Atwood's vocabulary of resistance, dissolution, citizenship, subjection, sovereignty, representation, and community is all widely disseminated, but it is all found in Lawson's *Politica*; and the *Friendly Debate* associates it all firmly with him. In the *Fundamental Constitution*, shared vocabulary makes Lawson, Locke, Atwood and Wildman(?) all seem to sing with one voice – but then even Plato can be roped into the choir. How much Lawson was used in contrast to these and other names, one cannot tell, but the fact that he is cited in such company shows clearly enough that he had become an exploitable authority. He was used either to structure events according to a dissolution theory, or alternatively to play a subordinate role in the formulation of a resistance theory. Despite the theories being differing responses to a thesis of rebellion, Lawson's name is now common to both and indicates how the line between them could be eroded.

[60] *Ibid.*, p. 101.   [61] Goldie, 'The Revolution of 1689', p. 531.
[62] Atwood, *Fundamental Constitution*, pp. 101–2.   [63] *Ibid.*, pp. 101–2.

14

Aftermath

Lawson's appearance as something of an authority in the final stages of the settlement crisis was made possible because, as it were, a widely distributed apanage of terms and attitudes passed through him. In doing so it was his own inheritance which destroyed traces of his distinctive identity. As Atwood exemplifies, he was merged with one who was to become infinitely more famous. Brief reference to two more texts will take the whole matter of Lawson's fading visibility one stage further. In 1702 a pair of anonymous and frivolous tracts concerning the rights of women were printed.[1] In the second of these the superiority of the male is reasserted. A series of what seem to be allusions to Lawson (when the author is in philosophical mood) prefigure an anecdote in which some apparently unemployed poets ('a pert company of candidates for the muses') rely on the authority of Lawson to subdue their landlady. Giving her 'messes of morality and lectures out of Lawson concerning the degrees of sovereignty and the Rights of a Woman', these loutish parodies of *real* majesty closely control the *personal* majesty of the 'old maid'.[2] Chauvinist or not, the author was probably hostile to the restrictive theories of government with which Lawson was associated; and manifestly a considerable familiarity with Lawson is assumed. Currency can have no better badge than inverted trivialisation.

The diffused voice of Lawson seems to sound behind much of Defoe's megaphonic *The Original Power of the People of England*, and indeed, conventionally enough, Defoe claims to be saying nothing new. Parliament represents the power of the people, and if this 'meets with a cess', or thrones become vacant, this power returns to the 'one happy centre of the great

---

[1] Anon., *Petticoat Government*; and Anon., *The Prerogative of the Breaches*. They were part of a voguish tradition of playful writing on the equality of woman, see e.g. *A Dialogue on Women*, 1696. Ian Maclean, *The Renaissance Notion of Woman*, Cambridge University Press, 1980, discusses parody literature of this sort as an offshoot of the Aristotelian theory of gender, and its difficulties.

[2] *Prerogative*, pp. 36–7. The prior allusions are to 'form' and 'matter' and to 'relates'.

circle of political order'.[3] All the power of Parliament is as the free representatives of the commons, but if Parliament should fail the people remain 'and while there is a people there may be a legal authority delegated'. Power is from God and it comes to 'the three heads' of the constitution from the people to whom it reverts if the constitution is in any way dissolved.[4] In the late revolution the King fled, the constitution was dissolved, and the people through a convention resettled the crown.[5] For Defoe, the corollary of dissolution and a prior community being able to resettle, is the continuing right of that community to defend itself even against those who are entrusted with governing power. If this is Lawsonian, and it seems almost as strongly Lawsonian as one could hope without the use of names and specific vocabulary, then it is Lawson refined to his activist implications. The tract interestingly maintains or exploits the sort of ambiguity that we have seen in Lawson's theory of representation (as well as Baxter's *Commonwealth*) and, like the *Politica*, does not rely upon a theory of contract. Defoe begins by using the vocabulary of irrevocable (virtual) representation. Originally, all people were a part of Parliament but, being too numerous, representatives were chosen to stand for the whole, who (turning directly to the present Parliament) 'are an abridgement of the many volumes of the English Nation'.[6] Yet later, these same representatives are delegates answerable to the whole.[7] 'The truth is, in right reasoning the first invasion made upon justice, either by the tacit or actual assent of the three heads of our constitution, is an actual dissolution of the constitution; and ... the people have a right to dispose the incumbant and commit the trust of government de novo.'[8] Lawson would hardly have been comfortable with such egregiousness, one suspects, but what matters here is how Defoe's argument illustrates the differing patterns of ideas that can come from a common terminological legacy – for the effect is not only to threaten Parliament, but to collapse a theory of dissolution into one of resistance. Lawson's work seems to lie behind Defoe, as it does behind Baxter. Yet only gradually, and with considerable hesitation along the way, is the *Politica* distilled to its activist potential, and its activist aspects assimilated to a language that is voiced against a present regime. Baxter's fears about Lawson in the *Political Catechise* are fully intelligible as reflections on the subsequent exploitation of the *Politica* rather than as judgements upon its author's intentions or political disposition. In realising this potential in Trimmer and Atwood,

[3] Defoe, *The Original Power of the People of England*, 1701, in *Works* with a Memoir by William Hazlitt, Clements, London, 1840, 2, p. 5.
[4] *Ibid.*, pp. 6 and 9.   [5] *Ibid.*, p. 9; cf. Tyrrell, *A Brief Enquiry*, pp. 54–5.
[6] Defoe, *Original Power*, pp. 5–6; cf. *Politica*, p. 340.   [7] Defoe, *Original Power*, p. 9.
[8] *Ibid.*, p. 10.

and then putatively in Defoe, we see not only Lawson's ambivalence or his definitional indifference towards resistance simplified, but also the erosion of important conceptual delineations he tried to maintain. The lines between settlement, failure, dissolution, and an ongoing right to resist or participate in government existed only insofar as they were maintained in a war of words, and Lawson was ultimately on the losing side. Overall, Lawson appears as a theorist of dissolution and governmental failure – and where he does not appear he seems most plausibly to lurk behind such theories of semantic circumnavigation. For the rest, he is taken out as a dissolution insurance policy by those running the conscious risk of a resistance theory. He appears as a resistance theorist only insofar as the distinction between dissolution and resistance is collapsed. Always contentious, it did collapse and this in a sense was a victory (with which we still live) for the Tories and non-jurors but it was an empty victory, for rebellion was an easier badge to wear in 1700 than in 1689 or 1670.

That we do live with what was, with respect to a sector of the vocabulary, a partially Tory victory, can be seen in our acceptance of the terminological conflations which Tories helped to bring about. We hardly notice a difference between 'revolt', 'rebellion' and 'resistance', 'subject' and 'citizen' whilst theories of dissolution or governmental failure are seen as part of a radical resistance movement.[9] Only in the light of this partially Tory-engineered elision of vocabulary can we fully see how modern liberal scholars have seen Lawson's theory of settlement and failure almost entirely in terms of a theory of resistance, even a radical one. This is irony to the point of travesty though such twists of lineal respectability should not surprise us. The real point is that if we are robbed of the requisite distinctions, it becomes doubly difficult to know what was going on.

The journey of the *Politica* then, from Baxter's *Commonwealth* to the *Original Power* of Defoe is a long and symptomatically significant one. Insofar as we can disengage a distinct role for the work in a larger pattern of change, it reveals the gradual exposure of a medieval and largely Italian incubus of active citizenry, but it begins and ends with a barely visible George Lawson. The public life of the *Politica* began with the work deeply entangled in the *Commonwealth*; it ends in the shadow of the *Two Treatises*. A little over a hundred years later Lawson was almost entirely unknown and Defoe's tract, which may have leaned heavily on the *Politica*, could

---

[9] See e.g. David Wootton, 'The Fear of God in Early Modern Political Theory', *Historical Papers*, Canada (1983), p. 66 where he writes of Buchanan's justification for revolt; Goldie, 'The Roots of True Whiggism', p. 211; James Tully, 'Current Thinking on Sixteenth- and Seventeenth-Century Political Theory', *Historical Journal*, 24, 2 (1981), where Lawson's theory is thought to be more 'conservative' than Locke's because the people can only 'revolt' in concert; why this is deemed more conservative than effective is a mystery to me.

be mistaken for a paraphrase of Locke. Brief authority had had its day, a textual diaspora all too well effected.

As Thomas Chalmers remarked of Defoe's short work, with touching innocence, 'Every lover of Liberty must be pleased with the perusal of a treatise, which vies with Mr Locke's famous tract in power of reasoning, and is superior to it in the graces of style.'[10]

Lovers of Lawson might feel, as if by a card trick of history, cheated.

---

[10] Cited in Defoe, *Works*, vol. 2, ed. Hazlett. For another variation: J. W. Gough claims that there is a strong similarity between Lawson and Bolingbroke – his evidence is from passages where Bolingbroke is citing Locke. See *Fundamental Constitution*, pp. 121–2, 186.

Part V

CONCLUSIONS

❧ 15 ❧

Between Hobbes and Locke

Yet another comparison between Hobbes and Locke: or at last, a sensible location for the *Politica*? Neither really, but Lawson began his public career with an attack on *Leviathan*, and his *Politica* fades from view in the shadow of Locke, so some debt is owed to the Hobbes–Locke multinational. This debt has accrued interest inasmuch as I have discussed Lawson and the Allegiance Controversy with hardly a mention of Locke. In the terms of the traditional historiography of political thought the central questions might still be seen to be whether Lawson really influenced Locke and if so what this might tell us about the elusive relationship between Locke and Hobbes.

Lawson, albeit reluctantly, was one of the first to contribute to the anti-*Leviathan* literature which was to rumble on throughout the century. The literature was politically and stylistically heterogeneous but, as Goldie has emphasised, it was largely held together by a common theological postulate. In this respect, Lawson was typical and perhaps helped set the tone, along with Hobbes's fellow exile John Bramhall, for the later huntings of *Leviathan*.[1] Like Hobbes, Lawson saw God as a sovereign power, but he could never be tied to a simplex specification of divinity. His earlier arguments with Baxter, and at one remove Twiss ('Amica diss.'), had denied the adequacy of any simple understanding of God, and the attack on *Leviathan* is explicitly on the political consequences of such 'simplexity'. An omnipotent arbitrary God provided the model, as it were, for an omni-potent arbitrary sovereign. Just as a simplex understanding of God is an oversimplification, so Hobbes's attempt to frame the whole complexity of political and social relationships into the notions of absolute subjection of subjects to a sovereign in the name of peace is a gross and dangerous distor-tion of the world. Hobbes is the great oversimplifier, taken to task for

[1] Mark Goldie, 'The Reception of Hobbes', In J. H. Burns, ed., *The Cambridge History of Political Thought*, 1450–1700, Cambridge University Press, forthcoming. Lawson's *Exam-ination* was preceded by John Bramhall, *A Defence of True Liberty*, 1655, and Alexander Ross, *Leviathan Drawn Out with a Hook*, 1653. Bramhall followed up again with *Castiga-tions of Mr. Hobbes*, and *The Catching of Leviathan*, 1658.

subverting or ignoring the vitally important notions of community, church, justice, tyranny and citizenship.

This simplifying propensity has a human as well as a conceptual dimension; Hobbes, maintains Lawson, had an insufficient respect for his inheritance. This is not to say that Lawson held the past as sacrosanct, but that he believed Hobbes would have made fewer errors had he not wielded an indiscriminate sword at the Gordian knot of tradition.[2] Thus he remarks, 'where Hobbes hath done ill none have done worse, where he hath done well many before him hath done better' (*Exam.* 78). Lawson's comments on Hobbes's positivism provide a central illustration of the conceptual and human facets of simplification – for law is an analogue of the divine. Lawson takes Hobbes to be a strict legal positivist, for whom law is simply a matter of what can be enforced by a sovereign authority, which through its promulgations becomes the arbiter of justice. Lawson's position is that such an understanding distorts the nature of law by taking an attribute for the whole and thus obscuring the difficulties of balancing enforcement with justice which an adequate definition should underline. The point is also that this duplex nature of law had been common knowledge for centuries, indeed since Aristotle who, as he accepts, is anathema to Hobbes (*Exam.* 92–4). Interestingly, however, Lawson adds that if Hobbes cannot arrive at an adequate understanding through Aristotle, he should at least be able to arrive at one through Marsilio. Here Lawson seems to be assuming Hobbes's familiarity with the Paduan and was exploiting what he took to be a central figure in a common inheritance. The corollary is that Hobbes, for all his huffing and puffing, was not so singular as he would pretend. The reference to Marsilio intimates the tip of a common iceberg of intellectual inheritance, with the disturbing currents of the Peloponnesian wars and the rarified logical empiricism of Ockham silent beneath the sea. As we might also expect from this, Lawson, although impatient, is not as hostile to Hobbes as many of his other critics. The Engagement Controversy provides some partial agreement; both accept a theory of indivisible sovereignty and Lawson accepts too a theory of social contract, if not Hobbes's highly individualistic (and anti-communal) working of it.

It should also be said that the *Examination* is a piecemeal study and insofar as it is in agreement with the *Politica* it is this work which, if indirectly, displays the fully considered areas of agreement and disagreement between a Hobbesian and Lawsonian understanding of politics; and as it

[2] Quentin Skinner, 'The Ideological Context of Hobbes's Political Thought', *Historical Journal*, 9 (1966), pp. 286ff., for the classic account of Hobbes's relationship to *de facto* theory; see also Goldie, on the controversy surrounding Sherlock in 'The Revolution of 1689 and the Structure of Political Argument', *Bulletin of Research in the Humanities*, 83 (1980), pp. 483ff. On Hobbes and Lawson see also C. Condren, 'Confronting the Monster: Lawson's Reactions to Hobbes', *Political Science*, 40 (1988), pp. 67ff.

floats on a fluid and far-reaching inheritance, which Lawson seems happy to recognise, his virtually ignoring Hobbes is a sort of poetic injustice. However, as I have indicated in an *ad hoc* way throughout, there are important differences between the *Examination* and the *Politica*. At this point these should be summarised as a prelude to indicating the extent of the ground Lawson shared, or came to share, with Hobbes by 1660. A theory of contract, important in the *Examination*, all but disappears in the *Politica*; the distinctions between *real* and *personal* majesty, subject and citizen, community and polity, emerge to take on greater significance, and such a close relationship that they constitute a virtual lexical field from which the whole syntagma of his theory is generated to impose a conceptual order upon the world. The individualism of Lawson's notion of majority (*Exam.* 26–7) is replaced by the corporate *valentior* (or *sanior*) *pars*. The activist rhetoric of a right to self-defence against tyrants, the intimations that they put themselves in a state of war with the people, all but disappear; and Lawson becomes at least equivocal on the right of resistance. Further, religion is clearly embraced as a cause of the Civil War, whereas in the *Examination* it seems to be dismissed as a hypocritical mask; and the notions of legislative, executive, and judicial, doubtfully applied to English circumstances in the *Examination*, are posited in the *Politica* as terms which define *personal* majesty *per se*. Whether these changes of tone, emphasis and logic are entirely due to the necessities of settlement, or whether the arrogant extremities of *Leviathan* created an over-reaction in Lawson, or whether to some extent confrontation with *Leviathan* helped Lawson redefine his position, one cannot tell. What does become clear, however, is that Lawson's *Politica* has more in common with *Leviathan* than the surface hostility of the *Examination* might lead us to suspect.

Both *Leviathan* and the *Politica* are powerful persuasives for peace, which is to say more than that their authors were prepared to exploit one of the most hallowed and resonant terms of political discourse. Hobbes has rightly been seen by modern scholars, as he was seen by his contemporaries, as a *de facto* theorist; and, as I have shown, there is a discernable *de facto* theme running through the *Politica*, carried over from the *Examination* and possibly the residue of Lawson's missing Engagement tract. It seems close to the work of Ascham, and Ascham recognised Hobbes to be of his ilk.[3] At the same time, this indicates that *de facto* theory should not be seen as a common body of doctrine but rather as a point of casuistical agreement; and Lawson certainly recognised that much more was needed for a general theory of politics. In this way, like Hobbes, he goes well

---

[3] Anthony Ascham, *On the Confusions and Revolutions of Government*, 1649; Marchmont Needham, *The Case of the Commonwealth Truely Stated*, 1650. See especially pp. 103ff.

beyond the scope of men like Ascham, Needham, Rous, and their opponents. Both Hobbes and Lawson developed fully fledged theories of legislative sovereignty and made these central to their works as a whole. We are so used to such theories of sovereignty that the significance of this point of agreement might be underrated. Not all who wrote about politics regarded sovereignty as a central issue – for some it had seemed negotiable and peripheral in the days of civil strife.[4] For Weston and Greenberg the emphasis on legislation alone would put both Hobbes and Lawson on the right side of the great divide between modern and medieval.[5] More specifically, both Hobbes and Lawson regarded sovereignty as indivisible, and the attempt to divide it as destructive. Hobbes's views on 'mixarchy' are well known, and despite Lawson's use of the expression 'mixed government', his are at one with them in both the *Examination* and the *Politica*. Lawson's mixed government, like Hobbes's 'artificial man', is a corporate body defined through its function. It was, in effect, Lawson's Hobbesian rescue of the notion of mixed monarchy that some writers later in the century found particularly suggestive. The corollary of indivisible sovereignty for both authors was the concept of a subject as definitionally subjected. Subject and sovereign are (conventionally enough) mutually defining.[6]

It is at this point, however, that Hobbes is apt to say, 'here endeth the lesson' and Lawson 'here beginneth our real problems'. Subjects we may be, but we may always be recognised under another *notion*. This deviation from shared defined relationships takes us in two further directions – to the problems of Erastianism and to resistance.

Hobbes was seen as an Erastian, and Lawson claims that the Erastians have never understood the issues involved in the relationships between church and state. Yet the general label of Erastian, even when not a term of abuse, is imprecise as there were distinguishable issues involved in its use – those surrounding indifference, and internality. When these are clarified, Hobbes and Lawson seem not to be so distinct, despite Hobbes's semantically simpler position.[7] If one accepted the almost inescapable English

---

[4] A point stressed by J. S. Morrill, *The Revolt of the Provinces: Conservatives and Radicals in the English Civil War, 1630–1650*, Allen and Unwin, 1976.

[5] C. C. Weston and J. R. Greenberg, *Subjects and Sovereigns*, Cambridge University Press, 1981, *passim*.

[6] For later examples: *The Case of Oathes Stated, State Tracts*, 1705, 1, pp. 340ff.; John Locke, *Two Treatises of Government*, ed. P. Laslett, Cambridge University Press, 1963, Book 2 'On Dissolution'.

[7] On the abuse, use and imprecision of the term see John Graham, 'Independent and Presbyterian', unpublished Ph.D. thesis, Washington University of St Louis, 1978, e.g., p. 258; John Marshall, 'The Ecclesiology of the Latitude Men, 1660–1689: Stillingfleet, Tillotson and Hobbism', *Journal of Ecclesiastical History*, 36, 3 (1985), pp. 401ff., gives further indirect support for the alignment of Hobbes and a writer like Lawson.

Protestant and evangelical distinction between internal and external acts and the distinction between necessity and indifference in matters of church government, then one was Erastian insofar as one pushed contentious issues under the heading of externality and indifference and settled such issues by invoking secular authority in the name of peace. Two distinctions are involved, then, each of which could be applied variously. Lawson accepted both and was clearly prepared to place a great deal under the auspices of indifference and externality and this pushes him closer to the Erastians than he might be prepared to admit in his speedy dismissal of them. Hobbes relies only on the distinction between the internal and external and this conceptual difference seems to open a bigger gap in theory than I suspect it did in practice. As Lawson's career indicates, he was able to accept as many state imposed ecclesiological changes as Hobbes lived through – all as a good Church of England man. Not too much stress should be placed on arguments from the remnants of biography. Lawson's latitudinarian capacity to accommodate himself within the Church of England may have been an application of precept – a precept which on various occasions might have been used to make him defect; but, in his isolated and protected world at More, he may not have had to accommodate himself at all in practice.

If, then, in Lawson's theory, the state could control the church (as long as it did so in terms of the right notions) to an extent pretty close to the satisfaction of Hobbes, what then of the grounds to resist the state's power? Hobbes recognises logically, if reluctantly, an individual's right to resist violently, but that right, as in Hunton, is sufficiently circumscribed to become socially insignificant. With Lawson the matter is more doubtful. There is a residual right similarly implied by his theory, but, as I have suggested, either he too accepts the logic with some reluctance as an unpleasant corollary of an intellectual inheritance he was adapting to more settling purposes; or, he was engaged in a more abstract and definitional enterprise. Or, on the basis of the definitional enterprise he made some attempt to resolve tensions in the name of peace, and in the requisite voice change failed to exclude the corollary of resistance. If the first (or third) possibilities are correct, then there is a crucial difference between Hobbes and Lawson, in that it is Hobbes's lack of a sense of community which vitiates his right to resist. Like poor Grendel after his accident, the naked individual may shake a fist at the failing sun but concerted action is rebellion. For Lawson, it is the very sense of community which makes resistance or rebellion cataclysmic. It is little wonder that he seems so hesitant about the exercise of a right to resist. If the second reading of the resistance *topos* in Lawson is correct, however, a further pattern of similarities is opened up between the *Politica* and *Leviathan*.

To begin with, Hobbes and Lawson similarly recognise a discrete realm of prudence. Granted, Hobbes reduces much to rules that he believes must lead to certain sorts of behaviour; but (and this had led to much dissatisfaction with his injunctions to follow the golden rule of obedience) he would not provide a restrictive abridgement of the sovereign's sphere of action and judgement. One can but trust to that judgement, and hope. Up to a point Lawson seems to have held a similar view (unless his prudential restrictions were to be adumbrated in the *Politica*'s second unpublished part). But it was only up to a point at which the subject *qua* citizen could exercise a judgement of his own. If the see-saw reading is correct, however, Lawson was attempting to specify the terms through which prudential judgement needed to be organised. He attempts, as it were, to provide more of an inescapable vocabulary to impress upon the book of prudence without destroying it with over-inscription. Sovereign, subject and citizen in all their dealings must be aware of the complexity of human political identity and the diversity of justifiable behaviour. His language was designed to insure this without pre-empting action.

Lawson, Hobbes, and their contemporaries shared presuppositions rooted in Aristotelian metaphysics, which may be summarised as the general belief that understanding required a public stable language, with a vocabulary sufficiently varied and precise to capture the intricacies of the subject-matter of discourse. Words thus hovered uncertainly between the creation and representation of meaning. Hobbes insists that all knowledge is predicated on the stability and adequacy of one's terms. His nominalism was elaborated in such a way as to stress creative arbitrariness in language's use, which I have suggested provided a sub-text to Lawson's remarks about 'imperious dictators and masters of words'.[8] In relative contrast, Lawson was apt to appeal to the tensions and complexity of the world as something that should be captured, not simplified, by definition. This, of course, was still to leave one reliant upon the concepts through which the world was seen and the creation of a conceptual aporia may have been the means chosen to make this clear. The complementary problems thrown up by these differing responses to the relationship between words and the world were to flow on through Locke, Hume, Kant, Nietzsche, Schopenhauer; to logical atomism at one extreme and the Wolf–Sapir hypothesis at the other. They must be touched on again in considering Lawson and Locke.

In the meantime, however, it can also be said that a broadly shared linguistic sensibility generated for Hobbes and Lawson alike a direct political consequence. For both, a political vocabulary was a function of political order – even if political order could only be understood through an appropriate battery of abstractions. *In extremis*, for Hobbes, political order could define

---

[8] Thomas Hobbes, *Leviathan*, ed. M. Oakeshott, Blackwell, 1960, part 1.

and circumscribe a public political discourse with central concepts such as justice taking on meaning only in the context of political rule.[9] Lawson too suggests that certain intimately related terms are meaningful only in the context of political form. Most noticeable amongst these are of course the notions of resistance and rebellion. This is a point which again, as I have indicated, helps explain the popularity of Lawson's work and the dissolution hypothesis in the late seventeenth century. For both men, only on the basis of a proper definitional foundation could a body of precept be built; and precept, each held, was particularly necessary in a confused world marked by striking political ignorance. The full complexity of the political was revealed through time, and for both men it was precept that had to make sense of – and have epistemological priority over – history. But in agreeing on this, each is at one with most of his world.

In the light of those underlying similarities, the differences between Hobbes and Lawson with respect to the particular pasts of England and classical antiquity, and the differing degrees to which the past is used to display the conceptual authority and guiding power of precept in their major works, becomes less significant. Hobbes saw the reading of classical history, especially Roman republican histories, as partially responsible for the Civil War, for they extolled the notion of active citizenship. In contrast, Hobbes subsumed the notion of citizenship entirely under that of subjection. Lawson went precisely to the antique and medieval Italianate notion of the *civis* to augment the lexicon. He did this less to encourage or justify resistance, than to capture a complete picture of the political expressed in near and distant history, a picture Hobbes was prepared to schematise in the interests of an iconography of peace.

Finally, it should be noted that in attempting to manipulate and reform the vocabulary of English political discourse, each relied upon a distinctive linguistic model; and in a world of unstable and still rapidly expanding vernacular and of numerous and unstable linguistic communities, it was probably something important to cling to. Hobbes relied explicitly on an image of mathematics and science which, especially in its evocations of arithmetical operators and simple numbers, suggested a self-contained conceptual world of discrete and simple finite elements well suited to the arbitrariness of his nominalism. Mathematics in effect provided a model for an ideal language of political understanding. In this, as in other ways, Hobbes showed himself to be a powerful figurative thinker. Now is not the place to discuss this much neglected aspect of his work; but the specific model

---

[9] *Leviathan*, 13, 15, 18. S.S.Wolin, *Politics and Vision*, Little Brown, Boston, 1960, gives a perceptive account of this.

of intellectual relationships chosen as the Key to the Kingdom of Man was itself one which increasingly deprecated and simplified the role of the figurative in language. This may help explain the discrepancy between the power of Hobbes's metaphors and his relegation of the role of metaphor in argument.

Lawson too used a model of intellectual relationships for political understanding. He turned, however, not to the new world of philosophy as science, but to the old one of philosophy as theology, and to rhetoric. The metaphorical structure of his work is sufficiently important to require further discussion in its own right, but in the immediate context it underlines some of the random oddity of reputation. The metaphor of theology and rhetoric afforded a more central role for figurative language than one drawn from Hobbesian science. It is the embrace of traditional modes of thought, more sophisticated in their treatment of the figurative than the aggressive new scientism, that may begin to make the lesser known Lawson now seem more modern than his overpoweringly famous contemporary.

Despite differences of political principle, conceptual vocabulary and mode of argumentation, Hobbes and Lawson belonged to much the same intellectual world. It was a world, as Lawson reveals far more clearly than Hobbes, which stretched back to what we call the Middle Ages. It was a world not so much rejected as destroyed in the processes of constant adaptation and idiolectic refinement. The adaptation was made difficult by the awesome disturbances of Reformation and Civil War and also by the fragmenting consequences of printing and the translation of a discriminate Latinate terminology into the vibrant instability of expanding vernaculars.[10] Given the linguistic presuppositions shared by Hobbes and Lawson, it is understandable that their political arguments show a common concern with the reformation of vocabularies and the spoiling manipulation of the words that might impose conceptual order on near chaos, or induce chaos from precarious order.

Locke is conventionally seen as standing towards the end of these troublesome transformations of political linguistics and yet it is the remarkable similarity between his words and Lawson's that has done more than anything

---

[10] This expansion of the vocabulary between 1450 and 1650 was remarkable, though the curve seems to have been greater rather earlier than dictionary definitions indicate. On this see R. W. McConchie, '"Wise and Learned Cunctation": Medical terminology, 1547–1612 and the *OED*', *Dictionaries*, 5, (1983), pp. 22ff. The full consequences however have not been explored with respect to political discourse, but contemporaries of Hobbes and Lawson were well aware of the expansion. See e.g. the *Vindex Anglicus*, 1644, *Harleian Miscellany*, 2, pp. 37–42; Hugh Ormsby-Lennon, 'The Dialect of those Fanatick Times; Language Communities and English Poetry 1580–1660', unpublished Ph.D. thesis, University of Pennsylvania, 1977, at length, for an interesting discussion of linguistic grouping.

else to give the *Politica* belated attention. Lawson was not, as the cliché might put it, a man ahead of his times; if the similarities are so striking then, was the process of transformation less clear and complete in Locke than we might think?

That John Locke was very familiar with the writings of Lawson can be reasonably well established. His diary records that he was lent a copy of the *Politica* in April 1679; and although Sylvester Brownover's initial catalogue of Locke's library in 1693 lists nothing by Lawson, Laslett and Harrison's fastidious bibliographical reconstruction shows that Locke owned all the published works of Lawson, including both editions of the *Politica*.[11] A family resemblance of varying degrees of proximity between the second of the *Two Treatises* and the *Politica* has been accepted for some time. At one extreme, Laslett has noted, but probably underplayed, a number of piecemeal similarities between the works; at the other, Maclean has stated with enthusiastic hyperbole that a paraphrase of the second of the *Two Treatises* could stand as a synopsis of the *Politica*. In claiming that Lawson solved the central constitutional problems of mixed monarchy a generation before Locke, Franklin seems much closer to Maclean than Laslett.[12] In the light of the work of all three authors, the similarities of constitutional theory between Lawson and Locke need less rehearsal here than the unnoticed ones between Lawson and Hobbes.

Nevertheless, it should be noted that the more famous of both Locke's and Lawson's works was preceded or prefaced by specific attacks on what we regard as absolutist thinkers; and, more important, that the hostility which resulted in similar constitutional theories was grounded in very similar theological beliefs: For both Lawson and Locke, God who made us owns us all; although we have rights and are obliged to obey the higher powers, absolute subjection is due only to the omnipotent divinity; all rights stem from duties to God. As Tully remarks of Locke, human beings are never isolated individuals, but exist and must be understood only in a context of

[11] M. Cranston, *John Locke, A Biography*, Longmans, London, 1957; A. H. Maclean, 'George Lawson and John Locke', *Cambridge Historical Journal*, 9, 1 (1947); S. Brownover, in Lovelace Collection; J. Harrison and P. Laslett, *The Library of John Locke*, Oxford, 1971, for all relevant details.

[12] See Laslett's *Notes* in Locke, *Two Treatises* 2, 96; also Richard Ashcraft, *Revolutionary Politics and Locke's Two Treatises of Government*, Princeton University Press, 1986, pp. 310–11; cf. 146, 211, 222; Maclean, 'George Lawson and John Locke', pp. 69–70, and presumably at greater length in the missing thesis, 1947; Julian Franklin, *John Locke and the Theory of Sovereignty*, Cambridge University Press, 1978, Introduction and chap. 3, citing the missing work: all reduced to a passing note in Carlo Viano, *John Locke; Dal Razzionalismo all Illuminismo*, Einaudi, Torin, 1970, p. 222; where Lawson is treated as one of the minor writers on division of powers whom Locke systematised.

relationship with God and with each other.[13] The social relationships central
to the thought of both Locke and Lawson are paradigmatically expressed
for each in the notion of a community. It is this which, constituted according
to the 'laws of nature' (Locke) or 'divine precept' (Lawson), is able to authorise particular political orders – all of which are introduced to lessen the
inconveniences of social living. Consent is of secondary importance in the
formulation of a community but becomes the principal criterion of legitimacy
in the formation of a political society. Both authors also distinguish between
tacit and express consent, a distinction required by the acceptance of a
doctrine of agency integral to the informing corporation image of community. With the introduction of a contingent political form, itself a corporate trust for Locke and Lawson, the community remains as a constituent
authority should that trust fail in any way. Both Locke and Lawson place
similar stress on legislation and the importance of due legal process. Both
believed in the need for a reformed and regularly convened Parliament.

If, then, one abridges the two works to a series of abstract propositions,
Maclean's comparison seems not so far-fetched, and in the absence of all
else (including Rutherford, Hunton, Milton, Althusius, the Levellers) it
would speak of a telling reliance of Locke upon Lawson. But abstract propositions devoid of the context of theoretical articulation and the problems
that the theorist confronted may well be uninformative and misleading,
and other names must get in the way. Considering the general shapes and
theoretical thrusts of the two works, there are important differences. About
half of Lawson's *Politica* is devoted to ecclesiology and a good deal of his
attention is given to weaving the mythology of the ancient constitution and
Civil War into a pattern of general precept. In contrast, the second of the
Two Treatises is uniformly more abstract and *sans* ecclesiology. To some
extent this indicates a rather different range of problems and a different
approach to their solution. In the cause of settlement Lawson had to come
to grips with the contentious symbolism of English history, whilst Locke
– writing after the destructive work of the royalist apologist and historian
Robert Brady – may have felt it simpler to avoid reference to that which
had been so effectively co-opted by his opposition.[14]

Furthermore, the second of the *Two Treatises* is a theory of social contract
and one in which property takes on a symbolic, amphibolous and centrally

[13] James Tully, *A Discourse on Property*, Cambridge University Press, 1982, e.g. p. 11. One
cannot, I think, draw too firm a line between Locke and Lawson in terms of an affirmation
of individual rights on self-defence, and scriptural command. Locke's right of individual
self-defence is rooted in a theology very similar to Lawson's and which is intimated in the
Examination. What we have is not two separate traditions, but two distinguishable repertoires
which have a very different balance in the *Politica* and the *Two Treatises*.
[14] J. G. A. Pocock, *The Ancient Constitution and the Feudal Law*, Norton, New York, 1957,
for the discussion of this hypothesis.

important role.[15] In contrast, although the *Examination* (72–3) presents
a contract theory and posits abuse of property as a criterion for appeal
against rulers, the *Politica* offers only a theory of trust; and propriety, in
some respects like Locke's concept of property (embracing degree and
right), does not constitute an organising principle for the argument. The
compression and simplification of vocabulary which seems to be represented
in this contrast is more clear, however, in two ways, with respect to
each man's notion of community. First, Locke does not employ the refine-
ments of *real* and *personal* majesty in order to insist on the ultimate authority
of the people (itself embracing Lawson's subject and citizen). This creates
less tension than in Lawson with respect to the potentially conflicting claims
to be housed under the notion of sovereignty; it may be that Locke was
following Pufendorf's suggestion that such a refinement was redundant in
conveying the simple point that when there is no government, there may
remain a people who can reconstitute another.[16] Secondly, although there
is a doctrine of agency in both Lawson and Locke, in the former the agents
are clearly a majority in the medieval sense – a corporate collectivity whose
existence is theoretically sustained by qualitative considerations, such as
rationality. This is not so obviously the case for Locke. Although the individualism in his work has been exaggerated, his use of majority seems to
be a simple, individualistic numerical majority of adult males. We are beginning to make a firm shift intimated in Leveller materials (and Lawson's
Examination) from people 'is' to people 'are' – something reinforced by
Locke's use of microcosmic illustrations to justify collective action. Tuck
is therefore right to emphasise a difference between Lawson and Locke here,
but it is by no means absolute or irrevocable, for the residual but potentially
significant criterion of rationality still haunts Locke's work.[17] A rational
being to some extent knows God's laws and may stand for weaker brethren.
The corporate metaphor has a less informing role in Locke than in Lawson;
individualism accompanies, or even constitutes its diminution.

There also seems to be something of a simplification in Locke's concluding
lines of the second of the *Two Treatises*, where it is argued that the majority
of the community may resume legislative authority for themselves, as well
as being able to erect a new form when the old has failed and power has

[15] See Laslett in Locke, *Two Treatises*, Introduction, for the symbolic importance of property.
I have touched on its amphibolous role in the context of linguistic simplification, *The Status
and Appraisal of Classic Texts*, Princeton University Press, 1985, chap. 8; for the most
systematic discussion see Tully, *A Discourse*.
[16] Pufendorf, *De jure*, trans. C. H. and W. A. Oldfather, Clarendon Press, Oxford, 1934,
Book 7, chap. 6.
[17] Richard Tuck, *Natural Rights Theories: Their Origin and Development*, Cambridge University Press, 1979, p. 144; James Tully, 'Current Thinking about Sixteenth- and Seventeenth-
Century Political Theory', *Historical Journal*, 24, 2 (1981), elucidating the point, pp. 482–3.

reverted to them. Locke's modification of this is marginally more Lawsonian, though Lawson would probably still have required that the terminology be supplemented rather than extended to refer also to the operations of community.[18]

Penultimately, the end to which each man's argument is directed is different. The second of Locke's *Two Treatises* is unquestionably, even aggressively, a theory of resistance couched revealingly and protectively in the idiom of self-(property) defence. The *Politica* is far more amelioratingly a theory of dissolution and resettlement. Finally, the *Two Treatises* are altogether more rationalistic. Much more of the political world, appropriately enough, is amenable to definitive principles for action. Although Locke recognises prudence, and even the suspiciously opaque realm of *arcana imperii*, that realm is closely mewed up, and woe be to any governor that tries to fly too far alone. Here Lawson is between Hobbes and Locke. The book of prudence, as it were, is neither like Hobbes's tome of near blank pages, nor Locke's revolutionary timetable; it is a sort of *Tristram Shandy* complete with text, stark pages and wavy lines.

In this context, both Locke and Lawson draw formally similar distinctions between conquest and usurpation. For both, conquest may be the operation of providence, whilst usurpation itself is never a matter of right. But whereas Lawson is content to remark that conquerors tend towards despotic forms of government, Locke attempts to restrict the area of despotic control. Beyond it the people may rise up 'shaking off a Power, which Force, and not Right hath set over any one, though it hath the Name of *Rebellion*, yet is no offence before God'.[19] Lawson too had noted that what was called rebellion was not necessarily so; however, his point was to discriminate formally between different abstract notions under which specific actions might be subsumed – and he did not illustrate with examples of either. Locke's argument is illustrated from the Bible and its point is to help undermine the force of the accusation of rebellion, which drew so heavily on biblical injunction. The difference in argumentative direction becomes even clearer as Locke turns directly to usurpation and tyranny.[20]

In analogous discussions, Lawson's point had been that although the act of usurpation was illegitimate the gaining and the exercise of usurped power must be distinguished; that power itself being good, its possession intimated some formal element of consent; and, in any case, the putative right of resistance must be weighed against obligation to power and considerations

[18] Locke, *Two Treatises* 2.243, 19–21; Tully, 'Current Thinking', p. 482, seems to be a victim of such conflations when writing of the individual's obedience to the community in Lawson. Lawson would insist on a distinction between obedience and loyalty or fidelity, for obedience only arises in the context of governmental form.
[19] Locke, *Two Treatises*, 2.196, 19–24.
[20] *Ibid.*, 2.197–210.

of prudence. Locke, however, does not make the old Lawsonian/Bartolan point about the acquisition and exercise of power, and rather than counselling prudence sets up the lack of an alternative appeal as a formal criterion for the exercise of the right, along with assurances that people do not exercise their rights frivolously.[21]

Both men regard the consent of the community as crucial to the foundation of a polity, but, whereas for example, Lawson writes, elliptically that no power is fully acquired until it is accepted, Locke (who might be providing an activist gloss upon Lawson), writes 'Nor can such an Usurper, or any serving from him, ever have a Title, till the People are both at Liberty to consent, and have actually consented to allow, and confirm in him the Power he hath till then Usurped.'[22] The time lag can clearly be considerable, the deliberations of the people weighty and redolent with the genuine possibility of exercising a right of resistance. There is no passage parallel to this in the *Politica*. In short, whilst both writers regard consent as a foundation for a legitimate political regime, Locke's stress more clearly than Lawson's is upon the right to withhold this consent. In dealing with tyranny Locke converts the right to resist into the established duty of self-defence, closer to the *Examination* than the *Politica*. Tyranny is the exercise of power to which there can be no right; if there is no alternative appeal against the actions of the tyrant, the tyrant dissolves a proper governmental relationship with the people who are thus placed in a state of war.[23] Locke's references to force in this context are to pure and immediate violence, this is not like Lawson's highly reified notion of force (papal authority) as the immoral reverse of power – which in any case he keeps free of such discussions. It is the violence of tyranny for Locke which, as it does for Atwood, both justifies resistance as self-defence and dissolves the government, making – in Lawson's predominantly nominal terms – resistance technically impossible. Such nominal delineations seem not to matter for Locke. His illustrations of the right to resist elaborated from the small-scale model of a petty robbery, effectively extend the notion of resistance not only to embrace self-defence but also to deal with circumstances beyond, though suggested

---

[21] *Ibid.*, 2.203–9. This is closer to Rutherford or Milton; and the issue of legal appeal seems intimated in Peter Martyr Vermigli, 'Commentary on Romans 13', in *Political Thought*, ed. R. Kingdon, Droz, Geneva, 1980, 15.10–11. Alberigo Gentili had asserted something very similar; the absence of a competent judge being a criterion of self-defence, *De jure*, 1, 13, 16; relying on Baldus, *Consilia*; see also Hunton, *A Treatise*, p. 17. Lawson clearly could have drawn on such a lineage.

[22] Locke, *Two Treatises*, 2.198, 16–20.

[23] *Ibid.*, 2.199. This is closer to Althusius than to Lawson's *Politica*. If this does not place Locke to 'the left' of his contemporaries, as Ashcraft quaintly puts it (*Revolutionary Politics*, p. 309), it does mean, as he argues, that there is a significant gap between Lawson and Locke, explicable partly with reference to Locke's notion of 'people'.

by, the strict Ramist compass of Lawson's political realm. In extension, the notion of resistance, tied as it is to the ample and all-encompassing notion of property, takes on a dominating role in the argument as a whole, with dissolution being seen largely under its aegis.[24] The causes of dissolution are all justifications for resistance, or erosions of the right of appeal which render self-defence an imperative. A distinctive dissolution thesis is vaporised. So, if Locke protects resistance from the accusation of rebellion, it is through its assimilation to self-defence.

Locke, we may say, from a body of common precept, conceptual vocabulary, and constitutional proposition orchestrates and exploits the sort of activism which is dampened or counter-balanced in the *Politica*. In part this is achieved through a series of terminological simplifications and extensions of meanings and the weakening of structural metaphors where Lawson had erected discriminate if only notional barriers, open to arbitrary employment. In part this is achieved by providing illustrations from small-scale social relationships amongst individuals beyond the formally considered political realm to which the concepts were still primarily to be applied, that is, to the corporate domain Lawson had called politics in the strict sense. Finally this is achieved also through the elevation of a notion of political right with property at its symbolic centre: right less certainly restricted in its scope by the emphases on political duty and prudence that accompany it in the *Politica*. The cumulative differences of emphasis and the strategies of argument that make them clear need no more elaboration if one reads the *Politica* as the victim of the very activist inheritance Locke recaptured and might even have partially abstracted from the pages of the *Politica* itself. Indeed, given Lawson's apparent attempts to offset citizen rights with subject duties, Locke may be turning critical attention largely to Lawson when he remarks that telling people they may decide matters for themselves when they are already in the hands of others is to offer relief when it is too late: 'this is in effect no more than to bid them first to be Slaves, and then to take care of their Liberty.'[25] Failing to see that the criticism might already have been made, I commented to much the same effect upon Lawson's apparent equivocations on the right of resistance.[26] Locke, too, thinking casuistically that the point of theory should be to guide and rationalise action, may have seen Lawson as equivocal where he needed to stand firm and be counted.

[24] Locke, *Two Treatises*, 2.211ff. which follows on from the discussion of tyranny. Laslett remarks of 2.216 that Locke could have had Hobbes in mind – one might add, or Grotius or Pufendorf, or Lawson, or no one specifically; cf. also John Nalson, *The Complaint of Liberty*, 1681, who keeps the terms property and life well apart. The elision was a perceived danger.
[25] Locke, *Two Treatises*, 2.220, 10–16.
[26] Condren, '*Sacra* Before *Civilis*', *The Journal of Religious History*, 11, 2 (1981), pp. 532–3.

A fragment of Locke's, unpublished until 1830, provides a succinct account of his practical rationale for theorising about society. The ethics of the schools, he states, tell us nothing of morality 'but only to understand their names, or to call actions as they or Aristotle does; which is, in effect to speak their language properly, the end of morality being to direct our lives'. Those who fail to produce the requisite credal directives are dismissed as but 'language masters'.[27] Lawson too had dismissed 'masters of words' in a context that suggests Hobbes was the target; but my see-saw reading of the resistance *topos* would indicate that Lawson would be as apposite a mark for Locke's dismissal of scholastic moral theory as anyone. Although, manifestly, Lawson believed in guiding people towards the good, rectifying terminological ignorance through fastidious and reciprocal delineation of necessary notions was a prior underlabouring task, and it was one more systematically evidenced in the *Politica* than anywhere in the *Two Treatises*. Unless, Lawson seems to urge, one masters his words one cannot hope to understand. To use Locke's phrase, how we may know presupposes how we should 'direct our lives'. Such understanding as Lawson offers, however, may forestall the sort of activist injunctions the enthusiastic Locke (and for that matter the admiring Humfrey) justified in the religious heat of the revolutionary moment of 1689. What appears, largely on the cobweb thesis, as a vital difference of emphasis, arguably becomes (on its alternative) a disparity of theoretical enterprise. Insofar as Lawson presents an insolubly duplex understanding of political being rather than a doctrine of political right, direct comparison with the *Two Treatises* may be tainted by *ignoratio elenchi*.[28] Thus aspects of the *Politica* may be considered in the light of Locke's own monument to philosophical underlabouring.

In *An Essay Concerning Human Understanding* we see Locke, Hobbes and Lawson, all masters of words, at one in a world of shared linguistic presuppositions, for it is a principal theme of *Book 3* that an adequate battery of sortal concepts is needed to do justice to the complexity and variety of the world. Although the definitional process *per se* is quite arbitrary, it should never be used to oversimplify.[29] Indeed, Lawson's notion of duplexity becomes in Locke's terminology rather like a 'complex idea' arising from the unification of mixed modes, phenomena he notes which

---

[27] 'Thus I Think' in Peter King, *Life of John Locke*, London, 1830, vol. 2, p. 127.
[28] If, as I am suggesting, Lawson is a more rigorous scholastic philosopher than Locke in his *Two Treatises*, I am not to be taken as insinuating he is really the better political theorist; neither am I contradicting my emphasis on rhetoric, as the persuasive dimension of discourse. I have little truck with the common nexus of views – philosophy equals logic; philosophy is inimicable to rhetoric; all good theory is philosophy. For discussion see C. Condren, *The Status and Appraisal of Classic Texts*, Princeton University Press, 1985, p. 10, chaps. 1 and 6. [29] Locke, *Essay*, 3.1.2; 3.11.9; 3.6.28.

are particularly prevalent in the realm of moral discourse.[30] What is crucial for Locke (despite the second of the *Two Treatises*), Hobbes and Lawson is that such terms are used with scrupulous precision and consistency.[31] Lawson's political animal, then, the subject/citizen is a complex rather than a simplex idea: and so rather than being a more moderate, or equivocal version of the second of the *Two Treatises*, the *Politica* may in this respect provide an exemplification of the sort of definitional phenomenon for which Locke finds an important place in the *Essay* in which the relationship between notions, as much, if not more, than the representation of things, is vital. Even here, however, a qualification is important, for the use of aporia as a means of circumscribing the complexities of the world in words does not come within Locke's purview. His attitude to metaphor being more at one with Hobbes, would make it difficult for him to see or accept such a definitional strategy. Here perhaps Lawson's world is falling into Locke's past.[32]

Now, these relative contrasts aside, the *Politica* and the second of the *Two Treatises* are still remarkably and importantly comparable; but the very attempt to trace patterns of usage from Baxter through to Humfrey and the Allegiance Controversy has shown that it would be very difficult to specify these as a pattern of influence or exclusive derivations from the man who really solved the constitutional problem of mixed monarchy in the seventeenth century. This must be somewhat anticlimactic, but the whole game of debt chasing with respect to Locke has been singularly inconclusive. This is partly, as it is with any thinker, a matter of explicating Locke's ideas from a largely common stock of words, and to do this is to engage in an interpretative and creative exercise couched in the idiom of empirical description. More specifically, however, the difficulty of debt chasing is acute because, as Michael Oakeshott remarked, Locke provided a masterful abridgement of English political experience.[33] Thus there are suggestions of Bilson, Fortescue, Hooker, Hunton, Stubbe, the Levellers, and even Baxter, many of which blend with Lawsonian mnemonics. Even if this family resemblance is particularly strong with respect to Lawson, and even if this is because Locke relied heavily upon him, the evidence must remain inconclusive. It is yet more so when one remembers that England was not, intellec-

---

[30] *Ibid.*, 3.5.6. For useful background discussion, Eugene F. Miller, 'Locke on the Meaning of Political Language', *Political Science Reviewer*, 9 (1970) pp. 163–93, esp. pp. 185–9 on the centrality of relational terms to politics, as opposed to terms of simple representation.
[31] Locke, *Essay*, 3.11.15–17.
[32] *Ibid.*, 3.10.34. In this way Locke's essay is firmly in the Baconian tradition of the *Magna instauratio* in its hostility to metaphor, conceit and *discordia concors*. See Melissa Wanamaker, *Discordia Concors*, Kenniket, New York, 1975, pp. 132–3.
[33] Michael Oakeshott, *Rationalism in Politics and other Essays*, Methuen, London, 1962, pp. 120–1.

tually speaking, an island and hence the experience of Locke encompassed the worlds of Pufendorf, Grotius, Calvin, Suarez, Marsilio, Aquinas, and Gerrard of Abbeville. These are all suggestive and slippery names and Locke could have relied on a writer like Pufendorf and still seemed English; he could have been ignorant of Gerrard of Abbeville and still have sounded like him.[34] It was this general difficulty of isolating exclusive relationships and weighing them against perceived difference that Levin misunderstood when he suggested that if originality is a criterion of classic status, then Locke has been lucky in his posthumous fate.[35]

To complicate matters further, however, much that can be said of Locke could be said of Lawson (excepting his luck). He too provided a fine abridgement of a neo-medieval, ancient and partially Anglicised inheritance – to the extent that through him we can see some of the conceptual problems of that inheritance captured in miniature. It is thus difficult to tie him down to an exclusive array of texts and concomitantly difficult to chart with certainty the pattern of his subsequent use, a pattern which, however, if it excludes Locke, must be reduced to the narrow certainty of the citation of his name. If we are to hazard anything more broad and ambitious than a catalogue of citations, we must be satisfied with a discrepancy between intellectual capacity, subsequent significance and between these and surviving evidence of use and contemporary importance.

None of this scepticism contradicts the assertion that Locke was probably very familiar with Lawson. The appeal however, may have been partially corroborative, as in some respects at least it seems to have been with Humfrey, for when Locke attacked Bagshaw in 1660 he already shared a range of theological and ecclesiological precepts with Lawson. He begins with a standard enough affirmation of God's absolute power in the elaboration of an argument in the neo-Erastian idiom of Lawson, and which is seen by some to be significantly Hobbist.[36] All power, he begins, comes

---

[34] On the one hand Locke has been accused by Hazlett of plagiarising Pufendorf, and he does sound a little like Gerrard of Abbeville. For brief comment see C. Condren, 'Rhetoric, Historiography and Political Theory: Some Aspects of the Poverty Controversy Reconsidered', *The Journal of Religious History*, 13, 1 (1984), p. 26. He has also been called a Puritan, a Thomist and Alan Gewirth has noted the similarities with Marsilio. See Gewirth, *Marsilius of Padua*, Columbia University Press, 1964, vol. 1, e.g., pp. 124, 164, 308. Familiarity with Lawson might help explain this, C. Condren, 'George Lawson and the *Defensor pacis*', *Medioevo*, 5–6 (1980), p. 612. For a valuable recent discussion of such themes see Janet Coleman, 'Medieval Discussions of Property: *Ratio* and *Dominium* according to John of Paris and Marsilius of Padua', *History of Political Thought*, 4, 2 (1983), pp. 209ff.
[35] M. Levin, 'What Makes a Classic Text in Political Theory: The Case of John Locke', *Political Science Quarterly*, 88 (1973).
[36] Locke, Lovelace Collection, Bodleian Library, MSS E7; in *John Locke, Two Tracts on Government*, ed. Philip Abrams, Cambridge University Press, 1967, and Introduction, p. 76, for a discussion of the similarities with Hobbes.

from God and is entrusted by him. The magistrate (regardless of the lesser issues of governmental form), argues Locke, has a right and must have the power in the interests of peace to control matters of religion which are external and indifferent. In contrast, the appeal to unlimited toleration and untrammelled freedom of conscience, and the propensity to stand upon the punctilios of religion have caused great mischief and are without any adequate biblical sanction. Granted there are inconveniences attending government and what is regarded as its yoke; but there is little in life that does not have advantage and disadvantage mixed.[37] We must consider the balance: the disastrous consequences of governmental absence from indifferent, as from other, matters outweigh the discomfort of the governmental burden. Bagshaw has taken the easy way of attacking something by seeing only 'the black side of the cloud'.[38]

Broadly, one may say that in the circumstances of 1660 – a fragile settlement at the nexus of centrifugal religious enthusiasms – Locke and Lawson shared fears of religious fragmentation and its civil consequences and shared also similar theological premises. In the *Politica*, however, such standard arguments and attitudes as Locke also digests are themselves balanced by the tolerant latitudinarianism which so appealed to Humfrey, and probably Baxter as he got older. But these do not appear until later in Locke, suggesting a balance between civil control and toleration.[39]

Be this as it may, Lawson could not have been in all ways a mere corroboration for Locke. Despite the theological and ecclesiological similarities and the shared fears and hope for a settlement, there are vital differences between Lawson and the Restoration Locke. These are directly related to the change from the Restoration to the Revolution Locke. First, in the Latin tract of 1661 – a more general statement of specific arguments directed against Bagshaw – Locke unequivocally reaffirms the requirements of subjection through either passive or active obedience, even when the intentions of the magistrate are nefarious. Now this is not quite so absolutist as it might seem, for Locke's extreme case leaves the actions consequent upon dubious

---

[37] Locke, MSS E7 in Abrams, *John Locke*, pp. 124–50; see p. 155 for another standard affirmation of sceptical ambivalence at one with Lawson, Donne, Machiavelli and Guicciardini. See above p. 125.

[38] *Ibid.*, p. 156, which has been seen as a particularly Hobbist passage. There is, of course, also a hint of Lawsonian duplexity, though it is less a matter of definitional necessity in Locke, than a plea for rhetorical fairness.

[39] There is no necessary contradiction in the change, as the rather misleading labels of conservative and liberal might imply. Locke, like Bagshaw, comes to pay more attention to the other side of the governmental cloud; and it should be remembered that if the early 'conservative' Locke is Hobbist, White, Hobbes's own early defender, saw him as a champion of toleration.

intent untouched.[40] Moreover, his arguments, however uncompromising, remain tied to the realm of indifference. Even so, this is much closer to Seth Ward than George Lawson. Secondly, and above all else, there is an effective denial of the notion of community beyond political society. Equal individuals, we are told, are incapable of forming a polity.[41] Labelling such a position is not straightforward. It is not really a Hobbist view, though it seems in some ways close to Baxter, but perhaps it is closest of all to John Hall.[42] What matters here is that it is decidedly un-Lawsonian, and as much at odds with the *Politica* as it is with the *Two Treatises*; for both of those works, the denial of community, the postulation of naked individuals equal and unsocialised before political subjection, denies the foundations of the works themselves.

We may say that at some stage, then, just as Locke lost his enthusiasm for the English monarchy's controlling interests in religion, especially as that particular governmental cloud drifted towards Rome, so too he found it necessary to rely upon and refurbish a concept of community as a means of challenging the claims of magistracy. In this change Lawson may have played a significant part precisely because of the religious affinities which already existed in 1660. The approximate play of similarities between Lawson and Locke suggests in effect that Locke may have taken a similar journey to Baxter, who also stepped back from an earlier enthusiasm for a neo-Erastian magistrate, and to John Humfrey who became increasingly involved in political actions uncongenial to the dictates of government. It would, of course, be nice to be able to date a turning-point here. 1673 might be a candidate, for it is difficult to imagine *On the Difference Between Civil and Ecclesiastical Government* being written in total ignorance of Lawson.[43] But to come full circle, we know that in April 1679, before Locke started the *Two Treatises*, and obscured all private traces of their creation, Lawson's *Politica* was in his possession. Possibly then, it was a watershed, at the head of the varied tributaries of a communal inheritance running back to the Apennine hills; but to go even this far would be to indulge the fantasy of one trying to dry out drowning books in neat and fixed progression, on the very edges of the sands of time.

---

[40] *An magistratis civilis...* in Abrams, *John Locke*, pp. 185ff., trans., pp. 210ff. As Locke, like Lawson, was highly sceptical about the possibility of knowing for certain what inner motivations were, this extremity is rather hypothetical.

[41] *An magistratis civilis...* esp. p. 200: if men are equal by virtue of common birth, then there can be no society, 'nulla vitae societas, nulla lex, nec republicae forma qua mortales inter se quasi in unum corpus coalescant nisi quisque prius libertatem illam (quam supponant) ...', the parentheses even cast doubt on pre-political liberty.

[42] Hall, *Of Government*, 1.8–9. It is difficult to see this as strictly Hobbist, rather it points to a difficulty in Hobbes's psychology – if men are as Hobbes describes them, how plausible is the view that they will divest themselves of their power?

[43] In Peter King, *The Life of John Locke*, London, 1830, 2 vols.

What then of the relationship between Hobbes and Locke? What of the transformation from medieval to modern in which Locke might seem to have such an important role? And what of the predicative vocabulary which might make the young conservative Locke seem so much like the moderate or radical Lawson?

Hobbes and Locke are habitually placed almost cheek by jowl and this has generated a series of hypothetical relationships between the two men all of which seem to assume that somehow it was Locke's duty to make his position clear on Hobbes. John Dunn, who provides a good and appealingly facetious account of the permutations, adds to the possibility that Locke was haunted by Hobbes.[44] Tully has suggested that the real answer is not in the *Two Treatises* but in the *Essay*.[45] Lawson's sharing so much with both men helps make a variety of relationships seem plausible, but it also suggests that Locke may have felt no obligation to come to grips with Hobbes. After all, Locke's principal political target was absolutism, especially of the Catholic strain. So, it was appropriate for him to attack Filmer because he could at least claim (though we might take this with a pinch of salt) that Filmer's views were so fashionable as to amount to a new orthodoxy. Regardless of how true this was, absolutist thinkers were apt to disengage themselves from Hobbes,[46] whose role was seen as that of the arch advocate of *de facto*ism, a maverick and potential embarrassment to high Church of England men who were eventually to wriggle towards compliance with a regime acceptable to Locke.[47] Since then some scholars have happily assimilated Hobbes to a somewhat contrived absolutist tradition and so lost some of the discriminate focus of religious polemic. Locke could afford to leave Hobbes on the edge of his vision, but given the similarity between his work and Lawson's he may also have felt, like Baxter, that Lawson had adequately dispatched Hobbes in any case. Had the Revolution Locke attacked Hobbes, however, he would I think have sounded very much like the Lawson of the *Examination*.

Much intellectual history focussed on the seventeenth century is a matter of shunting into view new or refurbished hypotheses about the nature of changes from medieval, or pre-modern, to modern and who are the engine drivers. The whole matter depends very much upon the selection of relative continuities to be traced. If we find ourselves redirected at some

---

[44] John Dunn, *The Political Thought of John Locke*, pp. 77ff.; Condren, 'Confronting The Monster', p. 82.

[45] Tully, *A Discourse*, p. 30.

[46] Sir George Mackenzie, *Ius Regium*, 1684; Nathaniel Johnstone, *The Excellence of Monarchical Government*, 1686; James Daly, *Sir Robert Filmer and English Political Thought*, Toronto University Press, 1979, pp. 149–50, for some perceptive remarks.

[47] Sherlock was a vindication of this as Goldie makes clear, 'The Revolution of 1689', see esp. annotated items 3 and 36.

textual point change, then we may mistake for a transformation what more aptly may be seen as the intersection of another winding if faltering branch line. Understandably, the question of who in particular really fires the engines of modernity and directs the trains is contentious. Conversely, there is a strong consensus that whoever they are, they are the 'radicals'. To be only a little unfair, we might not know the engine driver's name, but we know what he is. Yet the term radical seems accepted as having some classificatory and explanatory power (especially when projected as an 'ism') largely on an assumption of mutual understanding and approval. A latent ambiguity in the word reinforces this confidence, for with it we are apt to run together dramatic departure with political disposition, and so seem to locate the disposition that engineers the departure. Peripheral to their own times perhaps, the radicals are posthumously significant and in this (so it seems) lies an explanation for what we are now. Brief comment on the term and its siblings 'moderate' and 'conservative' provides a fitting point of transition for the final stage of this journey; for I have found none of them useful in trying to understand Lawson's text, or in disclosing the sort of changes with which it was involved; but, as I shall eventually suggest, the historiographical myopia all these words have induced with respect to the seventeenth century, is partially caused by the very kind of change on which Lawson's work does cast light.

If the *Politica* and its fate is indicative of any clear process of change, one can begin by saying that political argument was very much a matter of the trans-dispositional exploitation of a rich and contentious terminological inheritance of varying items which writers sought to promote, demote, co-opt and distribute at the expense of others. To such ends they drew on and slipped between differing modes of definition and selectively affected the intension of meaning. The overall drift in significant sectors of the vocabulary was for fewer words to do more work; for their areas of operation to eliquate and for concepts to fuse; and for precision to be more contingently dependent on variable predication, which, often lacking, generated ambiguity or indeterminant generality. Ironically, Lawson was, as it were, on the side of the conflationary modernising angels with respect to problems of governmental form, the significance of which he wished to demote, the types of which he ran together. In this way, he loosened the grip of Aristotelian nomenclature, suggesting flexible and empirically testable classifications for governmental systems. But where problems were really significant for him it was a different matter; and here, at the conceptual centre of his thought, he seems not to be a carrier of burgeoning modernity so much as a relic of rigour. Consider again the bland marginal *aperçu* in Starkey's second edition 'Subjects may defend their rights' (*Pol.* 93). Seemingly, the resistance-minded glossator saw no difference between subjects, citizens and people, and so provides as ironic and symptomatic an indication of the processes of semantic conflation, against which the *Politica* stood, as one could hope to find. Starkey's edition is a testimony to the perceived relevance of Lawson's work, and an epitaph to his enterprise. It is also a monument to the evanescence of ideas which change with reiteration and can transmogrify with even a marginal adjustment. Hardly surprisingly, little of this sort of conceptual transformation is captured by the deployment of formally anachronistic dispositional classifiers – radical, moderate, and conservative – insensible to the diversity of the conflationary process. On the one hand, Locke wanted, albeit passingly, to coalesce arbitrary government with prerogative.[48] On the other, it was royalists and non-jurors who wanted to assimilate rebellion and resistance. It was, additionally, a dispositionally odd alliance of Hobbes, Baxter and Humfrey (hardly to be imagined in the same railway carriage) which was intent on subsuming citizenship under the notion of subjection. For rather different purposes it was both Grotius and Locke who were instrumental in simplifying a very complex vocabulary of property;[49] Pufendorf who seems to collapse the duplex Lawsonian notion of majesty; and Locke, or possibly Milton, who wanted to subsume citizen and subject under an indeterminant notion of the people.

Moreover, it is difficult to see how, with any assurance, we can penetrate the rhetoric of seventeenth-century religious and political discourse when those engaged in it had a shared interest in disavowing radical change, and when most would claim to be moderate and even, as it were, conservative. 'As it were' is the important rider here; it is remarkable what 'radical' changes could be brought about in the name of tradition – people in Europe had hundreds of years practising this idiom of justification; but the terms conservative and radical were not a part of the political vocabulary.[50] One may go further: those whom we most happily call radicals – in the sense of those whom we consider were intending to effect radical changes – are very likely to be those who failed to deploy a rhetoric of tradition convincingly, those to whom the highly pejorative accusation of innovation has stuck. Examples of such accusation are legion. As John Jewel had remarked, innovation in matters touching religion was *a priori* improper. Not surprisingly it is one's enemies who sniff out newness, one's friends deny it with claims about maintaining or trying to re-establish the *status quo*; or with arguments about continuing the good old work of reformation. So Laud was accused of innovation and the Levellers also. Lawson levelled such

---

[48] Locke, *Two Treatises*, 2.210. Prerogative and arbitrary power constituted a rhetorical compound analogous to rebellion and resistance. The elision, however, is at odds with the earlier drift of his argument. Laslett notes the difference.

[49] Tully, *A Discourse*, p. 79.

[50] For further discussion with respect to a different coagulation of polemic see C. Condren, 'Rhetoric', at length.

accusation as did Milton; Filmer's works were condemned as new fashion; and those who employed a Lawsonian dissolution hypothesis in 1688–9 were alleged to be masking innovative tendencies, and smuggling in new models. The problem, as I have stressed before, is in penetrating the rhetoric to reach intention and disposition. Without attention to this rhetoric, conclusions about these hypothetically underlying phenomena are likely to be naïve as are conclusions concerning who really was radically innovative. The corollary is that it is difficult to see and pay adequate attention to the rhetoric of tradition if we approach it through a vocabulary of political disposition actually at odds with its operation. This we do in applying to it terms like radical, moderate and conservative as a set of relatively trouble-free, discriminate and objective terms. They apply to groups in nineteenth-century politics in a way that would not have been acceptable to the world before the eighteenth. They took their place in the lexicon as part of a process of refurbishing around the time of the French Revolution, albeit from established patterns of figurative use which provided an accommodating lubricant for their working. Such words as conservative and radical along with their close and even more misleading allies left, right and centre, having restructured the political domain to great effect, have themselves become metaphors in the historiographical domain with less happy consequence, unless, of course, we are seeking to extend the lineages of our own political dispositions. Something of the common pattern of this terminological interplay can be seen in microcosm in the metaphorical structure of Lawson's *Politica*, and that in turn may provide a clearer focus – or shunt into view yet another train of explanation for the fact that we no longer argue as people like George Lawson did.

16

Theory and historiography

Like traditions, intellectual contexts are tricky things lying at the heart of the historian's enterprise. Their specification is difficult because they are contingent upon the delineations structuring the world from which a given text is cast, a wet rag upon the present shore; upon the configurations within a given activity; and upon the rigidity of the delineations that keep one activity from flowing into another. It must sometimes seem that the lines are written only upon the water. So, what we may see now as *a political text* does not necessarily dredge up a clearly political intellectual context. Lawson's *Politica* is one such work, coming from a world in which, as John Pocock has stressed, the terms of politics were fluid, and the very notion of the political could be fugitive.[1] It was certainly not conceptually secure, self-evident or autonomous. When at the end of the century Richard More catalogued his books according to intellectual domain he used no classification of the political for his absolutist treatises, his regicide tracts, his Plato and his Machiavelli.

Not surprisingly, then, the texts that swirl suggestively around the *Politica* are both more and less than political: names such as Donne, Marvell, Scaliger, Andrewes, Tertullian eddy around it like Aristotle, Marsilio, Althusius, Machiavelli and Hobbes and by turns some shift from being corroborative background to specifically focussed context. If the delineations of the intellectual world are permeable, then understanding how adequately they may circumscribe intellectual contexts is a matter of exploring not only what happens within them but also what passes between them; and metaphorical interplay can wreck our understanding of the world. With respect to what happens within intellectual delineations, I have tried to

---

[1] 'What we have, then, is an extremely complex series of phenomena, testifying by its very incoherence to an explosion of political consciousness like few others of which there is record; something . . . susceptible to treatment in terms of articulation rather than theory. The great theories that emerged were – often consciously – experiments in the formation of new political and religious languages', 'Political Thought in the Cromwellian Interregnum', *W. P. Morrell: A Tribute*, ed. G. A. Wood and P. S. O'Connor, University Otago Press, Dunedin, 1973, p. 22.

locate the *Politica* in the ebb and flow of verbal manipulation; words were weapons and tools as well as, in part, the very means through which people could understand clearly anything going on around them. *If* an overall pattern emerges from the period discussed above, it is not quite what one would expect. Rather than an intension in the repertoires of political discourse, we find in a number of respects extension and elision of terminology. Accompanying this there is a victory for real definition over nominal – which itself must have helped reify the political into a more stable phenomenon, taking it closer to anatomy than theology.

The political, however, was a good deal less clear-cut and trouble-free as a domain than we are apt to assume; and we cannot hope to understand the seventeenth century and its 'political' discourse if we presuppose its autonomy or clear identity as we usually do. We do need to turn from what happens within to what passes between the political and its neighbouring domains, between which it could be so uncertainly suspended. Here, I believe, Lawson's *Politica* can be of enormously suggestive help.

A cry of frustration from the 'Amica dissertatio' reverberates through Lawson's *Politica*: 'So hard a thing it is to speak without *tropes*.' Lawson was a *metaforika* and, in an age of increasing plain style, an interestingly self-conscious one. Superficially, this alone might seem to diminish his theoretical significance – we have been taught long enough that metaphors are not arguments. Add to this the fact that Lawson's concerns were so much less secular than we expect of respectable post-medieval political theorists, and we might plausibly conclude by consigning Lawson back to obscurity.

Two recent and unrelated trends in scholarship should, however, make us reconsider. First there has been a noticeable stress on the importance of religion and medieval structures of thought in understanding the English Revolution.[2] For over a generation social causes have enjoyed a predominance incommensurate both with seventeenth-century perceptions of upheaval, and twentieth-century standards of proof. There has been a strong reaction and, to put the matter provisionally, most historians would now accept the religious commitment itself as an important *factor* in the explanation of the whole Revolution and the *emergence* of modern political awareness, although there seems a paradox here as modernity is so often held to involve a decline in religion.

Secondly, with respect to the philosophy of science, the mind, language, and anthropology, there has been a revived stress on the epistemological

[2] Brian Tierney, *Religion, Law and the Growth of Constitutional Thought*, Cambridge University Press, 1982; William Lamont, *Richard Baxter and the Millenium*, Croom Helm, London, 1979; Quentin Skinner, *The Foundations of Modern Political Thought*, Cambridge University Press, 1978; are all in different ways symptomatic of what Mark Goldie has referred to as a Figgisian revival.

significance of metaphor. It is being seen as a means of structuring perceptions; creating and sustaining conceptual fields; and of screening specific
problems.[3] Both trends are of relevance to understanding Lawson, and
he can in turn be of value in a respecification of the importance of religion
in the light of attention to metaphor.

Four principal distinguishable domains give rise to the metaphorical interplay in Lawson's *Politica*: the religious, the political, the legal, and that
constituted by the conceptual field of rhetorical and philosophical discourse
itself. Of course, the first three of these are the subjects of the *Politica*,
and the last is the means through which Lawson discusses them. There
is, then, in traditional Aristotelian and Quintilianesque terms a certain
decorum in their functioning also alternately as fields of metaphorical expansion and attraction. There is, in modern terms, no great angle of metaphor
involved. Functioning metaphorically rather than as the material objects
of discourse, they help explain Lawson's conceptual vocabulary, its problems, and the issues it seems to leave untouched.

To start with the most obvious case: from the outset Lawson uses the
lexicon of secular politics as an area of metaphorical expansion for ecclesiology. Thus a political identity is imposed upon the church by its predication
in terms of the state. This appears to be quite self-conscious and for Lawson
seems trouble-free because he takes the vocabulary of secular politics to
be coextensive with the political *per se*. At the same time, the political
is seen as a branch of theology; that is, it comes directly under the auspices
of the relationship between God and creation. Theology itself is thoroughly
informed by secular political terminology. God *governs* the universe; we
are the subjects of his power.[4] Politics may be a branch of theology, but
the theological is already politicised. Thus Lawson, amongst others, could
see a misconception of God at the heart of Hobbes's politics, and it is little
wonder that Lawson can look at the Bible as a book of *Politics* and describe
a church in the nomenclature of the state. Thus through a metaphorical
interaction between distinguishable domains he is able to establish two parallel conceptual taxonomies which can continue throughout the text to throw
light on each other. In this way, specifically, we can see how Lawson is
able to enjoy some of the benefits of contract theory – not least the notion

[3] Max Black, *Models and Metaphors*, Cornell University Press, Ithaca, 1962; Paul Ricoeur,
The Rule of Metaphor, Routledge, London, 1977; Bruno Laurentano, *Ambiguita e Meta-
phora*, Editioni Scientifiche Italiane, Naples, 1964; C. Turbayne, *The Myth of Metaphor*,
Yale University Press, 1962; Richard Rorty, *Philosophy and the Mirror of Nature*, Princeton
University Press, 1979; to say nothing of the deconstructionalist theories of De Mann and
Derrida, or the semiotics of Eco.
[4] A similar pattern of interplay between politics and the heavens goes back to Plato and Aristotle,
see G. T. R. Lloyd, *Polarity and Analogy*, Cambridge University Press, 1966.

that *personal* majesty is a trust – without explicitly elaborating a theory of contract. What is crucial here is that Lawson does not argue but assumes that there is in general (and in secular political terms) a community prior to any specific established polity; and that the collapse of a polity itself leaves the community intact. It need not be laboured further how central this is for Lawson. Here, however, I would suggest he is able to take so much for granted because, as it were, the ecclesiologically self-evident flows back to structure the conception of the secular. The direct analogue of the citizen is the believer and the New Testament does seem to show that a community of believers was prior to any formally structured church (the analogue of the state). Moreover, in the ecclesiological context, it seems absurd to suggest that one's status as believer is *per se* destroyed with the fall of a particular form of church, and even more absurd to suggest that the acquisition of the status of church member (subject) destroys one's status as believer. If so, then the pattern of metaphorical interplay between church and state would make it particularly easy for Lawson to hold, on the evidence of the analogue alone, that secular community is prior to and coextensive with specific political form, and that a subject must always be a citizen. In this way Lawson's theory of citizenship and community is strikingly circular; an example of what may be termed the prodigal's return. The vocabulary of state is used to describe the church which can then form a suggestive metaphor for secular relationships. He never escaped the circularity. Towards the end of his life Lawson wrote of prayer 'we must be loyal and obedient, and not like bare earthly worldlings, but like citizens of Heaven, for upon this condition we are admitted subjects of a heavenly Kingdom' (*Magna charta* 114).

Law, like religion, was both a problem within the domain of the political and a field of metaphoric expansion for understanding it. Lawson avoids contract, but makes use of trust, and a whole associated cluster of terms that shifted between politics and property law. The difficulty he had in controlling this, whilst capitalising on its seductively ordering capacities, has been made clear. If his work is typical, one can now ask whether contemporary scholarly debates over the role of the economic in the determination of political theory are all misconceived inklings of the wayward properties of figuration. Again the notion of the community and its representatives is drawn from a dominant and widespread medieval metaphor of legal corporation. It is the use of this informing metaphor, as I have suggested above, which explains the need to draw a distinction between tacit and express consent; it may be said that the standardised and troublesome terms within the realm of political discourse were, in a sense, the creatures of metaphorical interplay.

More than this, however, as one now might expect, the field of law informed religious discourse at least from the time of Tertullian.[5] Even the highest reaches of theological discourse were shaped by legal and juris-prudential idioms. Lawson was aware of precisely this. In the 'Amica disser-tatio', he remarks that when we speak of God's law, of obligation and judgement we are but using metaphors – but he does not then cease to use them.

From the perspective of comparing the religious and secular domains then, the legal may be seen as an almost immemorial common ground, although more generally it might be better to see a triadic relationship between three domains, each sustained in contradistinction to the others, but each living a precarious existence because of its susceptibility to its neighbour's stan-dardised terminology. However, this circulating structure or prodigal jour-neying of conceptual relationships, though generally relevant to the *Politica*, is too simple.

As I have already suggested, like Hobbes, Lawson used the conceptual field of intellectual discourse itself as an area of metaphorical expansion for understanding social actions and relationships. In particular he makes periodic use of the terminology of medieval philosophy and classical rhetoric as metaphors for the political. Thus the intersecting conventions of philo-sophy and rhetoric are more than just the medium for a message.

He draws an analogy between the concept of essence in philosophy and that of majesty in politics (*Pol.* 73); he uses the notion of *ad hominem* argument as a metaphor for the transmission of ecclesiastical office (*Pol.* 237). Henry VIII's acquisition of ecclesiastical power is referred to as a metonymous sleight of hand (*Pol.* 204). Perhaps the best example, how-ever, is the use of the rhetorical term synecdoche to express a representational relationship in politics (*Pol.* 340). The metaphor is at one with corporation imagery, but more obviously by fiat it alleviates the need to address questions of accountability. It was, finally, the analogue between the theological struc-ture of duplex argument ('Amica diss.') and the apparent confusions in Law-son's discussion of resistance, that led me to the conclusion that this whole topic may have been misconstrued by modern commentators. The duplex model of divinity may have been a suggestive metaphor for the legal fiction of the king's two bodies, and (in Lawson at least) for the political being's two bodies. It was an aporia at one with the *discordia concors* of the meta-physical poets who themselves discoursed upon politics and theology. If so, we should hardly be surprised: Man was created in the image of God and God was an absolute ruler of the universe.

---

[5] George Yule, *Puritans and Politics: The Religious Legislation of the Long Parliament*, Sutton Courtney, Oxford, 1982, p. 33, has felicitously described Tertullian as furnishing Christia-nity in the idiom of Roman Law.

Irrespective of this last interpretative possibility, one can say that the metaphorical interplay of politics, law, religion, and the discursive categories of philosophy and rhetoric, are central to understanding the *Politica*. But it is the typicality of this discursive fluidity which is suggestive here. For, in general terms, there was nothing unusual in the figurative interplay that the *Politica* displays.[6]

Indeed, one may go further and suggest that all the time we have some sense of differing discursive realms, figurative traffic must be looked for as vital to the conceptual furniture of our world, and instrumental to its transformation. A self-conscious attention to metaphor then is not only important to understanding how Lawson wrote, but also to how his political world was structured; and by extension to how our historiographical world attempts to come to grips with it. This is more than a matter of tidiness or stylistic decorum. It extends to the classificatory and predicative vocabulary constituent of historiography, and thus is a matter of how we see and write and the price paid for such discrimination in the currency of alternative perspectives being foreclosed and impossible issues opened up. Systematic attention to such matters takes us from historiography to the centre of the philosophy of history, and the shift is out of place here. Nevertheless it seems appropriate to intimate some possibilities immediately suggested by this work – and attention to metaphor invites reconsideration of the terms used habitually to understand the period commonly called (to invoke what is itself a complex metaphor) the English Revolution. I have already suggested that the plausible spatial images of centre and periphery must be treated with caution or scepticism when extended from economics and institutionalised politics, to intellectual life. At greater length I have argued that the metaphors of nineteenth-century political disposition are misleading and occlusive when projected on the residue of political rhetoric from earlier times. By the same token I would now suggest that we need to revise our understanding of the religious factor in the English Revolution. For talk of factors has unduly rigidified discursive fluidity; the factor metaphor has raised questions that cannot be answered and obscured the workings of metaphors within the surviving evidence which can be used to explain much. The difficulties that the articulate faced in the Revolution are quite lost if we try to separate factors (religious, constitutional, economic, ideological) and weigh them (as we should be able to) as discrete causes for a known

---

[6] The ubiquity of the interplay between the terminology of law, religion and politics needs little labouring, but see Cary J. Nederman, 'Aristotle as Authority: Alternative Aristotelian sources of late Medieval Political Theory', *History of European Ideas*, 8, 1 (1987), p. 39 which discusses Fortescue as an example of one who used rhetorical categories as political metaphors.

effect – namely, the rise of modern political thinking.[7] We would be better to see the seventeenth-century intellectual world comprised of resonant and reciprocally informing sets of terms and conventions of argument always capable of being carried over into other realms – the very existence of which are functions of adjacent patterns of discourse. This does not present a very stable picture, one in which problems could be separated and neatly contained. But this itself already helps explain how difficult it was to keep arguments from providence under control, how, as Morrill indicates, men might think political matters were negotiable only to find that having been carried over into religious issues they became intractable.[8] People could distinguish the political from the religious, but the structure of political discourse itself made their separation very difficult. For most, as for Lawson, politics was a branch of theology, but the theological world itself was largely a creature of politico-legal terminology.

And this in the largest sense they also knew: that it was one thing to distinguish another to separate. Lawson is by no means unusual in his emphasis on this. Yet the more we are able to separate firmly, the more abrupt and obvious metaphorical interplay becomes; the more we can be aware of its dangers and possibilities, the more metaphor itself can be contained. Mere distinction, however makes metaphorical interplay simple and potentially insidious and this itself helps maintain the fluidity of discourse as it is captured for example in the glass of Lawson's thought. Our capacity to separate where Lawson's world was apt only to distinguish indicates a reorganisation and a firming up of select and contingent lines of intellectual demarcation which may be seen as the failure to perpetuate a certain sort of metaphorical intercourse. It is, to a considerable extent (I would suggest), the failure to sustain a pattern of metaphorical interplay that we now see and rationalise as the *rise* of modern (and secular) political thinking. In the same way, it is the continuing fluidity of the distinguishable realms of political and historiographical discourse which has provided a constant though only half recognised source of metaphorical incursion which structures our perceptions of the past.

[7] Such an approach still seems to underpin C. C. Weston and J. R. Greenberg, *Subjects and Sovereigns*, Cambridge University Press, 1981, as it does more interestingly Michael Finlayson's theoretically self-conscious and salutary study, *Historians, Puritanism and the English Revolution*, Toronto University Press, 1984. Despite very timely attention to central items in the seventeenth-century historians' vocabulary (Puritanism and Revolution) he is still concerned to isolate and define the religious factor. His task is not made easier by confusing reification, metaphor and neologism and seeming to contradict himself on the epistemic status of the Revolution (cf. pp. 39 and 159–60).

[8] J. S. Morrill, *The Revolt of the Provinces: Conservatives and Radicals in the English Civil War, 1630–1650*, Allen and Unwin, London, 1976; Michael Mendle, *Dangerous Positions*, Alabama University Press, 1984, pp. 64ff. for a fine and succinct illustration of this figurative interplay and its escalating effect on argument.

Discursive incoherence caused by the failure to sustain a figurative structure of thought may not be a very edifying way of seeing the *emergence* of our own world but it may help explain why certain simplifications in the political vocabulary were necessary – if one takes away the corporate metaphor, the distinction between tacit and express consent begins to look difficult and puzzling; if one removes the rhetorical metaphor of synecdoche, the difference between officer and representative seems redundant. Lawson's careful distinctions between power and force, subject and citizen, community and polity, even *real* and *personal*, are all only fully intelligible in the context of the figurative traffic his world took largely for granted. Without it, they too become puzzling, or capable of rationalisation. Perhaps our unwillingness to draw a distinction between distinction and separation may stand symbolically for an important process of political conflation which was fought for and against during the seventeenth century. This is not to suggest some Vicoesque and pristine age of metaphorical thought; rather, that certain figurative patterns of the sort encapsulated in the *Politica* were undermined; others have been opened up in the constant if slowly shifting demarcations of the intellectual world.

The figurative circle characteristic of Lawson's work may have been broken, but analogous ones have been well rounded. In this light we should take colophonic note of the battles fought during the seventeenth century over the status of the metaphor itself. The hostilities to metaphor expressed by men such as Hobbes, the historian of the Royal Society, Sprat, and Baxter, were moves certainly to stabilise the language, but they were not really attempts to purge metaphor *per se*, rather to make specific and controllable a sort of metaphorical relationship authorised by older patterns of figuration. In some areas of discourse, the metaphorical continued to enjoy untrammelled authority. John Owen, who had no hesitation in writing off the metaphors of others as mere metaphors, insisted, in the style of Bunyan, that if the Holy Ghost could use metaphors, so we could now; and that plain language was fitting for men's truths, but, in the idiom of Valla, God's truths needed something more.[9] So discourse in the shadow of theology could enjoy its figurative privileges. It was this world to which Lawson belonged.

Hobbes, like Lawson, was a master *metaforika*, who saw with especial clarity the dangers of other people's figurative language and yet exploited his own with a merciless sense of decorum. This characteristic, however,

---

[9] Dr John Owen. Compare *The Doctrine of Justification by Faith*, London, 1677, pp. 7–8 for the Bunyanesque and Valla-like appeals to metaphor with *On Schism*, 1657, in *Works*, ed. Thomas Russell, 1828, vol. 19, p. 135 where the metaphor of the seamless robe of Christ is left to those without proper arguments; and *Truth and Innocence Vindicated*, *Works*, vol. 21, p. 171 where he proposes an Act of Parliament to control the metaphors of preachers.

was not, any more than it was for Lawson, an accident or prettifying addition to his argument. It was a way of focussing argument and *ipso facto* of avoiding or forestalling the emergence of other issues and a different range of terms, and of giving plausibility to his own conceptual armoury.

The war of words over the status of metaphor in its seventeenth-century form was part of the larger war fought over the co-option, distribution, promotion, destruction and dissipation of the conceptual inheritance which constituted the uncertain and drifting political domain. Lawson's *Politica* is a subtle and perceptive microcosmographia of these conflicts, and if it fought unsuccessfully against a range of lexical elisions – it displays a remarkable self-consciousness concerning the relationship between the words that conceptually form the political domain and the options for action seen under its auspices. As the political was largely subsumed by the theological, Lawson was also able to bring the medieval theologian's sensitivity to the creative, discriminating and even censoring capacities of metaphor in the maintenance or adjustment of this conceptual domain. Like Bunyan, Lawson knew that metaphors do not make us blind, but, somewhat like the censors Milton feared, they do kill reason in one eye. From Lawson we might learn to watch for the prodigal returning with the needle in his hand.

INDEX

Cambridge Studies in Early Modern British History

Titles in the series